CIVILIZATION IN ISLAM

CIVILIZATION IN ISLAM

Md. Irshad Khan

RANDOM

RANDOM PUBLICATIONS

NEW DELHI - 110 002 (INDIA)

Civilization in Islam

ISBN 978-93-51117-23-0

Published in 2015 in India by

RANDOM PUBLICATIONS

4376-A/4B, Gali Murari Lal, Ansari Road
New Delhi-110 002
Phone: +9111-43580356, 23289044
E-mail: randomexports@gmail.com; sales@randompublications.com; info@randompublications.com

Reprinted 2025

Type Setting by: Friends Media, Delhi-110089
Digitally Pritnted at : Replika Press Pvt. Ltd.

Preface

Islam was destined to become a world religion and to create a civilization which stretched from one end of the globe to the other. Already during the early Muslim caliphates, first the Arabs, then the Persians and later the Turks set about to create classical Islamic civilization. Later, in the 13th century, both Africa and India became great centres of Islamic civilization and soon thereafter Muslim kingdoms were established in the Malay-Indonesian world while Chinese Muslims flourished throughout China. Islam is a religion for all people from whatever race or background they might be. That is why Islamic civilization is based on a unity which stands completely against any racial or ethnic discrimination. Such major racial and ethnic groups as the Arabs, Persians, Turks, Africans, Indians, Chinese and Malays in addition to numerous smaller units embraced Islam and contributed to the building of Islamic civilization. Moreover, Islam was not opposed to learning from the earlier civilizations and incorporating their science, learning, and culture into its own world view, as long as they did not oppose the principles of Islam. Each ethnic and racial group which embraced Islam made its contribution to the one Islamic civilization to which everyone belonged. The sense of brotherhood and sisterhood was so much emphasized that it overcame all local attachments to a particular tribe, race, or language—all of which became subservient to the universal Brotherhood and sisterhood of Islam.

The global civilization thus created by Islam permitted people of diverse ethnic backgrounds to work together in cultivating various arts and sciences. Although the civilization was profoundly Islamic, even non-Muslim "people of the book" participated in the intellectual activity whose fruits belonged to everyone. The scientific climate was reminiscent of the present situation in America where scientists and men and women of learning from all over the world are active in the advancement of knowledge which belongs to everyone. The global civilization created by Islam also succeeded in activating the mind and thought of the people who entered its fold. As a result of Islam, the nomadic Arabs became torch-bearers of science and learning. The Persians who had created a great civilization before the rise of Islam nevertheless produced much more science and learning in the Islamic period than before. The same can be said of the Turks and other peoples who embraced Islam. The religion of Islam was itself responsible not only for the creation of a world civilization in which people of many different ethnic backgrounds participated, but it played a central role in developing intellectual and cultural life on a scale not seen before. For some eight hundred years Arabic remained the major intellectual and scientific language of the world. During the centuries following the rise of Islam, Muslim dynasties ruling in various parts of the Islamic world bore witness to the flowering of Islamic culture and thought. In fact this tradition of intellectual activity was eclipsed only at the beginning of modern times as a result of the weakening of faith among Muslims combined with external domination. And today this activity has begun a new in many parts of the Islamic world now that the Muslims have regained their political independence. Islamic civilization as a whole is, like other traditional civilizations, based upon a point of view: the revelation brought by the Prophet Muhammad is the “pure” and simple religion of Adam and Abraham, the restoration of a primordial and fundamental unity. The very word islam means both “submission” and “peace” or “being at one with the Divine Will.” Approximately 23% of the world’s population is Muslim. Current estimates conclude that the number of Muslims in the world is around 1.6 billion. Muslims are the majority in 49 countries, they speak about 60 languages, and come from diverse ethnic backgrounds. The two main denominations of Islam are the Sunni and Shia sects. They differ primarily upon of how the life of the ummah (“faithful”) should be governed, and the role of the imam.

This valuable book discusses the major features of Muslim society, including family life, Islamic law, economic practices, and government relations, and profiles Muslim life in each region of the world.

I thank all members of my team who have helped in the preparation of the book. My special thanks go to "Random Publications" who have published the book.

— *Md. Irshad Khan*

Contents

Chapter 1

Introduction

The Allah

Belief in La ilaha illallah or Tauhid has a far-reaching impact on our life:

(i) A believer in Tauhid surrenders himself completely to the Will of Allah and becomes His true servant and subject. Allah has created all that is on the earth and in the sky for the service of mankind. When a person surrenders himself to Allah's commands, he understands and appreciates that Allah has made all His Creation beneficial for him.

The Quran confirms this when it says, "Have you not seen how Allah has made all that is in the earth subservient to you?" (22:65) "Do you not see how Allah has harnessed whatever is in Heaven and whatever is on earth for you? He has lavished His bounties on you both apparent and hidden..." (31:20)

These two verses clearly indicate that Allah has created everything on the earth and in the sky for the service and comfort of humans. The blessing of being served by other objects and creatures is only apparent when we believe and practise Tauhid. This means we must be totally obedient to Allah.

(ii) It produce? in the believer a high degree of self-respect, confidence and contentment. He knows that he depends on none but Allah for the fulfilment of his needs. He firmly believes that Allah alone has the power to provide all his requirements and no one else has any power to do good or harm him.

When can a believer be confident and develop self-respect? He can be so only when he feels that he depends on none but His Creator for the fulfilment of his needs. He does not become worried because he knows that Allah will take care of all his needs if he is truly obedient.

(iii) This belief makes a believer humble and modest. He is never arrogant or haughty. He is fully aware that everything on earth belongs to Allah and he gains control over the rest of the creation only by being a subject of Allah. He also knows very well that whatever he has is from Allah. So there is no reason to be proud or arrogant.

(iv) Belief in Tauhid makes a believer dutiful and upright. The believer knows that he must carry out the commands of his Creator to succeed in this life and the life hereafter. This awareness keeps him away from neglecting his duties and from other sins.

(v) It makes a person brave and courageous. It removes from his mind the fear of death or concern for safety. The believer knows that it is Allah who will cause death at the appointed time and none but He can harm the believer's safety. So, if he obeys Allah, he has nothing to worry about. He goes on doing his duty without any fear.

(vi) A believer in Tauhid consciously feels himself to be part of the whole universe. He is the best of all creations of Allah — the Powerful Master of the whole universe. This belief broadens his horizon and his outlook expands.

(vii) It produces in a believer strong determination, patience and perseverance. The believer becomes single-minded and dedicates himself to seeking the pleasure of his Creator.

Think of a boat. It has a rudder which guides the boat's movement: with the rudder under control, the boat moves forward proudly over the waves, but if the boat is not controlled by the rudder, it is tossed in any direction by every wave.

Similarly, when a believer surrenders himself to Allah alone, he can go forward in the affairs of life without fear. But if he does not obey Allah, he has to obey false gods like the fear of losing his job, fear of danger, fear of hunger and the like. When someone believes in Allah alone, his life is not ruled by such fears.

(viii) The most important effect of the belief in La ilaha illallah is that it makes a person obey Allah's commands. A believer in

> Tauhid is sure that Allah knows and sees everything and he cannot escape Allah's ever-watchful eye for a single moment. In fact, Allah is nearer to him than his own jugular vein (50:16). So, a true believer does not commit a sin either secretly or in the darkness of the night because he has a firm conviction that Allah sees everything all the time.

A believer in Tauhid seeks the pleasure of Allah by making his actions reflect his beliefs. Belief without practice has no place in Islam.

We Muslims are believers in Tauhid. We are Allah's servants and subjects. Our faith must be reflected in our actions.

> **Al-Qadr :** *We believe that Allah has created the universe and He is its Absolute Controller and Regulator. Allah has fixed a set course for everything in the universe; this is called al-Qadr. Nothing can happen without the will and the knowledge of Allah. The destiny of every creature is already known to Allah.*
>
> *(25:2, 33:38)*

But this does not mean that man has no freedom of will. We know that man is the Khalifah (agent) of Allah on this earth. We also know that Allah does not force us to do anything. It is up to us to obey or disobey Him. Whether we will obey or disobey is known to Him. But the fact that Allah knows what we are going to do does not affect our freedom of choice. Man does not know what his destiny is. He has the free will to choose the course he will take.

We will be judged on the basis of our intentions on the Day of Judgement. If we follow Allah's guidance we will be rewarded; if not, we will be punished. By believing in al-Qadr we testify that Allah is the Absolute Controller of all the affairs of His universe. It is He Who decides what is good and what is bad.

Allah knows already the fate of all human beings. This does not mean that we can do whatever we like, as if it would make no difference to what happens to us. We must pay attention to the Divine Guidance provided by Allah the Almighty. He gave human beings free will. We can choose between right and wrong. We will be judged for our actions on earth on the Day of Judgement.

Allah knows everything. He is the only One Who can judge His subjects. He asks mankind to follow the Divine Guidance He has provided for man's fulfilment in the life-after-death. But it depends entirely on the mercy of Allah to judge who will be rewarded and who will not.

Allah knows what will happen to everyone, but we do not know. This fore-knowledge is one of His Divine qualities (as-sifat). Sometimes things happen that do not seem to make sense to us. Why do floods, hurricanes and earthquakes happen? Why do people starve to death in many countries around the world? Why do people suffer? What makes one man good and another a criminal?

We do not know all the answers to these questions. We have only a little knowledge of the universe, but Allah knows everything. We would be wasting time if we blamed Allah for the problems or the bad things that happen, simply because we do not seem to see the reasons behind them. We should have firm faith in the wisdom of our All-Knowing Creator, and help people in distress as much as we can.

We are unable to understand and interpret many of Allah's actions. It is meaningless to argue that human beings act without freedom and that we are forced to act the way we do. We decide for ourselves what we will do, and what we will not, and we are responsible for our own actions. This freedom of action does not contradict the foreknowledge of Allah.

What did You Learn?

Key Stage:

1. What do the following Arabic words mean:

   a. Malaikah; b. Kutubullah; c. Risalat; d. Akhirat
2. What does the word Tauhid mean?
3. Carefully read the words of Suratul Ikhlas what does it tell us about Tauhid?
4. Who is the Controller of the Universe?
5. Why do you think the presence of more than one Creator would cause problems?

Key Stage:

1. "Belief in Tauhid ought to change a person's life." Explain this statement, giving practical examples to clarify your answer.
2. "Tauhid, Risalat and Akhirat, summarise the whole of the Islamic system of life." Discuss this statement.
3. Group the seven basic beliefs of Islam into the three basic concepts and create a diagram of your own.
4. What is the Arabic word for each of the words listed below:

   a. Faith; b. Prophethood; c. The One; d. Oneness of Allah; e. Angels; f. Books of Allah; g. Declaration of Faith

5. Explain why belief in al-Qadr is so important in the life of a Muslim.

Key Stage:

1. Discuss the significance of the positive and negative aspects of Tauhid.
2. "Belief in Tauhid has to result in action in order to be effective." Justify this statement in your own words.
3. Give an outline of the Islamic belief that al-Qadr does not contradicts person's free will to choose between right and wrong.

Mission of the Prophet

Risalat is a channel of communication between Allah and mankind. Allah, the Most Merciful, has provided man with guidance to follow the right course and so make this world a happy and peaceful place to live in. There will be a great reward in the life-after-death for those who follow this guidance.

Since the beginning of the Creation, Allah has "sent His guidance for mankind through His chosen agents. These chosen people are called prophets (sing, nabi, pi. anbiyaa"). They asked the people of their time to obey and worship Allah alone. They taught, guided and trained the people to follow the way of Allah.

Prophets were human beings. We should never refer to them as the sons of Allah. Allah is One and He has no partner, son or daughter. It is a major sin to say that Allah has a son, daughter or partner.

The message of all the prophets is one and the same. As Allah is One, so is His message. The message is to worship Allah alone and to reject all false gods. "We did send Nuh (Noah) to his people, and he said 'My folk, worship Allah, you have no other god than Him. I fear for you the torment of an awful day.'" (7:59) In other words, all the prophets preached the message of:

La ilaha illallah (There is no god except Allah)

You may ask why we need guidance from Allah. The answer is simple: we human beings are weak and frail; we have no knowledge of the future and the knowledge we do have is limited. Also, we are not perfect. You can see that with so many weaknesses, we are unable to make any guidance for ourselves which can hold good for all times and all conditions. This is the reason why Allah has blessed us with guidance through prophets. Not only this, Allah has also sent books of guidance through some of His prophets (2:213,7:52). These prophets are also called messengers (sing. rasla).The Quran is the last book of Allah's guidance. We will learn about it later.

Allah sent prophets to every nation at different times (10:47, 13:7, 35:24). It was necessary to send prophets at different times to bring forgetful human beings back to the right path (as-Siratal Mustaqim).

The Messengers

According to a saying of Prophet Muhammad the number of prophets is one hundred and twenty-four thousand. The Quran mentions only the twenty-five most prominent by name:

> *As Muslims we must believe in all the prophets and messengers (2:285). Allah's guidance to mankind, which began with Adam was completed with Muhammad .*

We have already mentioned belief in Angels (Malaikah) in al-Imanul Mufassal.' Who are the angels? What do they do? Can we see them? How are they different from man?

Angels are a special creation of Allah. They have been created from divine light (Nur) to perform specific duties. By comparison Adam, the first man, was created from clay, and the Jinn from fire. Iblis, the devil, is from the Jinn. Some people think Iblis was the leader of the angels. This is not true according to the Quran (18:50).

Angels have been given the qualities and powers necessary to carry out their duties, but they do not have free will. They always obey Allah and can never disobey Him. Man, on the other hand, has been given free will and can choose between right and wrong. This is why man will have to account for his actions on the Day of Judgement.

Angels do what Allah commands them. They are the sinless servants of Allah's will. They help men in the use of free will. Man decides what to do and angels help him to carry out the decision. The duty of angels is to glorify and praise Allah. They never get tired. They are always ready to obey Allah. They do not need sleep, nor do they require the things a human being would need.

We cannot see angels unless they appear in human form. Angel Jibbrail once appeared in human form before a gathering of the companions of the Prophet. He came to teach them, but only the Prophet knew he was an angel. Angels can take any suitable appearance to carry out their duties.

There are many angels in the kingdom of Allah. Prominent among them are:

Jibbrail or Jibbrail (Gabriel)

Mikail or Mikal (Michael)

'Izrail (Malakul Mawt, also called Azrail)

Israfil : Jibbrail brought the revelation from Allah to Prophet Muhammad and to all the other prophets. 'Izrail — also called the 'Angel of Death' (Malakul Mawt) — is responsible for ending our life. Israfil will blow the trumpet at the time of the end of the world and on the Day of judgement.

Some angels are busy recording all that we do. They are called the Respected Scribes (Kiraman Katibin). Not a single word we say goes unrecorded (50:18).

Allah maintains His kingdom perfectly, and angels are His obedient servants. Angels will welcome in Heaven those of us who always obey Allah's commands and will throw the wrong-doers into Hell (39:71-74).

So far we have learned that we human beings are the servants of Allah and His agents on earth. But we need guidance to carry out our duties as Allah's agents. We are unable to guide ourselves because we have many weaknesses within us and we have very limited knowledge of the past, present and future. Only Allah is above all these shortcomings and He alone has the power to give us guidance that is suitable for all times and places. We know that Allah has not left us without guidance and that He has sent prophets to show us the right path in life. In addition to this, He has also sent books of guidance through some prophets — His messengers.

Allah's blessings are countless. He provides us with all that we need. Just imagine how wonderfully He arranges our growth in the tender and affectionate care of our parents from birth to youth. Who provides us with food when we are in our mother's womb? Who fills our mother's breasts with milk to suckle as soon as we are born? Allah, the Merciful, of course. Allah's greatest favour to mankind is His guidance contained in the revealed books. The pure, perfect and most useful knowledge comes only from Allah, the Wisest and the Greatest (2:146-147,4:163,53:1-6).

A Muslim believes in all the revealed books which are mentioned in the Quran. They are: the Tawrat (Torah) of Mosa (Moses), the Zabur (Psalms) of Daud (David), the Injil (Gospel) of Isa (Jesus) and the Quran revealed to Muhammad. The Quran also mentions the Suhuf of Ibrahim (Scripture of Abraham).

Of the divine books, only the Quran remains unchanged, preserved in its original form. The original Tawrat, Zabur and Injil no longer exist. The texts available today were written by their followers many years after the death of their prophets. The writers have changed and distorted Allah's words. They have mixed divine words with those of human beings.

The Bible, which is a collection of the books of the Old Testament and the New Testament, has been translated into English from available Hebrew and Greek manuscripts. A careful reader can easily find some of the additions and alterations made to them.

The Bible, as it is available today, has many errors in it. It is not a divine revelation. It contains numerous misleading misconceptions and false accounts of the prophets. The message of Allah sent through them was either lost or distorted, because of the neglect or folly of their followers. On the other hand, the Quran contains Allah's guidance for mankind in its original form and language, unchanged and undistorted. It restates in clear and unambiguous language the message of Allah which the followers of earlier prophets have lost. The message of the Quran is valid for all times and climes.

The Quran is a unique book. It is guidance from our Creator for all of mankind. It is the sacred book of Muslims and the main source of Law in Islam. Every word of the Quran is from Allah'. The Quran is the final revelation from Allah to mankind. The revelation to Prophet Muhammad began in the cave of Hira' in 610 CE. As we have said, the previous books sent to earlier prophets have not survived in their original form. Only the Quran remains unchanged. It is guidance for all of humanity until the end of the world. It is clearly very important that this book is preserved and kept free from human distortion.

No other book in the world can match the Quran in respect of its recording and preservation. The astonishing fact about this book of Allah is that it has remained unchanged even to a dot over the last fourteen hundred years. Allah the Almighty has Himself taken the responsibility of preserving the Quran. He says: "Surely, We have revealed this reminder (Dhikr) and Lo, We verily are its Guardian." (15:9) This verse shows that Allah revealed the Quran and He will protect it. Indeed, He has protected it from any change whatsoever, and His protection will Continue forever.

None except the Creator could have produced the unique verses of the Quran. Allah challenges humans and jinn together to produce anything similar to the Quran, whilst informing them that they will never be able to do it (2:23; 10:37-38; 17:88). This challenge remains, and will continue to remain, unanswered.

The Quran was recorded as soon as it was revealed under the personal supervision of Prophet Muhammad .The Quran exists today in its original form, unaltered and undistorted. It is a living miracle in the sense that it has survived so many centuries without suffering even the smallest change. Every word of it — every single letter and sound — is in the hearts and minds of thousands of Muslims who continue to memorise and recite it every day. No variation of text can be found in it. You can check this for yourself by listening to and comparing the recitation of Muslims from different parts of the world.

Arabic, the language of the Quran, unlike the languages of other revealed books, is a living, dynamic and very rich language. Millions of people all over the world use Arabic in their daily lives. This shows the relevance of the Quran and its universal usefulness even in today's world. Through the Quran our Creator speaks to us. It is a clear proof of His Sovereignty over the universe, and that He is All-knowing, All-aware. The subject matter of the Quran is Man and his ultimate goal in life. Its teachings cover all areas of this life and the life-after-death. It contains principles, teachings and guidance for every area of human activity. The theme of the Quran consists broadly of the three fundamental concepts of Tauhid, Risalat and Akhirat. Tauhid is the basic theme of the Quran. All the prophets of Allah called people towards Tauhid. The Quran gives a vivid description of the Paradise which will be awarded to the truly obedient servants of Allah. The severe punishment to be meted out to the evildoers is also described vividly in the Quran.

The Quran urges people to follow its guidance and teachings. The success of human beings on this earth and in the life-after-death depends on obedience to the teachings of the Quran. We cannot perform our duties as the servants of Allah and His agents if we do not follow the Quran. The Quran urges us to use our energies and wealth to establish the supremacy of Allah's Laws and remove all evils from the society in which we live.

The superb style of the Quran has a tremendous effect on its readers. It totally changes the pattern of life of those who believe and practice its teachings. It leaves a soothing effect on the mind of its reader, even if he does not fully understand its meaning. The incredible effect is hard to describe, it has to be experienced to really appreciate it.

Revelation, Collection and Compilation of the Quran : The Quran was revealed to Muhammad through the angel Jibbrail. It was sent down in stages and completed over a period of twenty-three years. Each and every word of the Quran was recorded as soon as it was revealed by Allah to the Prophet through the angel Jibbrail. The verses of the Quran were sent down at different times according to the needs of the early Muslims. Jibbrail carefully instructed the Prophet in which order the verses should be put together. The Quran is not put together in the order the verses were revealed, nor according to subject matter. Its order is according to the plan of Allah, and is yet another of its striking and unique characteristics.

The Prophet's secretary, Zaid bin Thabit, used to record them exactly as the Prophet told him. He would read back to the Prophet what he had recorded.

The Quran consists of 114 chapters (sing. Sarah, pl. Suwar). The short opening chapter, Suratul Fatiha is followed by the longest chapter of the Quran, Suratul Baqarah (The Cow), with 286 verses. The chapters gradually get shorter. The shortest chapter is the 108th chapter, Suratul Kawthar (The Abundance), which has just 3 verses. There are 6236 verses (sing. Ayah, pi. Ayat) altogether. Chapters revealed when the Prophet was living in Mecca are known as Makki (Meccan) and those revealed in Medina are called Medani (Medinan).

The Quran is also divided into 30 parts (sing. Juz', pl. Ajza') of roughly equal size, which is convenient for recitation purposes.

Many of the early Muslims memorised the Quran immediately after the verses were revealed. Some of the famous Huffaz (plural: persons who memorised the Quran; singular: Hafiz) were: Muadh bin Jabal, 'Ubadah bin as-Samit, Abu Darda', Abu Ayub al-Ansan and Ubay bin Kaab.

Shortly after the death of the Prophet in 632 CE, 'Umar suggested to the Khalifah, Abu Bakr, that the Quran be compiled in one volume. Up until then, the Quran was written down in separate sections. A committee was formed under Zaid bin Thabit to gather the material of the Quran into one volume.

Great care was taken to compile the Quran exactly as it had been recorded during the time of the Prophet. After careful checking and rechecking the work was completed. During the Khilafat of 'Umar, the copy was kept with Hafiah, one of the widows of the Prophet .

Later, many schools were established for the teaching of the Quran throughout the Muslim territories. During 'Umar's time, one such school in Damascus had sixteen hundred pupils under Abu Darda', one of the famous Huffaz.

As the Islamic state expanded, people in various places recited the Quran in their local dialect and accent. To avoid the possibility of any confusion or misunderstanding the Khalifah, 'Uthman, ordered the preparation of one standard version of the Quran to be written in the dialect of the Quraish. Prophet Muhammad was from the Quraish tribe. Zaid bin Thabit, 'Abdullah bin al-Zubayr, Said bin al- 'As and 'Abdur Rahman bin al-Harith were asked to prepare copies from the copy of Hafiah.

This farsighted action by 'Uthman made the uniform recitation of the Quran possible. Two original copies from the time of the Khilafat of 'Uthman still exist today — one in the Topkapi Museum in Istanbul, Turkey and the other in Tashkent, Uzbekistan. The National Library of Karachi, Pakistan has a photocopy of the Tashkent original.

The revelation of the Quran began in 610 CE at the cave Hira' on Mount Nar in Mecca. The first revealed verses are:

Iqra' bismi rabbikal ladhi khalaq,
Khalaqal insana min 'alaq.
Iqra' wa rabbukal akram,
Alladhi 'allama bil qalam.
'Allamal insana malam yalam.
"Read in the name of your Lord Who created,
Created man from something that clings.
Read, and your Lord is most generous,
Who taught by the pen,
Taught man what he did not know." *(96:1-5)*

The Quran was revealed over 22 years, 5 months and 14 days. The last verse of the Quran was revealed shortly before the Prophet's death:

Al yawma akmaltu lakum dinakum,
wa atmamtu 'alaikum nimaiti,
wa raditu lakumul islama dina.

"This day I have perfected your religion for you, and completed My favour upon you, and chosen for you Islam as your way of life." (5:3) Many Arabic words used in the Quran are almost impossible to translate into other languages, including English. However, with the help of the Ahadith and Surah (biography of the Prophet and his companions) translations of the Quran have been produced in many languages.

Muslims scholars have devoted years of study to explain and interpret the Quran in Arabic and other languages. These explanations and interpretations are called Tafasir (sing. Tafsir). They help us to understand the Quran. May Allah help us to understand His words and act on them.

Death is a natural event for all living things. It comes to every one of us. We will all die. The Quran says:

"Everyone shall die." *(3:185; 21:35; 29:57)*

Death brings an end to our temporary life on this earth. It is an occasion of sorrow and grief for the loved ones of the deceased. In Islam, people mourn for the dead person by reciting the Quran and saying prayers (dua). Islam asks us to keep in mind that death can arrive at any time. Only Allah knows when His servants will die. Death puts an end to our human body but it does not destroy our soul. The soul is taken away by the angel Malakul Mawt ('Izrail or Azrail) to Allah (32:11).

A person is sure to behave well and follow Allah's commands if he remembers death and the life-after-death.

In Islam, a dead body is ritually washed before it is buried. It is then covered with white sheets and fragrance is spread all over it. A funeral prayer is conducted before the burial. This prayer is called Salatul Janazah.

Day of Judgement

Akhirat : We have already mentioned the three most important beliefs in Islam: Tauhid (oneness of Allah), Risalat (Prophethood) and the Akhirat (life-after-death). Now we will look at the Akhirat.

Belief in Akhirat is vital for all Muslims. Our life on this earth is temporary. It is meant to prepare us for the Akhirat, which is never-ending. Life on this earth is meaningless if good actions are not rewarded and bad conduct not punished. Why attend school if bad behaviour goes unpunished and there's nothing at the end to reward all our efforts? In the same way, life on earth is meaningless if we don't face the consequences of our actions after death, standing in the majestic Court of justice of Almighty Allah on the Day of Judgement (Yawmul Akhir or Yawmuddin).

To prepare ourselves for this day, we need to follow the guidance given through the prophets. There would have been no need for prophets if there were no life-after-death.

There are people who do not care whether there is a life-after-death. Some do not even believe in it at all. These people will suffer terribly for their disbelief. A sensible person cannot possibly say there is no life-after-death. He can be doubtful but he will always be at a loss if his doubt proves untrue.

So, the safe course to follow is to believe in all that the prophets told people to believe. Not to care about Akhirat is a serious failing. We are certain that all human beings die, so it is quite reasonable to prepare for that eternal life which, no doubt, will follow death.

Doubts have been expressed by unbelievers about life-after-death. They cannot understand how Allah can raise men and women after death. But Allah can make human beings out of nothing so it is not difficult for Him to raise them after death (22:5-7; 36:77-79).

The Quran says:

> *"Does man think that we shall not assemble his bones? Yes, surely, yes, we are able to restore the very shape of his fingertips."* *(75:3-4)*

Life on this earth would not be peaceful, rather it would be horrible, if all people thought that there would be no life-after-death. There would be no restraint or control on what we do. Belief in Akhirat has a tremendous influence on the life of a Muslim. He knows that Allah is watching all his actions and he will have to account for them on the Day of Judgement. His conduct and behaviour will therefore be responsible, controlled and careful. He will always try to do those things which Allah will favour and give up those actions which will incur His punishment.

A Muslim believes that he will be rewarded in the life-after-death for all his good actions. He will live in Heaven, a place of eternal happiness and peace.

Wrong-doers will be punished on the Day of Judgement and will be sent to Hell, a place of severe punishment and suffering.

To prepare for that day and to be rewarded by Allah, the Merciful and the Kind, we need to do all that Allah demands of us and give up all bad habits and wrong actions. We can do this if we follow the guidance given to Muhammad by Allah. This is the safest course for our success in the Akhirat.

Messenger of God

Last Messenger

The earliest biographers of the Arabian Prophet, whose works are extant in Arabic, are Ibn-Ishaq (A.H. 151), Ibn-Hisham (A.H. 218),

Waqidi (A.H. 207), and Tabari (A.H. 310). Ismail Abulfida, Prince of Hamah, in Syria (A.H. 733), compiled a Life of Muhammad in Arabic, which was translated by John Garnier, Professor of Arabic at Oxford (A.D. 1723), and into English by the Rev. W. Murray, Episcopal clergyman at Duffus, in Scotland.' Dr. Sprenger of Calcutta commenced a Life of Muhammad in English, and printed the first part of it at Allahabad (A.D. 1851); but it was never completed. The learned author afterwards published his work in German in 1869. The only Life of Muhammad in English, which has any pretension to original research, is that by Sir William Muir of the Bengal Civil Service.

Muhammad (lit. the praised one), son of Abdul Muttalib, by his wife Amina, was born at Mecca at, August 29th, A.D. 570. He assumed the prophetic office at the age of forty, fled from Mecca at the age of fifty four, and died at Medina, June 9th, A.D. 632, aged sixty two.

The Hijrat, or Hegira (the flight from Mecca), which is the Muhammadan era, dates from July 16th, A.D. 622.

In forming an estimate of Muhammad's prophetical pretensions, it must be remembered that he did not claim to be the founder of a new religion, but merely of a new covenant. He is the last and greatest of all God's prophets. He is sent to convert the world to the one true religion We follow the prophet in his self-asserted mission from the cave of Hira to the closing scene, when he dies in the midst of the lamentations of his harem, and the contentions of his friends-the visions of Gabriel, the period of mental depression, the contemplated suicide, the assumption of the prophetic office, his struggles with Meccan unbelief, his flight to Medina, his triumphant entry into Mecca and we wonder at the genius of the hero.

We are not insensible to the beauties of the Quran as a literary production, and we admire its conceptions of the Divine nature, its deep and fervent trust in the power of God, its frequent deep moral earnestness, and its sententious wisdom.

Ever since human beings came into being they have been subject to certain disciplines of internal impulses and extraneous order which go together to determine human behaviour. However, the internal impulses can be tamed by the application of moral and spiritual discipline while the extraneous order is subject to the exercise of ever-developing human capabilities which result in the creation of better living conditions. As social relations grow and rules of social conduct are improved upon, the extraneous order becomes more and more conducive to human development.

Another basic factor that needs to be remembered is that both positive and negative traits are embedded in the human being and that they have a pivotal role to play in the shaping of one's personality. But these too are controlled by human consciousness. The more it develops the more responsive are the positive qualities in dominating the negative aspects; the less it is developed the more negative aspects tend to dominate the positive qualities of man.

These three essential features of human life — man's internal impulses, extraneous order and the negative and positive traits — are a person's constant companion, and the success or failure of a person in life depends upon their successful or unsuccessful utilization.

In such a situation the individuals who are left alone in the maze of life with no system of guidance and relief are likely to falter or get frustrated. As a result they contribute to unbalancing the society and leading it to social disruption. In these circumstances persons who do not consider themselves answerable to society for their actions form themselves into exploiting classes by monopolizing the means of production and become unbearable in their oppression upon the weaker and poorer sections of society which, in fact, are their creation. At this stage the conscientious and daring among the people rise to the occasion and initiate a class struggle to free the lower classes from the shackles of the upper classes. Such people are present in every society and they have been making their presence felt to a smaller or greater extent. When, however, inspite of these efforts by conscientious people deterioration exceeds certain limits, and the social structure itself becomes rotten beyond redress, Prophets are sent to restructure society on a more modern, forward-looking and enlightened pattern.

This process of re-educating humanity had been going on at various stages of history throughout the world till finally a stage arrived when, after a long process, the human intellect had developed appropriately and had shed its false notions and idiosyncrasies to quite an extent. At this stage in the pre-industrial era Prophet Muhammad (Peace be upon him) came on to the scene of history. The last of the Prophets was thus sent to perfect the system of life under Divine guidance.

The role played by Prophet Muhammad (Peace be upon him) needs to be correctly defined if we are to understand the true nature of his greatness, and if we wish to follow, in the right spirit and with devotion to his august person, his teachings and the directions set by him. In the past many centuries not much has been done in this regard by the Muslims in general and the religious elite in particular except to eulogise the Prophet's person and pay lip-service to his achievements.

The true intent and bearing of his teachings have not been spelt out by the 'religious' guides and Muslim rulers because they were not true to their faith and had their own vested interests to serve, which they had deceitfully created. Their interests required that the people be kept ignorant about the revolutionary character of these teachings. Thus they tailored Islam to their own requirements and to their personal benefit. They formed it into a protective barrier to safeguard the interests of the few *jagirdars* and moneyed barons as against many poor people who were being suppressed by them. They created an upper class who seized the means of production, which was state property, and deprived the masses of education, good health and decent living. They dispossessed the people of their ownership of the means of production, their share in state power and their right to administer their own affairs. Our present social structure stands at this very level. The greatness of Prophet Muhammad (Peace be upon him), and for that matter of all the Prophets, lies in that they stood for the oppressed as against the oppressors, for the exploited as against the exploiters, for the interests of the masses as against those of the vested interests, for collective benefit as against individual advantages.

Having gone through this basic premise in the introductory study made above we would now venture to elucidate some of the important features of the Prophets' call to Islam which stand as part of his personality and which must be emulated by all human beings, Muslims as well as others.

The foremost feature of Prophethood is truthfulness and consistency between words and actions. The other features are: simple living as against pompous life-style; making full use of one's intellectual capabilities and sense of understanding in day-to-day affairs while not being led away by emotional viewpoints and slogans; developing collective wisdom among the people and acquiring as well as spreading knowledge to the utmost; standing up against all kinds of tyranny and siding with the oppressed poor; doing justice to everybody and in all circumstances; doing a good turn to as many people as one can by helping them to stand upon their own feet and helping those in distress with no desire for any benefit in return; freeing oneself from the influence of those forefathers who were wrongdoers and instead finding fresh solutions to modern requirements; not following the evil path of immodesty, injustice and violence. Thus the solutions to modern problems have to be framed in the light of the Holy Quran, the Prophet's Sunnah, other Holy Scriptures and the scientific literature produced in later periods of history. Prophet Muhammad's objective was clearly to evolve a system of life by which the human race would live in peace, harmony and freedom and that social equality and universal fraternity could become a reality.

We must, however, understand that the exemplary qualities of Prophet Muhammad (Peace be upon him) enumerated above cannot be imbibed unless we first of all demolish the existing social structure of our country which is based on economic and political exploitation of the masses by initiating a thorough struggle at the people's level; it is not enough to resort to mere reformatory measures. This is necessary because otherwise this socio-economic set-up will not allow any room for the suppressed people to work for amelioration of their lot, and to develop their personalities, through material, moral and spiritual advancement.

This is precisely why Prophet Muhammad (Peace be upon him) concentrated on three things: First and foremost he put forth the message of Truth that Allah Almighty is the Creator of the universe, that He is the absolute ruler and lawgiver as well as the Sustainer of the whole living world and that He should be accepted as such by the human beings. They should strive to come nearer to Him and earn His love by assimilating to some extent a few of His attributes such as love, forgiveness, providing sustenance to the needy, alleviating suffering and illness and improving things around them in order to serve their fellow-beings. His second message was that the purpose of creation of humankind is to evolve a system of life that will be instrumental in establishing a just social order in which each person will be a source of succour, enlightenment and peace of mind for the other. Such a productive and orderly life could only be fostered by shedding selfishness, lust for power and wealth and the urge to usurp others' rights. The third message that was translated into action by him was to change the existing social order based upon exploitation of the labour of the numerous downtrodden by the few who had appropriated the means of production which, legitimately, is the common property of the people. Such social structure had curtailed the opportunities of economic development from reaching the hands of the majority of the people, and denied their basic human rights. This third message, in fact, constitutes the programme for realizing the first two objectives.

In view of what has been explained above it can be said authoritatively that Prophet Muhammad (Peace be upon him) was a "Prophet of Revolution". The salient features of this revolution are:

1. Breaking up of the grip of exploiter landed and moneyed classes, and their accomplices the religious elite, over the oppressed poor.

2. Eradicating poverty and ignorance.
3. The State guaranteeing basic human rights and freedoms.
4. Doing away with religious intolerance and inculcating instead the spirit of cooperation, fraternity and mutual understanding at the human level.
5. Organizing the society on progressive lines while keeping in view the principle that exploitation of the weak, and oppression against them in any form whatsoever, was not to be allowed.
6. Carrying out all human affairs, be they family or state affairs, on the basis of mutual consultation and consensus.
7. Granting equal rights and uniform social status and dignity to every one while considering no one inferior to the other on account of wealth or position in society. The sole criterion for determining a higher status in society was to be one's contribution towards betterment of society.
8. Developing the individual into a beacon of excellence, both morally and spiritually, so that he or she is able to contribute in a committed manner to the building up of society.
9. Spreading this message of Islam to the four corners of the world and working for a world-revolution in the realm of intellect and learning.

It is thus imperative on us to follow this path set for humanity by Muhammad and other Prophets (Peace be upon them) and by the Holy Books, irrespective of caste, colour or creed. This is the only way we can make this earthly abode of ours into an abode of peace and piousness and, in the long run, convert it into a heaven of bliss, beauty and serenity.

This path can be followed by us only by getting rid of the dogmatic, fanatical and sectarian interpretation of Islam, that goes to divide rather than unite people and creates gruesome monopolies to the detriment of the common man, by pulling down the overbearing feudal structure and replacing it with a just socio-economic order. This great task can only be accomplished by setting up an organization consisting of scrupulous and dedicated persons of all denominations who expressly believe in Allah, who accept the Quran and the life-example of Prophet Muhammad (Peace be upon him) as their guide in all matters and are prepared to carry out a long struggle for bringing about a democratic revolution in order to put back the downtrodden people on the seat of power.

Nearest Companions

The Caliph, or Khalifa (i.e., the vicegerent of the Prophet), is the sovereign dignity amongst Muhammadans, vested with absolute power. The word more frequently used for the office in Muhammadan works of jurisprudence is Imam (leader), or Imam-ul-Azam (the great leader). It is held to be an essential principle in the establishment of the office, that there shall be only one Caliph at the same time; for the Prophet said: -"When two Caliphs have been set up, put the last to death and preserve the second, for the last is a rebel" (vide Mishkat, bk. xvi. chap. i.) According to all Sunni Muhammadan books, it is absolutely necessary that the Caliph be "a man, an adult, a sane person, a free man, a learned divine, a powerful ruler, a just person, and one of the Quraish" (i. e. of the tribe to which the Prophet himself belonged). The Shias, of course, hold that he should be one of the descendants of the Prophet's own family; but this is rejected by the Sunnis and Wahabis. The condition that the Caliph should be of the Quraish, is very important; for thereby the present Ottoman Sultans fail to establish their claims to the Caliphate.

After the deaths of the first five Caliphs, - Abu Bakr, Umar, Uthman, Ali, and Hasan,-the Caliphate, which is allowed by all parties to be elective, and not hereditary, passed successively to the Umayyads and Abbasides. The temporal power of the Abbaside Caliphs was overthrown by Houlakon Khan, son of the celebrated Chengiz Khan, A.D. 1258; but, for three centuries, the descendants of the Abbaside, or Baghdad, Caliphs resided in Egypt, and asserted their claim to the spiritual power.

The founder of the dynasty of Ottoman Sultans was Uthman, the son of a tribe of Oghouz Turks, a powerful chief, whose descendant, Bazazet I, is said to have obtained the title of Sultan from one of the Abbaside Caliphs in Egypt, A.D. 1389. When Salim I, conquered Egypt (A.D. 1516), it is asserted that he obtained a transfer of the title of Caliph to himself from one of the successors of the old Baghdad Caliphs. It is, however, a mere assertion; for the title and office being elective, and not hereditary, it was not in the power of any Caliph to transfer it to another. Force of circumstances alone compelled the ruler of the Ottoman Empire to assume the position, and has induced his subjects to acquiesce in the usurpation.

Perception of God

The name of the Creator of the universe in the Quran is Allah, which is the title given to the Supreme Being by Muhammadans of every race and language. It is called the special, or essential, name of God, the *ism-i-zat;* all other names being considered merely *ism-i-sifat,* or attributes, of which there are said to be ninety-nine.' It is supposed to have been derived from the word *ilah,* a deity or god, with the addition of the definite article al, thus Al-ilah, The God. But Imam Hanifa says that, just as God's essence is unchangeable so is His name, and that Allah has always been the name of the great Eternal Being (vide Ghyas-ul-Loghat). It appears to be an Arabic rendering of the Hebrew 98 e.d., God. It is expressed in Persian and Hindustani by the word Khuda, derived from the Persian Khud (self); the self-existing one.

The Muhammadan belief in the existence of God is expressed in the first part of the well known confession of faith, La-ilaha Illallaho, "There is no deity but God," the interpretation of which occupies so prominent a place in all treatises of divinity.

The following is an interpretation of the Muslim belief in the existence and nature of God, by the famous scholastic divine, Imam Ghazzali, in his book entitled Al Maqsud-ul-asna, an extract from which Ockley has translated from Pococks Specimen Historiae Arabum:

"Praise be to God the Creator and Restorer of all things; who does whatsoever he pleases, who is Master of the glorious throne and mighty force, and directs his sincere servants into the right way and the straight path; who favoureth them, who have once borne testimony to the unity, by preserving their confessions from the darkness of doubt and hesitation; who directs them to follow his chosen apostle, upon whom be the blessing and peace of God; and to go after his most honourable companions, to whom he hath vouchsafed his assistance and direction which is revealed to them in his essence and operations by the excellencies of his attributes, to the knowledge whereof no man attains but he that hath been taught by hearing. To these, as touching his essence, he maketh known that he is one, and hath no partner; singular, without anything like him; uniform, having no contrary; separate, having no equal. He is ancient, having no first; eternal, having no beginning; remaining for ever, having no end; continuing to eternity, without any termination. He persists, without ceasing to be; remains without falling, and never did cease, nor ever shall cease to be described by glorious attributes, nor is subject to any decree so as to be determined by any precise limits or set times, but is the First and the Last, and is within and without.

He, glorified be his name, is not a body endued with form, nor a substance circumscribed with limits or determined by measure; neither does he resemble bodies, as they are capable of being measured or divided. Neither is he a substance, neither do substances exist in him; neither is he an accident, nor do accidents exist in him. Neither is he like to anything that exists, neither is anything like to him; nor is he determinate in quantity nor comprehended by bounds, nor circumscribed by the differences of situation, nor contained in the heavens. He sits upon the throne, after that manner which he himself hath described, and in that same sense which he himself means, which is a sitting far removed from any notion of contact, or resting upon, or local situation; but both the throne itself, and whatsoever is upon it, are sustained by the goodness of his power, and are subject to the grasp of his hand. But he is above the throne, and above all things, even to the utmost ends of the earth; but so above as at the same time not to be a whit nearer the throne and the heaven; since he is exalted by (infinite) degrees above the throne no less than he is exalted above the earth, and at the same time is near to everything that hath a being, nay, 'nearer to man than their jugular veins, and is witness to everything though his nearness is not like the nearness of bodies, as neither is his essence like the essence of bodies.

Neither both he exist in anything, neither doth anything exist in him; but he is too high to be contained in any place, and too holy to be determined by time; for he was before time and place were created, and is now after the same manner as he always was. He is also distinct from the creatures by his attributes, neither is there anything besides himself in his essence, nor is his essence in any other besides him. He is too holy to be subject to change, or any local motion; neither do any accidents dwell in him, nor any contingencies befall him; but he abides through all generations with his glorious attributes, free from all danger of dissolution. As to the attribute of perfection, he wants no addition of his perfection. As to being, he is known to exist by the apprehension of the understanding; and he is seen as he is by an ocular intuition, which will be vouchsafed out of his mercy and grace to the holy in the eternal mansion, completing their joy by the vision of his glorious presence.

He, praised be his name, is living, powerful, mighty, omnipotent, not liable to any defect or impotence; neither slumbering nor sleeping, nor being obnoxious to decay or death. To him belongs the kingdom, and the power, and the might. His is the dominion, and the excellency, and the creation, and the command thereof. The heavens are folded up in his right hand, and all creatures are couched within his grasp. His excellency consists in his creating and producing, and his unity in communicating existence and a beginning of being. He created men and their works, and measured out their maintenance and their determined times. Nothing that is possible can escape his grasp, nor can the vicissitudes of things elude his power. The effects of his might are innumerable, and the objects of his knowledge infinite.

He, praised be his name, knows all things that can be understood, and comprehends whatsoever comes to pass, from the extremities of the earth to the highest heavens. Even the weight of a pismire could not escape him either in earth in heaven; but he would perceive the creeping of the black pismire in the dark night upon the hard stone, and discern the motion of an atom in the open air. He knows what is secret and conceals it, and views the conceptions of the minds, and the motions of the thoughts, and the inmost recesses of secrets, by a knowledge ancient and eternal, that never ceased to be his attribute from eternal eternity, and not by any new knowledge, super added to his essence, either inhering or adventitious.

Allah's Will

He, praised be his name, doth will those things to be that are, and disposes of all accidents. Nothing passes in the empire, nor the kingdom, neither little nor much, nor small nor great, nor good nor evil, nor profitable nor hurtful, nor faith nor infidelity, nor knowledge nor ignorance, nor prosperity nor adversity, nor increase nor decrease, nor obedience nor rebellion, but by his determinate counsel and decree, and his definite sentence and will. Nor doth he wink of him that seeth, nor the subtlety of him that thinketh, exceed the bounds of his will; but it is he who gave all things their beginning; he is the creator and restorer, the sole operator of what he pleases; there is no reversing his decree nor delaying what he hath determined, nor is there any refuge to man from his rebellion against him, but only his help and mercy; nor hath any man any power to perform any duty towards him, but through his love and will.

Though men, genii, angels and devils, should conspire together either to put one single atom in motion, or cause it to cease its motion, without his will and approbation they would not be able to do it. His will subsists in his essence amongst the rest of his attributes, and was from eternity one of his eternal attributes, by which he wiled from eternity the existence of those things that he had decreed, which were produced in their proper reasons according to his eternal will, without any before or after, and in agreement both with his knowledge and will, and not by methodising of thoughts, nor waiting for a proper time, for which reason no one thing is in him a hindrance from another.

Allah's Hearing and Sight

And he, praised be his name, is hearing and seeing, and heareth and seeth. No audible object, how still soever, escapeth his hearing;

nor is any thing visible so small as to escape his sight; for distance is no hindrance to his hearing, nor darkness to his sight. He sees without pupil or eyelids, and hears without any passage or ear, even as he knoweth without a heart, and performs his actions without the assistance of any corporeal limb, and creates without any instrument, for his attributes (or properties) are not like those of men any more than his essence is like theirs.

Furthermore, he doth speak, command, forbid, promise, and threaten by an eternal, ancient word, subsisting in his essence. Neither is it like to the word of the creatures, nor doth it consist in a voice arising from the commotion of the air and the collision of bodies, nor letters which are separated by the joining together of the lips of the motion of the tongue. The Quran, the Law, the Gospel, and the Pslater, are books sent down by him to his apostles, and the Quran, indeed, is read with tongues, written in books, and kept in hearts; yet as subsisting in the essence of God, it doth not become liable to separation and division whilst it is transferred into the hearts and the papers. Thus Moses also heard the Word of God without voice or letter, even as the saints behold the essence of God without substance or accident. And that since these are his attributes, he liveth and knoweth, is powerful and willeth and operateth, and seeth and speaketh, by life and knowledge, and will and hearing, and sight and word, not by his simple essence.

He, praised be his name, exists after such a manner that nothing besides him hath any being but what is produced by his operation, and floweth from his justice after the best, most excellent, most perfect, and most just model. He is, moreover, wise in his works, and just in his decrees. But his justice is not to be compared with the justice of men. For a man may be supposed to act unjustly by invading the possession of another; but no injustice can be conceived of God, inasmuch as there is nothing that belongs to any other besides himself, so that wrong is not imputable to him as meddling with things not appertaining to him. All things, himself only excepted, genii, men, the devil, angels, heaven, earth, animals, plants, substance, accident, intelligible, sensible, were all created originally by him. He created them by his power out of mere privation, and brought them into light, when as yet they were nothing at all, but he alone existing from eternity, neither was there any other with him.

Now he created all things in the beginning for the manifestation of his power, and his will, and the confirmation of his word, which was true from all eternity. Not that he stood in need of them, nor wanted them; but he manifestly declared his glory in creating, and producing, and commanding, without being under any obligation, nor out of necessity. Loving kindness, and to show favour, and grace, and beneficence, belong to him; whereas it is in his power to pour forth upon men a variety of torments, and afflict them with various kinds of sorrows and diseases, which, if he were to do, his justice could not be arraigned, nor would he be chargeable with injustice. Yet he rewards those that worship him for their obedience on account of his promise and beneficence, not of their merit nor of necessity, since there is nothing which he can be tied to perform; nor can any injustice be supposed in him, nor can he be under any obligation to any person whatsoever. That his creatures, however, should be bound to serve him, ariseth from his having declared by the tongues of the prophets that it was due to him from them. The worship of him is not simply the dictate of the understanding, but he sent messengers to carry to men his commands, and promises, and threats, whose veracity he proved by manifest miracles, whereby men are obliged to give credit to them in those things that they relate."

Chapter 2

Rise of Islamic Civilization

Because of its comprehensive and integralistic approach—which is the demand of its unique Philosophy of Unity, the Holy Quran reconciles the elements of value in Rationalism and Empiricism, affirms the reality of both rational and the empirical (XXII:62; VI:73; etc.)—of course, in accordance with the status of each, demands belief in the Unseen (11:3) as well as in the Seen (111:190; etc.), i.e., in the supra-sensible as well as in the sensible, and synthesises the Ideational and the Sensate, projecting thereby a perfect and sound *Integralistic* or *Idealistic Culture.*

Literature

The Holy Quran came not to add one more to the list of the world's religions, or to merely correct certain notions taught by the different religions in respect of the *religious aspect* of human life; but—and that is extremely important for our notice—it came to impart a correct philosophy of *Culture* and, beyond that, to lay the foundations of a new *Civilisation.* The existence of socio-political dimension in the Holy Prophet Muhammad's spiritual struggle, in contrast to the other-worldly character of the spiritual struggle said to have been waged by Holy Prophet Jesus (Peace be on him!), was in response to the demands to the former's all-comprehending Message and Mission, whose range covered the entire area of human thought and behaviour: from the problems of the individual to the problems of the healthy growth of human civilisation.

And a new civilisation did come into existence—a balanced civilisation conceived in terms of the realisation of Piety, Truth, Justice, Love, Beauty, Wisdom and Service to Humanity, and based on the concept of integralistic or idealistic culture, as distinct from the pre-Quranic ideational and the modern sensate cultures, of the East and the West respectively—as already noticed. Just to give an idea of what type of civilisation emerged in history under the impact of Islam, we may give here only its briefest account, and that too qualified by the following considerations:

(i) Because of what we shall emphasise later about the intimate relation between the Islamic and the modern Western civilisation, we shall confine ourselves to that period wherein the Islamic civilisation matured in its different dimensions and we shall lay greater emphasis on its, what might be called, sensate aspects. Of course, their Islamic ethico-religious foundations as well as the concomitant high spiritual and moral tone of the Muslims in general—in spite of the deviations of certain members of the aristocracy—are unchallengeable.

(ii) We shall state the facts on the authority of a non-Muslim historian, Will Durante, who is one of the most recent writers on the subject, as also a devout Christian and fanatically anti-Islam— the latter qualification standing guarantee against any misgiving as to the authenticity of the account in respect of the merits of Islamic civilisation.

(iii) It is impossible to make the account in any degree comprehensive because of the extreme dearth of source-materials, as Will Durante himself admits:

"It is a pity that we know these three centuries (750-1050) of Arabic efflorescence so imperfectly. Thousands of Arabic manuscripts in science, literature, and philosophy, lie hidden in the libraries of the Muslim world; in Constantinople alone there are thirty mosque libraries whose wealth has been merely scratched; in Cairo, Damascus, Mosul, Baghdad, Delhi are great collections not even catalogued; an immense library in the Escorial near Madrid had hardly completed the listing of its Islamic manuscripts in science, literature, jurisprudence, and philosophy. What we know of Muslim thought in those centuries is a fragment of what survives; what survives is a fragment of what was produced; what appears in these pages is a morsel of a fraction of a fragment." *(The Age of Faith,* p. 257).

The Islamic Civilisation in its Age of Glory, Will Durante observes (The Age of Faith, pp. 179-343):

"In the Quran, are rules not only for manners and hygiene, marriage and divorce, and the treatment of children, slaves, and animals, but also for commerce and politics, interest and debts, contracts and wills, industry and finance, crime and punishment, war and peace. Muhammad did not disdain commerce....He threatened hell to lying or cheating merchants; denounced monopolists and speculators who 'keep back grain to sell at a high rate'; and bade the employer 'give the labourer his wage before his perspiration dries'. He prohibited the taking or giving of interest (ii, 275, iii, 130). No reformer ever more actively taxed the rich to help the poor. Every will was expected to leave something to the poor; if a man died intestate his natural heirs were directed to give a part of their inheritance to charity (iv, 8)....he improved the position of woman....

"Muhammad's ethic transcended the limits of the tribe...Distinction of rank or race, so strong among the tribes, was diminished by similarity of belief, 'If a negro slave is appointed to rule you, hear and obey him, though his head be like a dried grape'. It was a noble conception that made one people of diverse nations scattered over the continents.... Muhammad (taught)...."Let there be no violence in religion'. 'If they embrace Islam they are surely directed; but if they turn their backs, verily to the belongs preaching only'. 'Give a respite to the disbelievers. Deal thou gently with them'.....'Kill not the old man who cannot fight, nor young children, nor women'.....'Fight in the way of Allah against those who fight against you, but begin not hostilities. Allah loveth not aggressors'.

The Quran....gave to simple souls the simplest, least mystical, least ritualistic, of all creeds, free from idolatry and sacerdotalism. Its message raised the moral and cultural level of its followers, promoted social order and unity, inculcated hygiene, lessened superstition and cruelty, bettered the condition of slaves, lifted the lowly to dignity and Pride, and produced among Muslims (barring the revels of some caliphs) a degree of sobriety and temperance unequalled elsewhere in the white man's world. It gave men an uncomplaining acceptance of the hardships and limitations of life, and at the same time stimulated them to the most astonishing expansion in history.

"Civilisation is a union of soil and soul—the resources of the earth transformed by the desire and discipline of men....All these were busy in Islam....The orange tree the Arabs introduced it to Syria, Asia Minor, Palestine, Egypt, and Spain, from which countries it pervaded southern Europe. The cultivation of sugar-cane and the refining of sugar were likewise spread by the Arabs....and were brought by Crusaders to their European states. Cotton was first cultivated in Europe by the Arabs. These achievements on lands largely arid were made possible by organized irrigation; here the caliphs made an exception to their principle of leaving the economy to free enterprise; the government directed and financed the maintenance of the greater canals.

".....Under Muslim rule western Asia attained a pitch of industrial and commercial prosperity unmatched by western Europe before the sixteenth century.

"The state left industry and commerce free, and aided it with a relatively stable currency. Ibn Hawqal (c. 975) describes a kind of promissory note....from the Arabic work *sakk* for this form of credit is derived our work *check*. Investors shared in financing commercial voyages or caravans..... Monopolies were illegal.....

"....In general the Muslim seems to have excelled the Christian in commercial morality, fidelity to his word, and loyalty to treaties signed....normally the Muslim was the soul of courtesy, humanity, and tolerance...In general Muslim society was one of excellent manners....

"If we may believe the traditions, *Muhammad, unlike most religious reformers, admired and urged the pursuit of knowledge*.....Education began as soon as the child could speak.....At the age of six some slave children, some girls, and nearly all boys except the rich (who had private tutors) entered an elementary school....Tuition was normally free....Elementary education aimed to form character, secondary education to transmit knowledge....Tuition in these colleges was free, and in some cases government or philanthropy paid both the salaries of the professors and the expenses of the students... .students would travel from one end of the Muslim world to another to meet the mind of a famous teacher....When a visitor entered a Muslim city he took it for granted that he could hear a scholarly lecture at the principal mosque at almost any hour of the day.

"....The first paper-manufacturing plant in Islam was opened at Baghdad in 794 by al-Fadl, son of Harun's vizier. The crate was brought by the Arabs to Sicily and Spain, and thence passed into Italy and France....The invention facilitated the making of books wherever it went. Yaqubi tells us that in his time (891) Baghdad had over a hundred booksellers.

"Most mosques had libraries, and some cities had public libraries of considerable content and generous accessibility. About 950 Mosul had a library, established by private philanthropy, where students were supplied with paper as well as books. Ten large catalogues were required to list the volumes in the public library at Rayy. Basra's library gave stipends to scholars working in it....When Baghdad was destroyed by the Mongols it had thirty-six public libraries. Private libraries were numberless; it was a fashion among the rich to have an ample collection of books....princes like Sahib ibn Abbas in the tenth century might own as many books as could then be found in all the libraries of Europe combined...in a thousand mosques from Cordova to Samark and scholars were as numerous as pillars, and made the cloisters tremble with their eloquence; the roads of the realm were disturbed by innumerable geographers, historians, and theologians seeking knowledge and wisdom... .the conquerors showed such tolerance that of the poets, scientists, and philosophers who now made Arabic the most learned and literary tongue in the world only a small minority were of Arab blood.

"....Ibn Qutaiba (828-89) was one of many Muslims, who attempted to write a *history of the world*....Muhammad al-Nadim produced in 987 an *Index of the Sciences (Fihnstal- 'ulum),* a bibliography of all books in Arabic, original or translated, on any branch of knowledge.... we may estimate the wealth of Muslim literature in his time by noting that not one in a thousand of the volumes that he named is known to exist today.

"....Abul-Hasan Ali al-Masudi, an Arab of Baghdad, travelled.....He gathered his gleanings into a thirty-volume encyclopaedia....Al-Masudi survived omnivorously the geography, biology, history, customs, religion, science, philosophy, and literature of all lands from China to France...he summarized his views on science, history, and philosophy in a *Book of Information,* in which he suggested an evolution 'from mineral to plant, from plant to animal, and from animal to man'.

"Algebra....owes its name to the Arabs, who extensively developed this detective science....Al-Khwarizmi contributed effectively to five sciences............ he wrote on the Hindu numerals; compiled astronomical tables which, as revised in Muslim Spain, were for centuries standard among astronomers from Cordova to Changan; formulated the oldest trigonometrical tables known; collaborated with sixty-nine other scholars in drawing up for al-Mamun a geographical encyclopaedia; and in his *Calculation of Integration and Equation* gave analytical and geometrical solutions of quadratic equations. *This work,* now lost in its Arabic form, *was translated by Gerard of Cremona in the twelfth century, was used as a principal text in European universities until the sixteenth century, and introduced to the West the word algebra (al-Jabr*—'restitution', 'completion'. (Thabit ibn Qurra (826-901).... achieved fame in astronomy and medicine, and became the greatest of Muslim geometers....

"The Caliph al-Mamun engaged a staff of astronomers to make observations and records, to test the findings of Ptolemy, and to *study the spots on the sun.* Taking for granted the sphericity of the earth, they measured a terrestrial degree by simultaneously taking the position of the sun from both Palmyra and the plain Sinjr; their measurement gave 56-2/ 3 miles—half a mile more than our present calculation; and from their results they *estimated the earth's circumference* to approximate 20,000 miles. *These astronomers proceeded on completely scientific principles: they accepted nothing as true which was not confirmed by experience or experiment.* One of them, Abu'l-Farghani, of Transoxiana, wrote (c. 860) an astronomical text which remained in authority in Europe and Western Asia for 700 years. Even more renowned was al-Battani; his astronomical observations, continued for forty-one years, were remarkable for their range and accuracy; he determined many astronomical coefficients with *remarkable approximation to modern calculations*—the precession of the equinoxes at 54.5" a year, and the inclination of the ecliptic at 23° 55'. Working under the patronage of the early Buwayhid ruler of Baghdad, *Abu 7 Wafa....*discovered the third *lunar vartidation 600 years before Tycho Brahe. Costly instruments were built for Muslim astronomers: not only astrolabes and armillary spheres,* known to the Greeks, but quadrants with a radius of thirty feet, and sextants with a radius of eighty. The astrolabe, much improved by the Muslims, reached Europe in the tenth century, and was *widely used by mariners till the seventeenth.* The Arabs designed and constructed it with aesthetic passion, making it at once an instrument of science and a work of art.

"Even more important than the charting of the skies was mapping of the earth.... Suleiman al-Tajir—i.e., the merchant—about 840 carried his wares to the Far East; an anonymous author (851) wrote a narrative of Suleiman's journey; this oldest Arabic account of China antedated Marco Polo's *Travels* by 425 years. In the same century Ibn Khordadhbeh wrote a description of India, Ceylon, the East Indies, and China, apparently from direct observation; and Ibn Hawqal described India and Africa. Ahmad al-Yaqubi, of Armenia and Khurasan, wrote in 891 a *Book of the Countries,* giving a reliable account of Islamic provinces and cities, and of many foreign states. Muhammad al-Muqaddasi visited all the lands of Islam except Spain, suffered countless vicissitudes, and in 985 wrote his *Description of the Muslim Empire*—the greatest work of Arabic geography before al-Biruni's *India.*

"Abu al-Rayhan Muhammad ibn Ahmad al-Biruni (973-1048) shows the Muslim scholar at his best. Philosopher, historian, traveller, geographer, linguist, mathematician, astronomer, poet, and physicist—and doing major and original work in all these fields....His first major work (c. 1000) was a highly technical treatise—*Vestiges of the Past... .his attitude was that of the objective scholar, assiduous in research, critical in the scrutiny of traditions and texts* (including the Gospels), *precise and conscientious in statement,* frequently admitting his ignorance, and promising to pursue his inquiries till the truth should emerge. In the preface to the Vestiges he wrote like Frances Bacon: 'We must clear our minds....from all cause that blind people to the truth—old custom, party spirit, personal rivalry of passion, the desire for influence'....In 1030 he published his masterpiece, *History of India....His* interest extended to nearly all the sciences. He gave the best medieval account of the Hindu numerals. He wrote treatise on the astrolabe, the planisphere, the armillary sphere; and formulated astronomical tables for Sultan Masud. He took it for granted that the earth is round, noted 'the attraction of all things towards the centre of the earth', and remarked that astronomic data can be explained as well by supposing that the earth turns daily on its axis and annually around the sun, as by the reverse hypothesis. He speculated on the possibility that the *Indus valley had been once the bottom of a sea.* He composed an extensive lapidary, describing a great number of stones and metals from the natural, commercial and medical points of view. He determined the specific gravity of eighteen precious stones, and laid down the principle that the specific gravity of an object corresponds to the volume of water it displaces. He found a method of calculating, without taborious additions, the result of the repeated doubling of a number... .He contributed to geometry the solution of theorems that thereafter bore his name. He composed an encyclopaedia of astronomy, a treatise on geography, and an epitome of astronomy, astrology, and mathematics. He explained the workings of natural springs and artesian wells by the *hydrostatic principle* of communicating vessels.

"Chemistry as a science was almost created by the Muslims... .the Sarcinas introduced precise observation, controlled experiment, and careful records. They invented and named the alembic (al-anbiq), chemical analysed innumerable substances, composed lapidaries, distinguished alkalis and acids, investigated their affinities, studies and manufactured hundreds of drugs.... 'The most famous of the alchemists was Jabir Ibn Hayyan (702-65), known to Europe as Gebir....'The hundred or more works attributed to him.....were translated into Latin, and strongly stimulated the development of European chemistry....

"....(Muslims) developed in alchemy that experimental method which is the greatest pride and tool of the modern mind. When Roger Bacon proclaimed that method to Europe, five hundred years after Jabir, he owned his illumination to the Moors of Spain, whose light had come from the Muslim East.

"The remains of Muslim biology in this period are scant. Abu Hanifa al-Dinawari (815-95) wrote a *Book of Plants*... .adding many plants to pharmacology. Muhammadan botanists knew how to produce new fruits by grafting....Othman Amr al-Jahiz (d. 869) propounded *a theory of evolution like al-Masudi's : life had climbed from mineral to plant, from plant to animal, from animal to man.*' The mystic poet Jalal ud-Din (Rumi) accepted the theory....

".....The Muslims established the first apothecary shops and dispensaries, founded the first medieval school of pharmacy, and wrote great treatises on pharmacology. Muslim physicians were enthusiastic advocates of the bath, especially in fevers and in the form of the steam bath. Their directions for the treatment of smallpox and measles could scarcely be bettered today. Anaesthesia by inhalation was practised in some surgical operations; hashish and other drugs were used to induce deep sleep....Medical instruction was given chiefly at the hospitals. No man could legally practice medicine without passing an examination and receiving a state diploma; druggists, barbers, and orthopedists were likewise subject to state regulation and inspection. The physician-vizier Ali ibn Isa organized a staff of doctor to go from place to place to tend the sick (931); certain physicians made daily visits to jails; there was an especially human treatment of the insane.

".....Ali ibn Isa, greatest of Muslim oculists, whose Manual for Oculists was used as *a text in Europe till the eighteenth century.*

"The outstanding figure in this human dynasty of healers was Abu Bekr Muhammad al-Razi (844-926), famous in Europe as Rhazes he wrote some 131 books, half of them on medicine, most of them lost. His *Kitab al-Hawi* (*Comprehensive Book*) covered in twenty volume every branch of medicine. Translated into Latin as *Liber continues,* it was probably *the most highly respected and frequently used medical textbook in the white world for several centuries;* it was one of the nine books that composed the whole library of the medical faculty at the University of Paris in 1395. His *Treatise on Smallpox and Measles* was a masterpiece of direct observation and clinical analysis; it was the first *accurate study of infectious diseases,* the first effort to distinguish the two ailments. We may judge its influence and repute by the forty English editions printed between 1498 and 1866. The most famous of al-Razi's works was a ten-volume survey of medicine, the *Kitab al-Mansuri....* Gerard of Cremona translated it into Latin; the ninth volume of this translation, the *Nonus Almansoris was a popular text in Europe till the sixteenth century.*

".....Islam knew its greatest philosopher and most famous physician as Abu Ali al-Husein ibn Sina (980-1037)....he found time to write a hundred books, covering nearly every field of science and philosophy....He translated Euclid, made astronomical observations, and devised an instrument like our vernier. He *made original studies of motion, force, vacuum, light, heat and specific gravity. His treatise on minerals was a main source of European geology until the thirteenth century. His remark on the formation of mountains is a model of clarity:* 'Mountains may be due to two different causes. Either they result from upheavals of the earth's crust, such as might occur in violent earthquake; or they are the effect of water, which, cutting for itself a new route, has denuded the valleys. The strata are of different kinds, some soft, some hard; the winds and waters disintegrate the first kind, but leave the other intact. It would require a long period of time for all such changes to be accomplished... .but that water has been the main cause of these effects is proved by the *existence of fossil remains of acquatic animals on many mountains'.*

"Two gigantic production contain Avicenna's teaching: the *Kitab al-Shifa....an* eighteen-volume encyclopaedia of mathematics, physics, metaphysics, theology, economics, politics, and music; and the *Qanun-fi-l-Tibb,* or *Canon of Medicine,* a gigantic survey of physiology, hygiene, therapy, and pharmacology, with sundry excursions into philosophy. .He conceives medicine as the art of removing an impediment to the normal functioning of nature....The *Qanun,* translated into Latin in the twelfth century, *dethroned al-Razi, and even Galen, as the chief text in European medical schools; it held its place as required reading in the universities of Montpelier and Louvain till the middle of the seventeenth century.*

"....Avicenna....His influence was immence: it reached out to Spain to mold Averroes and Malmonides, and into Latin Christendom to help the great Scholastics; it is astonishing how much of Albertus Magnus and Thomas Equines goes back to Avicenna. Roger Bacon called him 'the chief authority in philosophy after Aristotle'; and Equines was not merely practising his customary courtesy in speaking of him with as much respect as of Plato.

"....Abu Yusuf lbn Isaq al-Kindi was born in Kufa about 803.... studying everything, writing 265 treatises about everything— arithmetic, geometry, astronomy, meteorology, geography, physics, politics, music, medicine, philosophy he struggled to reduce health, medicine, and music to mathematical relations. *He studied the tides, sought the laws that determine the speed of a falling body, and investigated the phenomena of light* in a book on Optics which *influenced Roger Bacon.*

"Thirtynine works of al-Farabi survive....One work....strikes us with its original force: *Al-Medina al-Fadila—The Ideal City*....the only right is might. Al-Farabi counters this view with an appeal to his fellow men to build a society not upon envy, power, and strife, but upon reason, devotion and love.

"....From the Alhambra in Spain to the Taj Mahal in India, Islamic art overrode all limits of place and time, laughed at distinctions of race and blood, developed a unique and yet varied character, and expressed the human spirit with a profuse delicacy never surpassed.

"Muslim architecture, like most architecture in the *Age of Faith,* was almost entirely religious... Nevertheless, though the remains are scant, we hear of bridges, aqueducts, fountains, reservoirs, public baths, fortresses, and turreted walls built by engineer-architects... The Crusaders found excellent military architecture at Aleppo, Baalbek, and elsewhere in the Islamic East, learned there the uses of machicolated walls, and took from their foes many an idea for their own incomparable castles and forts. The Alcazar at Seville and the Alhambra at Granada were fortresses and palaces combined.

"We probably own this splendour of ornament to the Semitic prohibition of human or animal forms in art: as if in compensation, the Muslim artist invented or adopted an overflowing abundance of nonrepresentational forms. He sought an outlet first in geometrical figures— line, angle, square, cube, polygon, cone, spiral, ellipse, circle, sphere; he repeated these in a hundred combinations, and developed them into swirls, guilloches, reticulations, *entralacs,* and stars; passing to floral forms, he designed, in many materials, wreaths, vines, or rosettes of lotus, acanthus, or palm tendrils or leaves; in the tenth century he merged all these in the arabesque; and to them all, as a unique and major ornament, he added the Arabic script.

"The brightest name of Muslim Egyptian science is that of Muhammad ibn al-Haitham, known to medieval Europe as Alhazen.... We know that al-Haitham chiefly by his *Kitab al-Manazir,* or *Book of Optics;* of all medieval productions this is probably the most thoroughly scientific in its method and thought. *Al-Haitham studied the refraction of light though transparent mediums like air and water and came so close to discovering the magnifying lens that roger Bacon, Witelo, and other Europeans three centuries later based upon his work their own advances toward the microscope and the telescope.* He rejected the theory of Euclid and Ptolemy that vision results from a ray leaving the eye and reaching the object; rather 'the form of the perceived object passes into the eye, and is transmitted there by the transparent body'—the lens.

He remarked the effect of the atmosphere in increasing the apparent size of sun or moon when near the horizon; showed that through atmospheric refraction the light of the sun reaches us even when the sun is as much as nineteen degrees below the horizon; and on this basis he *calculated the height of the atmosphere* at ten miles. He analysed the correlation between the weight and the density of the atmosphere, and the effect of atmospheric density upon the weight of objects. He studied with complex mathematical formulas the action of light on spherical or parabolic mirrors, and through the burning glass. He observed the half-moon shape of the image, during eclipses, on the wall opposite a small hole made in the window shutters; *this is the first known mention of the camera obscure, or dark chamber, on which all photography depends. We could hardly exaggerate the influence of al-Haitham on European science. Without him Roger Bacon might never have been heard of; Bacon* quotes him or refers to him at almost every step in that part of the *Opusmalius* which deals with optics' and Part VI rests almost entirely on the findings of the Cairene physicist *As late as Kepler and Leonardo European studies of light were based upon al-Haitham 's work.*

"'Never was Andalusia so mildly, justly, and wisely governed as by her Arab conquerors'. It is the judgement of a great Christian Orientalist, whose enthusiasm may require some discounting of his praise; but after due deduction his verdict stands... .al-Maqqari gives a *hundred examples of the justice, liberality, and refinement of the Umayyad rulers of Spain.* They were certainly an improvement upon the illiberal Visigothic regime that had preceded them. Their *management of public affairs was the most competent* in the Western world of that age. *Laws were rational and humane, and were administered by a well-organized judiciary. For the most part the conquered in their internal affairs, were governed by their own laws and their own officials. Town were well policed; markets, weights and measures were effectively supervised. A regular census recorded population and property. Taxation was reasonable compared with the*

imposts of Rome or Byzantium. The revenues of the Cordovan caliphate under Abd-er-Rahman III reached 12,045,000 gold dinars ($57,213,750)—*probably more than the united governmental revenues of Latin Christendom; but these receipts were due not so much to high taxes as to well-governed and progressive agriculture, industry, and trade.*

"....The Arab for the most part left the actual work of agriculture to the conquered; however, they used the latest manuals of agronomy, and under their direction agricultural science developed in Spain far in advance of Christian Europe.

"....Christians and Muslims intermarried freely; now and then they joined in celebrating a Christian or Muslim holiday, or used the same building as church and mosque....Clerics and laymen from Christian Europe came in safety and freedom to Cordova, Toledo, or Seville as students, visitors, or travellers.

"....Cordova....*extraordinary general prosperity....* streets were paved, had raised side walks, and were lighted at night; one could travel for ten miles by the light of streets lamps, and along an uninterrupted series of buildings....was *the focus and summit of Spanish intellectual life, though Toledo. Granada, and Seville shared actively in the mental exhilaration of the time.* Muslim historians picture the Moorish cities as beehives of poets, scholars, jurists, physicians, and scientists; al-Maqqari fills sixty pages with their names. Primary schools were numerous, but charged tuition; Hakam II added twenty-seven schools for the free instruction of the poor. Girls as well as boys went to school; several Moorish ladies became prominent in literature or art. Higher education was provided by independent lecturers in the mosques; their courses constituted the loosely organized University of Cordova, which in the tenth and eleventh centuries was second in renown only to similar institutions in Cairo and Baghdad. Colleges were established also at Granada, Toledo, Seville, Murcia, Almeria, Valencia, Cadiz. The technique of paper-making was brought in from Baghdad, and books increased and multiplied. Muslim Spain had seventy libraries, rich men displayed their Morocco bindings, and bibliophiles collected rare or beautifully illuminated books........ *Scholars were held in awesome repute in* Muslim Spain, and were consulted in simple faith that learning and wisdom are one.

".....Abu Muhammad Ali ibn Hazm (994-1064), besides serving as vizier to the last Umayyads, was a theologian and historian of great erudition. His *Book of Religions and Sects,* discussing Judaism, Zoroastrianism, Christianity, and the principal varieties of

Muhammedanism is *one of the world's earliest essays in comparative religion... Maslama* ibn Ahmad (d. 1007), of Madrid and Cordova, adapted the astronomic tables of al-Khwarizmi to Spain.....*Ibrahim al-Zarqali* (c. 1029-87) *of Toledo made an international name by improving astronomical instruments; Copernicus quoted his treatise on the astrolabe;* his astronomical observations were the best of his age, and *enabled him to prove for the first time the motion of the solar apogee with reference to the stars;* his 'Toledan Tables' of planetary movements were used throughout Europe. *Abul Qasim al-Zahrawi* (936-1013), physician to Abd-er-Rahman III, was honoured in Christendom as Abulcasis; he stands at the top of Muslim surgeons; his medical encyclopaedia, *al-Tasrif* included three books on surgery which, translated into Latin, *became the standard text of surgery for many centuries. Cordova was in this period the favourite resort of Europeans for surgical operations.*

"....*Cairo, Alexandria, Jerusalem, Baalbek, Aleppo, Damascus, Mosul, Emesa, Tus, Nishapur, and many other cities boasted of colleges; Baghdad alone had thirty in* 1064. A year later Nizam ul-Mulk added another: the Nizamiya; in 1234 the Caliph Mustansir founded still another, which in size, architecture, and equipment surpassed all the rest; one traveller called it the most beautiful building in the city. It contained four distinct law schools, in which qualified students received free tuition, food, and medical care, and a monthly gold dinar for other expenses; it contained a hospital, a bathhouse, and a library freely open to students and staff. Women probably attended college in some cases, for we hear *of a Shaikha*—a lady professor—whose lectures....drew large audiences (c. 1178)... .Muhammad al-Shahrastani, in a *Book of Religions and Sects* (1128) analysed the leading faiths and philosophies of the world, and summarized their history; *no contemporary Christian could have written so learned and impartial a work.*

"Europe knows Persian Poetry chiefly through Omar Khayyam... .*His Algebra,* translated into French in 1857, *made significant advances* both on al-Khwarizmi and on the Greeks; its partial solution of cubic equations has been judged 'perhaps the very highest peak of medieval mathematics'. Another of his works on algebra (a manuscript in the Leyden Library) studied critically the postulates and definitions of Euclid. In 1074 the Sultan Malik Shah commissioned him and others to reform the Persian calendar. The outcome was a calendar that required a day's correction every 3770 years—slightly more accurate than ours....

"Jalal-ud-Din Rumi (1201-73)....wrote several hundred poems. The shorter ones, collected in his *Divan* or *Book of Odes,* are marked by such depth of feeling, sincerity, and richness, yet naturalness, of imagery as place them *at the top of all religious poetry composed since the Psalms.* Jalal's main work, the *Mathnawi-i-Ma'nawi* (Spiritual Couplets), is a....religious epic outweighing in bulk all the legacy of 'Homer'.

"The Muslims continued, in this period (1057-1258), *their unchallenged ascendancy in science.* In mathematics the most signal advances were made in Morocco and Azerbaijan; we see here again the range of Islamic civilization. In 1229 Hasan al-Marraqushi (i.e., of Marraqesh) published tables of sines for each degree, and tables of versed sines, arc sines, and arc cotangents. A generation later Nasir ul-Din al-Tusi (i.e., of Tus) issued the first treatise in which trigonometry was considered as an independent science rather than an appendage to astronomy his *Kitab shakl al-qatta* remained without a rival in its field until the *De Triangulis* of Regiomontanus two centuries later. *Perhaps Chinese trigonometry,* which appears in the second half of the thirteenth century, *was of Arabic origin.*

"The outstanding work of physical science in this age was the *Kitab Mizanal-hikmah*....written about 1122 by....Abu'l Fath al-Khuzini. It gave a history of physics, *formulated the laws of the lever,* compiled tables of specific gravity for many liquids and solids, and *proposed a theory of gravitation as a universal force drawing all things towards the centre of the earth.* Water wheels....were improved by the Muslims; the Crusaders....introduced them into Germany.

"In 1081 Ibrahim al-Sahdi of Valencia constructed the oldest known celestial globe, a brass sphere 209 millimetres (81.5 inches) in diameter; upon its surface, in forty-seven constellations, were engraved 1015 stars in their respective magnitudes. *The Giralda of Seville* (1190) *was an observatory as well as a minaret; there Jabir ibn Aflah made the observations* for his *Islah al-Majisti,* or *Correction of the Almagest* (1240). The same reaction against Ptolemaic astronomy marked the works of Abu Ishaq al-Bitruji (Alpetraglus) of Cordova, who *paved the way for Copernicus* by destructively criticizing the theory of epicycles and eccentrics through which Ptolemy had sought to explain the path and motions of the stars.

"The age produced two geographers of universal medieval renown. Abu Abdullah Muhammad al-Idrisi was born at Ceuta (1100), studied at Cordova, and wrote in Palermo, at the behest of King Roger II of Sicily, his *Kitab al-Rujari (Roger's Book).* It divided the earth into seven climatic zones, and each zone into ten parts; each of the seventy parts was illustrated by a detailed map; these maps were the *crowning achievement of medieval cartography, unprecedented* in fullness, accuracy, and scope. *Al-Idrisi, like most Muslim scientists, took for granted the sphericity of the earth.* Rivalling him for the honour of being the greatest medieval geographer was Abu Abdullah Yaqut (1179-1229)....he completed his *Mu'jam al-Buldan* (1228)—a *vast geographical encyclopaedia* which summed up nearly all medieval knowledge of the globe. Yaqut included almost everything—astronomy, physics, archaeology, ethnography, history, giving the *coordinates of the cities* and the lives and works of their famous men. Seldom has any man so loved the earth.

"Botany, almost forgotten since Theophrastus, revived with the Moslems of this age. Al-Idrisi wrote a herbal, but stressed the botanical rather than merely the medicinal interest of 360 plants. Abu'l Abbas of Seville (1216) earned the surname of al-Nabati, the botanist, by his studies of Plant life from the Atlantic to the Red Sea. *Abu Muhammad ibn Baitar of Malago* (1190-1248) *gathered all Islamic botany into a vast work of extraordinary erudition, which remained the standard botanical authority till the sixteenth century,* and marked him as the greatest botanist and pharmacist of the Middle Ages. *Ibn al-Awan of Seville (1190) won a like pre-eminence in agronomy;* his *Kitab al-Falaha (Book of the Peasant)* analysed soils and manures, described the cultivation of 585 plants and fifty fruit trees, explained methods of grafting, and discussed the symptoms and cures of plant diseases. This was the *most complete treatment of agricultural science* in the whole medieval period.

"In this as in the preceding age the Muslims produced the leading physicians of Asia, Africa, and Europe. They excelled especially in opthalmology....Operations for cataract were numerous. Caliphate ibn abi-Mahasin of Aleppo (1256) was so confident of his skill that he operated for cataract on a one-eyed man. Ibn Baitar's *Kitab al-jami'* made medicinal-botanical history; it listed 1400 plants, foods, and drugs, 300 of them new; analysed their chemical constitution and healing power; and added acute observations on their use in therapy. But the greatest name in this acme of Muslim medicine is Abu Marwan ibn Zuhr (1091-1162) of Seville, known to the European medical world as Avenzoar. He was the third in six generations of famous physicians, all of one family line, and each at the top of his profession. His *Kitab al-Tasir,* or *Book of Simplification of Therapeutics and Diet,* was written at the request of his friend Averroes, who (himself the greatest philosopher of the age) considered him the

greatest physician since Galen. Ibn Zuhr's forte was clinical description; he left classical analyses of mediastinal tumours, pericarditis, intestinal tuberculous, and pharyngeal paralysis. Translation of the *Tasir* into Hebrew and Latin *deeply influenced European medicine.*

"*Islam led the world also in the equipment and competence of its hospitals.* One founded by Nur-ud-din at Damascus in 1160 gave free treatment and drugs during three centuries: for 267 years, we are told, its fires were never extinguished. Ibn Jubayr, coming to Baghdad in 1184, marvelled at the great *Bimaristan Adadi,* a hospital rising like some royal palace along the bank of the Tigrish; here food and drugs were given to the patients without charge. In Cairo, in 1285, Sultan Qalun began the *Maristan al-Mansur,* the greatest hospital of the Middle Ages. Within a spacious quadrangular enclosure four buildings rose around a courtyard adorned with arcades and cooled with fountains and brooks. There were separate wards for diverse diseases and for convalescents; laboratories, a dispensary, outpatient clinics, diet kitchens, baths, a library, a chapel, a lecture hall, and particularly pleasant accommodation for the insane. Treatment was given gratis to men and women, rich and poor, slave and free' and a sum of money was disbursed to each convalescent on his departure, so that he need not at once return to work. The sleepless were provided with soft music, professional storytellers, and perhaps books of history. *Asylums for the care of the insane existed in all the major cities of Islam.*

"....Muhammedanism produced its greatest theologian, the Augustine and the *Kant of Islam.* Abu Hamid, *al-Ghazali* was born at Tus in 1058....wrote his most influential book—*Tahafut al-Filasifa (The Destruction of Philosophy).* All the arts of reason were turned against reason. By a 'transcendental dialectic' as subtle as Kant's.... *seven centuries before Hume, al-Ghazali reduced reason to the principle of causality, and causality to mere sequence....In* his *Ihya Ulum al-Din (Revival of the Sciences of Religion)* he expounded and defended his renovated orthodoxy with all the eloquence and fervour of his prime; never in Islam the sceptics and the philosophers encountered to vigorous a foe....

"Abu Bakr (Europe so Abubacer) ibn Tufail (1107-1185)....found time to write, among more technical works, the most remarkable philosophical romance in medieval literature *(Hayy ibn Yaqzan).* It took its title from ibn Sina, and (through Ockley's English translation in 1708) *may have suggested Robinson Crusoe to Defoe.*

"....Known to Islam as *Abu al-Walid Muhammad ibn Rushd* (1126-98), and to medieval Europe as Averroes—the most influential figure in Islamic Philosophy.....In 1169 Averroes was appointed chief justice of Seville; in 1172 of Cordova....His work in medicine has been almost forgotten in his fame as a philosopher; he was, however, 'one of the greatest physicians of his time', *the first to explain the function of the retina,* and to recognize that an attack of smallpox confers subsequent immunity. *His encyclopaedia of medicine (Kitab al-Kulliyat fil Tibb),* translated into Latin, *was widely used as a text in Christian universities...* he added several works of his own on logic, physics, psychology, metaphysics, theology, law, astronomy and grammar....*Malmonides owed in Averroes' steps* in seeking to reconcile religion and philosophy.

In Christendom the Commentaries (of Averroes), translated into Latin from Hebrew, fed the heresies of Siger de Brabant, and the rationalism of the School of Padua, and the threatened the foundations of Christian belief. *St. Thomas Equines* wrote his *Summae* to stem this Averroistic tide; but he *followed Averroes* in the method of his Commentaries, in divers interpretations of Aristotle....*Roger Bacon marked Averroes next to Aristotle* and Avicenna, and added....' The philosophy of Averroes today (c. 1270) obtains the unanimous suffrage of wise men. *"The influence of Islam on Europe was varied and immense."* (All italics, present writer's).

The present civilisation is, in respect of its merits, the continuation of the Islamic civilisation, with the difference that theocentricism, integralism and comprehensiveness have dropped off under the stress of certain well-known historical circumstances, culminating in its transformation into a purely sensate civilisation. However, its tragic inadequacy and diseased condition is now being taken notice of by all sane-thinking Westerners, together with the necessity of adopting the Islamic philosophy of civilisation for restoring the balanced accommodation of all the values and thereby reverting to the original Islamic civilisation from which it sprang up. The thick curtain of hatred against Islam, nurtured assiduously for centuries by a scheming priesthood, is the only obstacle. But the goodness of human nature is bound to win the day, and the yearnings of the human soul for Truth and Beauty and Justice are bound to attain realisation. The light of reality has already begun to shine forth, as manifested in the following considered judgement of Prof. H.A.R. Gibb, the famous British orientalist:

> *"....In its foundations we have seen that Islam belongs to and is an integral part of the larger Western society. It is the complement and counterbalance to European*

> *civilisation, nourished at the same springs, breathing the same air. In the broadest aspect of history, what is now happening between Europe and Islam is the reintegration of western civilisation, artificially sundered at the Renaissance and now reasserting its unity with overwhelming force. The student of history, though fearfully conscious of the pitfalls of analogy, cannot help recalling two earlier moments in this secular process of creative interaction between the two halves of the western world. It was the glory and the greatness of the Roman Empire that it united them under its imperium and that from that unity were born the spiritual forces which have governed the course of Western history ever since. Halfway between that age and ours occurred the first great intellectual adventure of Islam, when it absorbed the heritage of Hellenism and brought it to a new flowering, the seeds from which contributed to the Renaissance in Europe.*

"The process could not end there. It is going on before our very eyes, on a wider and vaster scale, though the contrast offered by the Islamic world as a whole to the amazing technical progress of Europe may still blind us to it; and it may be that the sequel will be the same, that we must wait upon the Islamic society to restore the balance of Western civilisation upset by the one sided nature of that progress... .At all events Islam stands side by side with Europe in distinction from the true Oriental societies of India and the Far East....for the fullest development of its cultural life, particularly of its spiritual life, Europe cannot do without the forces and capacities which lie within Islamic society

"Within the Western world Islam still maintains the balance between exaggerated opposites. Opposed equally to the anarchy of European nationalism and the regimentation of Russian communism, it has not yet succumbed to that obsession with the economic side of life which is characteristic of present-day Europe and present-day Russia alike.

Its social ethic has been admirably summed up by Professor Massignon: 'Islam has the merit of standing for a very equalitarian conception of the contribution of each citizen by the tithe to the resources of the community; it is hostile to unrestricted exchange, to banking capital, to state loans, to indirect taxes on objects of prime necessity, but it holds to the rights of the father and the husband, to private property, and to commercial capital. Here again it occupies an intermediate position between the doctrines of bourgeois capitalism and Bolshevist communism'.

"But Islam has a still further service to render to the cause of humanity : It stands after all nearer to the real East than Europe does, and it possesses a magnificent tradition of inter-racial understanding cooperation. No other society has such a record of success in uniting in an equality of status, of opportunity, and of endeavour so many and so various races of mankind....*Islam has still the power to reconcile apparently irreconcilable elements of race and tradition. If ever the opposition of the great societies of East and West is to be replaced by cooperation, the mediation of Islam is an indispensable condition It its hands lies very largely the solution of the problem with which Europe is faced in its relation with the East.*

If they unite, the hope of a peaceful issue is immeasurably enhanced. But if Europe, by rejecting the cooperation of Islam, throws it into arms of its rivals, the issue can only be disastrous for both."

Besides the above judgement of H.A.R. Gibb, the verdict of Arnold J. Toynbee, the fanatical crusader against Islam and zealous upholder of Christian cause, is also worthy of note. He says *(Civilisation on Trial,* London, 1957; pp. 87, 88, 205-209):

> *"What value are we to place on Islam ourselves?....Islam's creative gift to mankind is monotheism and we surely dare not throw this gift away...* .Islam remains, with a mighty spiritual mission still to carry out....(*Italics, present writer's).*
>
> *"Two conspicuous source of danger—one psychological and the other material—in the present relations of this cosmopolitan proletariat (—i.e., westernised humanity—) with the dominant element in our modem Western society are race consciousness and alcohol; and in the struggle with each of these evils the Islamic spirit has a service to render which might prove, if it were accepted, to be of high and social value.*
>
> *"The extinction of race consciousness as between Muslims is one of the outstanding moral achievements of Islam, and in the contemporary world there is as it happens, a crying need for the propagation of this Islamic virtue.....It is conceivable that the spirit of Islam might be the timely reinforcement which would decide this issue in favour of tolerance and peace.*

> *"As for the evil of alcohol, it is at its worst among primitive populations in tropical regions which have been 'opened up' by Western enterprise... .the fact remains that even the most statesmanlike preventive measures imposed by external authority are incapable of liberating a community from a social vice unless a desire for liberation and a will to carry this desire into voluntary action on its own part are awakened in the hearts of the people concerned. Now Western administrators, at any rate those of 'Anglo-Saxon' origin, are spiritually isolated from their 'native wards by the physical 'colour bar' which their race-consciousness sets the conversion of the natives' souls is a task to which their competence can hardly be expected to extend; and it is at this point that Islam may have a part to play.*
>
> *"In these recently and rapidly 'opened up' tropical territories, the Western civilisation has produced an economic and political plenum and, in the same breath, a social and spiritual void....*
>
> *"Here, then, in the foreground of the future, we can remark two valuable influences which Islam may exert upon the cosmopolitan proletariat of a Western society that has cast its net round the world and embraced the whole mankind; while in the more distant future we may speculate on the possible contributions of Islam to some new manifestation of religion."*

The Christians

Before closing this discussion, it is necessary to attend to the Jewish-Christian allegation, referred to in the present work on different occasions, that, as one Orientalist has worded it, "Islam is the bastard child of Judaism and Christianity", and hence whatever is good in the value-system of the Islamic civilisation is in bondage to the Biblical civilisation. In that connection we may give here a brief review of the civilisation nurtured on an international level by Christianity, under the Biblical civilisational value-system, since its coming to power and until the Renaissance in western Europe brought about by the Islamic civilisation—whereafter the West adopted a secularistic and free-thought approach. We shall present here its basic characteristic features, leaving out certain vital facts for being dealt with in the next chapter under different headings; and our review, here again for avoiding all possibilities of doubt as to accuracy and authenticity, will be submitted in the words of a devout and eminent Christian historian of that civilisation, i.e.. Will Durante. Projecting it as 'Civilisation in the Age of Faith', he says *(The Age of faith,* pp. 44-843):

> *"The foster mother of the new civilisation was the church....There is an epic grandeur, sullied with superstition and cruelty, in the struggle of the new religion to capture, tame and inspire the minds....to forge a uniting empire of faith....*
>
> *"....In paganism the family had been the social and religious unit; it was a loss that in medieval Christianity this unit became the individual.*
>
> *"....the status of woman was hurt by the doctrine.... that woman was the origin of sin and the instrument of Satan.*
>
> *"The Church did not condemn slavery. Orthodox and heretic, Roman and barbarian alike assumed the institution to be natural and indestructible....slavery continued throughout the Middle Ages, and died without benefit of clergy.*

"Next to determination of faith, the greatest power of the Church lay in the administration of sacraments—ceremonies symbolising the conferment of divine grace....More important was the sacrament of penance....According to the Gospel (Matt, xvi, 19; xviii, 18), Christ had forgiven sins, and held endowed the apostles with a similar power to 'blind and loose'. This power, said the Church, had descended by apostolic succession from the apostles to the early bishops, from Peter to the popes; and in the twelfth century the 'power of the keys' was extended by bishops to the priests.... Absolution in confession removed from sin the guilt that would have condemned the sinner to hell.. .The Church claimed the right to remit such punishments....The Church commissioned certain ecclesiastics usually friars, as *quaestiarii* to raise funds by offering indulgences in return for gifts, repentance, and prayer. These solicitors....developed a competitive zeal....they exhibited real or false relics to stimulate contributions and they kept for themselves a due or undue part of their receipts.

"The official prayers of the Church were often addressed to God the Father; a few appealed to the Holy Ghost, but the prayer of the people were addressed mostly to Jesus, Mary, and the saints. The Almighty was feared....Jesus was closer, but He too was God, and one hardly ventured to speak to Him face to face....It seemed wiser to lay one's prayer before a saint certified by canonization to be in a heaven, and to beg his or her intercession with Christ....Every nation, city, abbey, church, craft, soul, and crisis of life had its patron saint, as in pagan Rome it had a god....The Church arranged an ecclesiastical calendar in which everyday celebrated a saint; but the year did not find room for the 25,000 saints that had been canonized by the tenth century. The calendar of saints was to familiar to the people that the almanac divided the agricultural year by their names. Many saints received canonization through the insistent worship of their memory by the people or the locality, sometimes against ecclesiastical resistance. Images of the saints were set up in churches and public squares, on buildings and roads, and received a spontaneous worship. ...With so many saints there had to be many relics—their bones, hair, clothing, and anything that they had used.

Every altar was expected to cover one or more such sacred memorials....The churches of Constantinople, before 1204, were especially rich in relics, they had the lance that had pierced Christ and was still red with His blood, the rod that had scourged Him, many pieces of the True Cross enshrined in gold, the 'sop of bread' given to Judas at the Last Supper, some hairs of the Lord's beard, the left arm of John the Baptist....In the sack of Constantinople many of these relics were stolen, some were bought, and they were peddled in the West from church to church to find the highest bidder. All relics were credited with supernatural powers, and a hundred thousand tales were told of their miracles. Men and women eagerly sought even the slightest relic, or relic of a relic, to wear as a magic talisman—a thread from a saint's robe, some dust from a reliquary, a drop of oil from a sanctuary lamp in the shrine. Monasteries vied and disputed with one another in gathering relics and exhibiting them to generous worshippers, for the possession of famous relics made the fortune of an abbey or a church.

The 'translation' of the bones of Thomas a Becket to a new chapel in the cathedral of Canterbury (1220) drew from the attending worshippers a collection valued at $300,000 today. So profitable a business enlisted many practitioners; thousands of spurious relics were sold to churches and individuals; and monasteries were tempted to 'discover' new relics when in need of funds. The culmination of abuse was the dismemberment of dead saints to that several places might enjoy their patronage and power... .The worship of God as Lord of Hosts and King of Kings inherited Sematic and Roman ways of approach, veneration, and address; the incense burnt before altar or clergy recalled the old burnt offerings; aspersion with holy water was an ancient form of exorcism; processions and illustrations continued immemorial rites; the vestments of the clergy and the papal title of *pontifex maximus* were legacies from pagan Rome. The Church found that rural converts still revered certain springs, wells, trees and stones; she thought it wiser to bless these to Christian use than to break too sharply the customs of sentiment. So a dolmen at Plouret was consecrated as the chapel of the Seven Saints, and the worship of the oak was sterilized by hanging images of Christian saints upon the trees. Pagan festivals dear to the people, or necessary as cathartic moratoriums on morality, reappeared as Christian feasts, and pagan vegetation rites were transformed into Christian liturgy. The people continued to light midsummer fires on St. John's Eve, and the celebration of Christ's resurrection took the pagan name of Eostre, the old Teutonic goddess of the spring.

The Christian calendar of the saints replaced the Roman *fasti;* ancient divinities dear to the people were allowed to revive under the names of Christian saints; the Dea Victoria of the Basses-Alpes became St. Victoire, and Castor and Pollux were reborn as St. Cosmas and Damian....The finest triumph of this tolerant spirit of adaptation was the sublimation of the pagan mother-goddess cults in the worship of Mary. Here too the people took the initiative. In 431 Cyril, Archbishop of Alexandria, in a famous sermon at Ephesus, applied to Mary many of the terms fondly ascribed by the pagans of Ephesus to their 'great goddess' Artemis-Diana; and the Council of Ephesus in the year over the protests of Nestorius, sanctioned for Mary the title 'Mother of God'. Gradually the tenderist features of Astarte, Cybele, Artemis, Diana, and Isis were gathered together in the worship of Mary. In the sixth century the Church established the Feast of the Assumption of the Virgin into heaven, and assigned it to August 13, the date of ancient festivals of Isis and Artemis.

Mary became the patron saint of Constantinople and the imperial family; her picture was carried at the head of every great procession, and was (and is) hung in every church and home in Greek Christendom. Probably it was the Crusades that brought from the East to the West a more intimate and colourful worship of the Virgin....Just as the sternness of Yahveh had necessitated Christ, so the justice of Christ needed Mary's mercy to temper it. In effect the Mother—the oldest figure in religious worship— became the third person of a new Trinity knights vowed themselves to her service, and cities gave her their keys....The Church had made great festivals of the events in Mary's life—the Annunciation, the Visitation, the Purification (Candlemas), the Assumption.

"...In Christian theory the whole human race had been tainted by the sin of Adam and Eve. Said Gratian's *Decretum* (c. 1150), unofficially accepted by the Church as her teaching, 'Every human being who is conceived by the coition of a man with a woman is born with original sin, subject to impiety and death, and therefore a child of wrath'; and only divine grace, and the atoning death of Christ, could save him from wickedness and damnation....*The preaching of this doctrine ....gave many medieval Christians a sense of inborn impurity, depravity, and guilt,* which coloured much of their literature before 1200.

"....By the age of sixteen the medieval youth had probably sampled a variety of sexual experiences. Pederasty....reappeared....In 1177 Henry, Abbot of Clairvaux, wrote of France that 'ancient Sodom is springing up from her ashes'....The Penitentials—ecclesiastical manuals prescribing penances for sins—mention the usual enormities, including bestiality; as astonishing variety of beasts received such attentions....Cases of incest were numerous. Premarital and extramarital relations were apparently as widespread as at any time between antiquity and the twentieth century....Rape was common....Knights who served high born dames or demoiselles for a kiss or a touch of the hand might console themselves with the lady's maids; some ladies could not sleep with a good conscience until they had arranged this courtesy. The Knight of La Tour-Landry....if we were to believe him, some men of his class fornicated in church, nay, 'on the altar'; and he tells of 'two queens which in Lent, on Holy Thursday... .took their foul delight and pleasance within the church during divine service'. William of Malmesbury described the Norman nobility as 'given over to gluttony and lechery', and exchanging concubines with one another lest fidelity should dull the edge of husbandry. Illegitimate children littered Christendom, and gave a plot to a thousand tales. The heroes of several medieval sagas were bastards—Cuchulain, Arthur, Gawain, Roland, William the Conqueror, and many a knight in Froissar's Chronicles.

"Prostitution adjusted itself to the times. Some women in pilgrimage, according to Bishop Boniface, earned their passage by selling themselves in the towns on their route. Every army was followed with another army, as dangerous as the enemy. 'The Crusaders', reports Albert of Aix, 'had in their ranks a crowd of women wearing the habit of men; they travelled together without distinction of sex, trusting to the chances of a frightful promiscuity'....The university students, particularly at Paris, developed urgent or imitative needs, the *files* established centres of accommodation....In Rome, according to Bishop Durand II of Mende (1311), there were brothels near the Vatican, and the Pope's marshals permitted them for a consideration. The Church showed a human spirit toward prostitutes....A council at Rouen, in the eighth century, invited women who had secretly borne children to deposit them at the door of the church, which would undertake to provide for them; such orphans were brought up as serfs on ecclesiastical properties. A law of Charlemagne decreed that exposed children should be the slaves of those who rescued and reared them ....Penalties for adultery were severe; Saxon law, for example, condemned the unfaithful wife at least to lose her nose and ears, and empowered her husband to kill her. Adultery was common notwithstanding.

"....Feudal masters seduced female serfs at the cost of a modest fine; he who 'covered' a maid 'without her thanks'—against her will—paid the court three shillings. The eleventh century, said Freeman, 'was a profligate age', and he marvelled at the apparent marital fidelity of William the Conqueror, who could not say as much for his father. *'Medieval society'*, said the learned and judicious Thomas Wright, *'was profoundly immoral and licentious"*.

"....In the Middle Ages....men, good and bad, lied to their children, mates, congregations, enemies, friends, governments, and God. Medieval man had a special fondness for forging documents. He forged apocryphal gospels....he forged decretals as weapons in ecclesiastical politics; loyal monks forged charters to win royal grants for their monasteries, Archbishop Lanfranc of Canterbury, according to the papal Curia, forged a charter to prove the antiquity of his see, schoolmasters forged charters to endow some colleges at Cambridge with a false antiquity; and 'pious frauds' corrupted texts and invented a thousand edifying miracles.

Bribery was general in education, trade, war, religion, government, law. Schoolboys sent pies to their examiners; politicians paid for appointments to public office, and collected the necessary sums from their friends; witnesses could be bribed to swear to anything; litigants gave presents to jurors and judges....perjury was so frequent that trial by combat was sometimes resorted to in the hope that God would identify the greater liar.

Despite a thousand guild and municipal statutes and penalties, medieval craftsmen often deceived purchasers with shoddy products, false measures, and crafty substitutes. Some bakers stole small portions of dough under their customers' eyes by means of a trap door in the kneading board; cheap cloths were secretly put in the place of better cloths promised and paid for; inferior leather was 'doctored' to look like the best; stones were concealed in sacks of hay or wool sold by weight; the meat packers of Norwich were accused of buying measly pigs, and making from them sausages and pudding unfit for human bodies. Berthold of Regensburg (c. 1220) described the different forms of cheating used in the various trades, and the tricks played upon country folk by merchants at the fairs.

"....*Once at war, Christians were no gentler to the defeated, no more loyal to pledges and treaties than the warriors of other faiths and times. Cruelty and brutality were apparently more frequent in the Middle Ages than in any civilisation before our own.*

"....In all classes men and women were hearty and sensual; their festivals were feasts of drinking, gambling, dancing, and sexual relaxation; their jokes were of a candour hardly rivalled today; their speech was freer, their oaths vaster and more numerous. Hardly a man in France, says Joinville, could open his mouth without mentioning the Devil.

"....begging flourished....Mendicancy reached....a scope and pertinacity unequalled today except in the poorest areas of the Far East.

"*Cleanliness,* in the Middle Ages, *was not next to godliness.* Early Christianity had denounced the Roman baths....and its general disapproval of the body had put no premium on hygiene. The modern use of the handkerchief was unknown....One result of the Crusades was the introduction into Europe of public steam baths in the Muslim style.

"....In the thirteenth century, the chamber pots of Paris were freely emptied from windows into the street....People eased themselves in courtyards, on stairways and balconies, even in the palace of the Louvre.

"....The commonest meat was pork. Pigs ate the refuse in the streets, and people ate the pigs.

"*Drunkenness was a favourite vice of the Middle Ages, in all classes and sexes.* Taverns were numerous, ale was cheap. Beer was the regular drink of the poor, even at breakfast. Monasteries and hospitals north of the Alps were normally allowed a gallon of ale or beer per person per day... .A customal of the abbey of St. Peter in the Black Forest includes some tender clauses: 'When the peasants have unladen the wine, they shall be brought into the monastery, and shall have meat and drink in abundance. A great tub shall be set there and filled with wine.....and each shall drink....and if they wax drunken and smite the cellarman or the cook, they shall pay no fine for this deed; and they shall drink so that two of them cannot beat the third to the wagon'.

"....*Gambling was not always forbidden by law;* Siena provided booths for it in the public square.

"....The French and Germans in particular were fond of the dance....Dancing could become an epidemic: in 1237 a band of German children danced all the way from Erfurt to Arnstadt; many died en route; and some survivors suffered to the end of their lives from St. Vitus' dance, or other nervous disorders.

"....Several persons, of any age or sex, might sleep in the same room. In England and France all classes slept nude.

"Does the general picture of medieval Europe support the belief that religion makes for morality? Our general impression suggests a wider gap between moral theory and practice in the Middle Ages than in other epochs of civilisation. Medieval Christendom was apparently as rich as our own irreligious age in sensuality, violence, drunkenness, cruelty, coarseness, profanity, greed, robbery, dishonesty, and fraud. It seems to have outdone our time in the enslavement of individuals....It surpassed us in the subjection of women; it hardly equalled us in immodesty, fornication, and adultery, or in the immensity and murderousness of war. Compared with the Roman Empire from Nerva to Aurelius, *medieval Christendom was a moral setback.*

"....*The intellectual virtues naturally declined in the Age of Faith;* intellectual conscience (fairness with the facts) and the search for truth were replaced by zeal and admiration for sanctity, and sometimes unscrupulous piety.....The *civic virtues suffered* from concentration on the after life....Perhaps *hypocrisy,* so indispensable to civilisation, *increased in the Middle Ages* as compared with the frank secularism of antiquity, or the unabashed corporate brutality of our time." (All italics, present writer's).

Cultural Movements

A civilization worthy of the name should promote a dual objective—the perfection of the individual, and the perfection of society or of relation between man and man, and that this was possible only where a civilization was inspired by and rested on a culture which normally operated for the progress of the individual and the progress of society at large.

The Fundamentals

In applying this principle to Islam, the question poses itself: What is the process which Islam recommends for man to achieve such a dual objective? In other words, what is the line of action man has to pursue or the principle of movement one has to observe in life in order to promote the two objects together? And then, arises the question: Are the two objects ends in themselves, or are they to lead on to any further or ultimate objective?

Before we undertake to ascertain the answer which the Quran furnishes to these questions, it seems necessary to know what view the Quran takes of human life, and of life, in general. Is life worth living or is one to seek refuge from it? Is it static or is it dynamic? Is it circumscribed by any period, or is it continuously growing from state to state? In other words, is the life of man to terminate with what is called "death," or is it to continue in another state? I have posed the questions for the obvious reason that the programme of life one may have to pursue in the present will be dictated by one's belief in one of the alternatives presented here.

If one should believe that life is to terminate with death, the character of the programme which such a belief will warrant will necessarily be different from the programme agreeable to a belief that the life lived on earth is not to end with death but has to continue in a new form on yet another plane or in a new state. Further, if one should believe that he has been born with a stigma attached to his soul of some sin committed by some remote ancestor or by himself in a previous birth, the line of action one will have to assume toward perfection will be yet different from every other.

Now what is the view which the Quran takes of human life? It divides its course into two broad periods. The first period consists of two stages. One is the stage of man in the making. This is the stage of evolution of the human species, or the stage leading to the emergence of the Biblical Adam and Eve. The second stage is the stage of his reproduction and multiplication. What follows thereafter from the emergence of the child from its mother's womb till it grows and crosses the threshold of death and passes on into a further phase of life, is covered by the second period of life envisaged by the Quran.

In regard to the first of the two stages covered by the first period, the Quran suggests that the bringing into being of man was not a sudden event in creation but that on the other hand it was the result of a lengthy process. Says the Quran:

> *"He it is who hath formed you by successive stages" (Q. 71:14) "And it is He Who hath created man of water." (Q. 25:54) "And God hath caused you to spring forth from the earth like a plant." (Q. 71 :17)*

In respect of the second stage in the first period or of man's reproduction, says the Quran:

> *"Now of fine clay have We created man: then made We the moist germ a clot of blood; then made the clotted blood into a piece of flesh, then made the piece of flesh into bones, and We clothed the bones with flesh; then brought forth man of yet another make—blessed therefore be God, the Most Excellent of makers." (Q. 23:12-14)*

"This is He Who hath made everything which He hath created in perfect form; and began the creation of man with clay:

'Then ordained his progeny from germs of life, from despised water:

> *Then shaped him, and breathed of His spirit into him, and gave him hearing and seeing and hearts; what thanks do ye return?" (Q. 32:7-9)*

What is noteworthy in this phase of the process is what the Quran calls the "breathing of God's spirit" into man as he emerges from his mother's womb.

The second period in the life of man begins with this emergence from his mother's womb and continue after death opening for him a new phase of existence. In respect of this period and particularly of what has to follow death, the Quran states:

> *"Thinketh man that he will be left to drift? Was he not a mere embryo in the seminal elements? Then he became a clot; then (God) shaped and fashioned and made of him a pair, male and female, Is not He able to bring the dead to life" (Q. 75:3-40)*
>
> *"What think ye of (the seed, the germ of life) that ye spill?*
>
> *Is it ye who create it? or are We its creator?*
>
> *It is We Who have decreed that death should be among you;*
>
> *Yet are We not thereby hindered from replacing you with others, your likes or from producing you again in a form which ye know not!*
>
> *Ye have known the first creation: Will ye not then reflect?" (Q. 56:58-62)*

> *It needs not therefore that I affirm by the sunset redness, And by the night and its gatherings, And by the moon when at her full, That from state to state shall ye assuredly be carried onward.* (Q. 84:19)

Such is the vision which the Quran presents of the course of life man has to take. His present state of life is to be succeeded by another state growing out of it, and followed by yet another and yet another in succession. Life thus viewed is a linear line and not a cycle and allows no return to a previous existence, as that will demonstrate a retrogression and not a movement forward. The essential function of Divinity as the Quran asserts is to disclose itself "every moment in fresh glory" (Q. 55:29), and likewise the primary function of human life is to march on from state to state, from one lower to one higher in an endless linear movement. Any line of action or programme of life which the Quran might suggest for him in his earthly sphere, or the role he has to fulfil, will not be intelligible or bear any meaning until we know whether the movement forward, the movement envisaged in the Quranic assertion, 'from state to state shall ye assuredly be carried forward", is a movement in which man will have the option to participate and even propel it, or is it a mere biological movement, as during the initial or first period of human life leading to the emergence of man through his mother's womb, a movement in which the man in the making has had no conscious share?

If the second period of his course in life is also wholly biological, then the entire edifice of religion or what is prescribed by it for human guidance falls to the ground. For, the biologist sees no future for man after his death. In fact, he has not so far developed the courage to accompany the dead into the grave and continue his biological research, nor has he cultivated an open mind on the possibility of a future for man. He is definite that after death there is no further life for man. On the other hand, the Quran is emphatic in its assertion that from state to state man will assuredly be carried onward. If it is so, the question will repeat itself: Is this process simply biological pushing man blindly forward from one physiological mound to another ? If it is so, where comes in the value of any plan of life prescribed for man by the Quran, since he is to serve only as a meek material in an inexorable biological process and is to have no voice in his movement. This is an issue which needs careful examination before we proceed any further. Let us first see what Muslim thinkers in the past have said on the subject.

The late Sir Muhammad Iqbal in his memorable work, *The Reconstruction of Religious Thought in Islam,* takes a biological view of the course of human life as visualised by the Quran, and quotes in his support a striking passage from the great mystic, Jalaluddin Rumi. Says he:

"It was only natural and perfectly consistent with the spirit of the Quran that Rumi regarded the question of immortality as one of biological evolution, and not a problem to be decided by arguments of a purely metaphysical nature, as some philosophers of Islam had thought. The theory of evolution, however, has brought despair and anxiety instead of hope and enthusiasm for life to the modern world. The reason is to be found in the unwarranted modern assumption that man's present structure, mental as well as physiological, is the last word in biological evolution, and that death, regarded as a biological event, has no constructive meaning. The world of today needs a Rumi to create an attitude of hope and to kindle the fire of enthusiasm for life. His inimitable lines may be quoted here:

"First man appeared in the class of inorganic things.
Next he passed therefrom into that of plants.
For years he lived as one of the plants,
Remembering naught of his inorganic state so different;
And when he passed from the vegetal to the animal state,
He had no remembrance of his state as a plant,
Except the inclination he felt to the world of plants,
Especially at the time of spring and sweet flowers,
Like the inclination of infants towards their mothers,
Who know not the cause of their inclination to the breast.
Again the great Creator, as you know,
Drew man out of the animal, into the human state,
Thus man passed from one order of nature to another,
Till he became wise and knowing and strong as he is now,
Of his first souls he has now no remembrance,
And he will be again changed from his present soul."

Interesting and attractive as is the vision of the evolution of man presented here, the point should not be overlooked that the primary purpose of the Quran is not to give any factual account of the rise and development of man as might be upheld by the discoveries of science. The statements of the Quran touching the subject do lend themselves to biological interpretation; but they certainly do not substantiate the view advanced by Rumi that before man assumed his present form, he had to live in succession as an inorganic substance, a plant, and an animal, or that he will replace his present form by that of an angel, and so forth, as he states in another passage which I shall have occasion to present to you in a few moments. The Quran does postulate that man is the result of an evolutionary process and that this process will continue even after what is called 'death', but does not posit or specify any distinct progressive biological stages therein such as specified by Rumi.

As we have already noticed, the Quran divides the movement of human life into two broad periods. Firstly, there is the period of man's making till he emerges from the mother's womb. This is the period which the Quran refers to in the verse:

> *"It is He Who hath formed you by successive stages."*
> *(Q. 71:14).*

'The period which begins with this moment when, as the Quran states, the spirit of God having been breathed into him, he receives the gift of hearing and seeing and feeling and thinking, (Q. 15:29) and continues his course of life thereafter crossing the line of what is termed 'death' is the period that matters.

It is this which the Quran has in view when it asserts: 'from state to state shall ye assuredly be carried onward." (Q. 84:19). It is in relation to this phase of life or movement that the Quran utters the following words of caution:

> *"Those who believe and do right: Joy is for them, and bliss their journey's end."* *(Q. 13:29)*
>
> *"Those who strive in our way, we shall show them the way."* *(Q. 29:69)*
>
> *"Whosoever followed the right course, it is only for the good of his own soul that he doth so; and whosoever followed the wrong course doth so to its own hurt. No soul charged with its own responsibility shall bear another's responsibility."* *(Q. 17:15)*
>
> *"I will not suffer the work of any among you that worked, whether male or female, to be lost."* *(Q. 3:194).*
>
> *"By the soul and Him who balanced it and infused into it the sense of discrimination between the wrong and the right, happy is he who keepeth it pure and unhappy is he who corrupted it."* *(Q. 91:7-10)*

"And whatever suffering ye suffer, it is what your hands have wrought." (Q. 42:30)

"Man shall have nothing but what he strives for." (Q. 53:39)

The earlier movement leading to the emergence of the child from its mother's womb is indeed a biological process—a process of which the emerging child has had no conscious apprehension and consequently no conscious share in its own making. But the subsequent is clearly indicated by the Quran to be a conscious movement propelled and controlled, for good or ill, by one's own self. The terms employed by it to distinguish the one from the other bear out the distinction suggested. In the one, *'atwaran'* is the expression used, and in the other *'tabaqan an tabaqin."* In the one, the Quran states that by successive stages of growth and development or moulds, man has been made; whereas in the other, it states that from one *'Tabaq'* or from one lower plane or state to one higher plane or state, man will assuredly be carried onward. The two terms connote two different types of development. The former refers to a physiological process as in the mother's womb. The biological mould or form or *'tawr'* is completed in the emerging child which thereafter merely expands its physical dimensions till death overtakes them. But the 'spirit of God,' which, as the Quran points out, is 'breathed' into him as he emerges from his mother's womb endowed with the talent to hear and see and feel and think, gathers increasing consciousness and develops an individuality. It is this individuality or personality or ego, as it is styled by philosophy, which is addressed by the Quran in the verse: "From state to state shall ye assuredly be carried onward." It is that which does not disappear with the disappearance of its physical mould. It assumes an independent existence the moment it discards its temporary physiological appurtenance. It is the development of this personality or ego on which the Quran concentrates all its attention. It gives man the heartening assurance that "from state to state, shall he assuredly be carried onward," if only he conforms to the laws of life guided by the sense of balance set in his very nature.

The question may incidentally arise here: what after all is this spirit of God breathed into man as he emerges out of the womb of his mother, and assumes an individuality or personality or ego? Is it any extraneous element infused into the body as the child emerges out of its mother's womb? Or, is it an off-shoot of the body itself, fashioned in its very form at a certain stage in its formation, permeating it through and through and holding it together, and composed of something so delicately elusive or fine that the science of biology, as it has developed so far, cannot apprehend it or bring it within its purview—an offshoot of the body possessing the talent to develop, at first through the instrumentality of the body itself, an individuality such as might outlive it, and thereafter live on its own? An answer to this is not possible to attempt in the absence of any direct aid from science. Nor is that necessary to our purpose.

Our interest here is in the progress which this human personality, the ego or the soul of man has to make in his march of life, and not in what it consists of. It is enough to know from the Quran that it is styled a spirit breathed by God into the body of man, and that it is called upon to take a consciously active interest in its own movement both here and hereafter. Even if this process is biological, in its structural setting as Mawlana Rumi envisages, the function of human personality, as recommended by the Quran, is to control and regulate the process of its own movement forward from state to state without wilfully creating for itself hindrances, and suffering a set-back in consequence. For, the Quran makes it clear that man has the option to make use of all the laws of nature to advance or retard his pace in life.

And He hath subjected to you all that is in the heavens
and all that is in the earth all is from Him.

Verily, herein are signs for those who reflect. (Q. 45:13)

It is this fact of life or assumption that has to determine the role man has to fulfil in life or the principle which should govern his movement in life in order that he might move forward from state to state, from one lower to one higher plane, towards perfection.

What then is the role which the Quran assigns to man in the scheme of things and what equipment does it offer him to fulfil the role and move forward in life from state to state? The figurative language and the imagery employed by the Quran to denote the role reminds me of a similar picture afforded by the English poet, Matthew Arnold, in his lines entitled "Revolutions:"

Before man parted for this earthly strand,

While yet upon the verge of heaven he stood,

God put a heap of letters in his hand,

And bade him make with them what word he could.

And man has turned them many times : made Greece, Rome, England, France:—Yes, nor in vain essayed, way after way, changes that never cease. The letters have combined: something was made.

Indeed something was made; but the poet in sorrow exclaims:

"Ah! an inextinguishable sense

Haunts him that he has not made what he should,

That he has still, though old, to recommence, Since he has not yet found the word God would.

And empire after empire, at their height of sway, have felt this boding sense come on,

Have felt their huge frames not constructed right

And dropped, and slowly died upon their throne."

That was Arnold's approach, evidently inspired by St. John's : 'In the beginning was the Word and the Word was with God, and the Word was God.' Here the purpose of man was to find out the Word. On the other hand, a reflex process is what is revealed by the Quran. It does not suggest that God merely 'put a heap of letters into man's hand when he parted for this earthly strand and bade him to make with them what word he could.'

It affirms that the 'Word' itself was shown to him and its meaning explained. Indeed, lest he forget its structure and composition, this very word was transfixed into his nature, bidding him to preserve it therein and not play with its letters and disturb their arrangement, so that he might live in peace with himself and in peace with his external world of relations and fulfil his role in life. And what is the role assigned to him? States the Quran:

> *"And when thy Lord said unto the angels : Lo, I am about to place a vicegerent in the Earth, they said : Wilt thou place therein one who will do mischief and shed blood, while we, hymn Thy praise and extol Thy holiness? He said : Surely, I know that which ye know not."*
>
> *"And He taught Adam all the names, then showed the objects to the angels saying : "Inform me of the names of these, if ye are in the right."*
>
> *"They said : Glorious art Thou : we have no knowledge save that which Thou hast taught us. Surely, Thou alone art the Knower, the Wise;"*
>
> *"He said : 'O Adam; you inform them of their names' and when he had informed them of their names, He said : 'Did I not tell you that I know the secrets of the heavens and the earth?' "* (Q. 2:30-33)

Thus rendered conscious of the purpose of creation and of the 'names' or the meaning of things, or the laws of their existence, it followed as a corollary that man should affirm the unity of existence sustained by his creator, the Lord of all being.

> *"And when thy Lord took out from the loins of Adam's children their progeny, and made then affirm (saying) Am I not your Lord? They said : Yea! We affirm." (Q. 7:172)*
>
> *So equipped, man's nature found itself agreeable to bear the trust of vicegerency.*
>
> *"Verily, we proposed to the heavens and to the mountains to receive the trust, but they shrank from receiving it and were afraid of it. Man alone undertook to bear it." (Q. 33:72)*

The 'undertaking' was, on the face of it, not an easy affair. The Quran is struck by its very audacity as the continuation of the verse suggests : "Lo! how unfair and harsh was man to himself!—Not aware of what exactly he undertook." But the purpose of his creation was nevertheless to carry him "onward from state to state" towards the state of perfection. But to lessen the pang implicit in the ordeal and to help him bear the burden of the trust undertaken, and to keep the life intended for him, or the letters of the 'Word' revealed to him, in proper form, says the Quran, a sense of balance was set in his nature and he was told that his march upward would depend on what use he makes of it.

> *"Allah it is Who hath sent down the Book of Truth, and the Balance." (Q. 42:17)*
>
> *"By the soul and Him Who balanced the same and infused into it the sense of discrimination between the wrong and the right, happy is he who keepeth it pure, and unhappy is he who corrupted it." (Q. 91:7-10)*
>
> *During the early stage or before the 'spirit of God' is breathed into him, or during the stage of his making, no responsibility is attached to man, since he is not conscious of the movement. The question of responsibility arises the moment consciousness begins to be at play. The first phase of his life in this second period which closes with what is called 'death' is the basic stage of preparation for all subsequent stages. It is the stage of freedom of will and action, or of willing cooperation with the laws of life, helped by the balance set in the*

> *nature of man. What follows is but a continuation of it. 'Your creation and resurrection are but like a single moment.'* *(Q. 31:28)*

Even in this stage, the stage ushered in by death, the march onward is conditioned by a conscious effort appropriate to every new move. This is implicit in the urge one will feel there for what the Quran calls "light" and more and more of it. "Our Lord! perfect for us our light" (Q. 66:8) will be the perennial prayer of the aspirant. Every fresh instalment of light acquired or vouchsafed is thus a new state of life, accompanied by 'death' that necessary concomitant of life, the birth-pang ushering in a new state of existence. "It is We Who have decreed that death should be among you" (Q. 56: 60). "Blessed is He Who hath created death and life to test which of you is best in point of endeavour" (Q. 67:2). Throughout, the spiritual purpose persists. The movement is a conscious movement.

It is this aspect, the spiritual, which the Quran desires to emphasise for the guidance of man, and not exactly the biological. That this aspect also was probably present in Rumi's mind, notwithstanding his biological obsession as displayed in his lines quoted by Sir Mohammed Iqbal, is clear from a restatement of the same biological process in the following lines:

> *I died as a mineral and became a plant,*
> *I died as plant and rose to animal,*
> *I died as animal and I was man.*
> *Why should I fear death? When was I less by dying?*
> *Yet once more I shall die as man, to soar,*
> *With angels blest; but even from angelhood,*
> *I must pass on : all except God doth perish.*
> *When I have sacrificed my angel-soul,*
> *I shall become what no mind e'er conceived*
> *Oh, let me not exist! For non-existence*
> *Proclaims in organ tones : "To Him we shall return."*

Here the biological process, even as Rumi conceives it, is rendered dependent upon a conscious effort, upon the 'sacrifice' as he states, of a lower nature in search of a higher. And that is essentially a conscious spiritual process, and applies equally well to the life in the present lived in its material set up and to the life to follow which is expected to be wholly a matter of the spirit.

Such is the course of life which the Quran envisages or outlines for man. It is for man to traverse this course with steady steps if he is to profit by life. The way to do it is to conform to the way of God or the laws of life at work in Nature. Says the Quran:

> *"Turn steadfastly to the way of devotion, the way laid by God, for which man by his nature hath been fitted. There is no altering in the way laid by God. That is the right way of devotion (or religion). But most people know it not".* *(Q. 30:30)*

The Law of Movement at work in life to which man is to conform for his progress in life. But this law does not operate unilaterally in Nature. It works in conjunction with another fundamental law of life to produce order and harmony in life. This other Law is what I may call the Law of Unity in life. Indeed, the Law of movement subserves this other law to let life disclose itself every moment in fresh glory which in reality is its function. (Q. 55:29). The implication here for man is clear. He has been fitted by his nature to make progress in life in every direction possible for him, by pressing into his service all the provisions of the earth and the forces of nature.

But the Quran makes it clear to him that no progress made by him will operate for his ultimate good unless it is expressed in terms of the good of every living object on earth who, in the language of the Prophet of Islam, form together the 'Family of God.' That is what the Quran calls *'amal-i-saleh'* or the righteous mode of living, which alone at the organizational level, can afford to man a civilized order of life. The two laws of life are therefore to work hand in hand, if life is to give a united happiness for mankind. This Principle of Unity as sponsored by the Quran, I shall take up for consideration in my next lecture.

Campaign and the Theories

Administration of Justice before Islam : Before Islam the Arabs of the Hijaz were wandering Bedouins with no organised government. They started as tribes; when the number of tribes increased they were divided into sub-tribes and were identified by the names of the branches and families comprising a tribe. The only tie which bound members of the same tribe to each other was that of blood. Those who came from the same stock, or thought they did, comprised a tribe and came to have, both individually and collectively, the right of defence against another tribe.

While this obligation devolved on the whole tribe, it was the responsibility of an individual to participate in common defence and submit loyally to the traditions of a tribe. Each tribe had its own Shaykh or Chief who was the symbol of sovereignty. This sovereignty was bestowed on him by the tribe and did not belong to him as a hereditary right, although the birth of an individual in the house of a chief weighed considerably in his election to the leadership of the tribe. The other factors were his age and wisdom. The Shaykh represented the tribe in its external relations with other tribes. His only source of strength was public opinion in his own tribe because he had no standing army or any other executive organisation to carry out his administration.

Each tribe, in addition to the supreme chief, had a judge who settled cases referred to him in accordance with the traditions of the tribe. In arriving at a decision, however, he often used his own judgment and that is where his reputation was affected by his personal experience and wisdom. The institution of the judge was, however, neither established nor sacrosanct. The Bedouins sometimes took a case to a judge, sometimes to a diviner, and at other occasions to somebody else who was known for his personal wisdom. Nevertheless, the institution did exist, although it was not binding on any member of the tribe to take a case to a judge. Even where cases were referred to him the judgment was not binding on the contending parties.

There were no hard and fast rules about the jurisdiction of this court nor did it have any executive authority. The only source it looked for an implementation of its ruling was public opinion in the tribe which made it difficult for any member to overide or ignore the judgment pronounced by a judge in a given case. These judges had no written law to guide them nor was there any unwritten code of well-established conventions. They depended mostly on the traditions and customs of their tribe which were founded partly on experience and partly on beliefs and superstitions inherited from Judaism.

We read of numerous conflicts between chiefs of different tribes where we find the quarrel being ultimately referred to a third person who acts as a judge. He could be more properly called an arbitrator because the two contending parties agreed to choose a judge. Al-Bukhtari tells us of a criminal case a little before the appearance of Islam. A man from Banu Hashim, a branch of the Quraish, was employed as a camel-driver by a man from another branch of the Quraish. While the camel-driver was passing by on business, somebody else from Banu Hashim asked him for the loan of a rope to fasten the saddle girth of his camel. The Hashimi camel-driver lent his fellow Hashimi the shackle rope of one of his camels. On his return the employer of the Hashimi camel-driver questioned him about the missing rope.

In the argument that followed the employer fatally struck the camel-driver and left him dying. Before, however, the camel-driver breathed his last he managed to find a passerby from the Yemen whom he charged with the task of telling the story of his death to Abu Talib, the head of Banu Hashim. The employer of the camel-driver was sent for by the chief. At first he denied the charge but Abu Talib firmly told him: "You have killed one of us. I give you three alternatives: either give us a hundred heads of camels, or let fifty persons from your tribe swear on oath that you did not kill the camel-driver. In case you refuse either of the alternatives the only course left to us is to kill you." This story shows the influence exercised by the tribal chief over the affairs of the tribe. It also shows that in a given case recourse could be had to more than one legal remedy.

The administration of justice differed from tribe to tribe in accordance with the degree of civilisation attained by it. Mecca before Islam had attained a fair degree of progress in administration, part of which was the maintenance of justice. Different administrative duties were assigned to ten leading men from ten different sub-tribes. Among these was the maintenance of justice which was entrusted, before Islam, to Abu Bakr. He was in charge of blood-money penalties, and compensation.

The alliance of Fudul signified the agreement of a number of sub-tribes of the Quraish, who agreed that neither an alien nor a citizen would be wronged in Mecca, irrespective of his status as a free man or a slave. In case of a man being wronged, in violation of this agreement, the tribe pledged itself to back the aggrieved party and secure justice for him even though it meant payment from their own pocket. Similarly, the tribal laws in Medina before Islam were relatively more progressive because of the presence of the Jews who had with them the Tawrat and the commentary which contained numerous laws and judgments. The Arabs in Medina before Islam were, so to say, more or less subject to the Jewish code.

After Muhammad declared himself Prophet, he lived for thirteen years in Mecca and ten in Medina. The ten years after the migration to Medina are the constructive period, where legislation in Islam is concerned. During these ten years various laws were promulgated by the Quran and a large body of the Hadith, in explanation of the laws of the Quran, became available. These two sources, the Quran and the Sunnah, were the main sources of legislation in Islam.

The Quran was revealed in parts over a period of some twenty-three years. About two-thirds of the Quran was revealed in Mecca and about one-third in Medina. A careful study of the verses revealed in Mecca would establish that during this period hardly any legislation—civil, criminal, or personal—was promulgated. This part of the Quran is addressed primarily to the ethics of religion and lays down clearly and firmly the principal tenets of the faith. It inculcates moral virtues like justice, charity, gratitude, observance of promises, and fear of God. In brief it lays down the moral code for a chaste life. On the negative side it prohibits murder, adultery, the burying alive of daughters born in a family, the breaking of promises, cheating in weights and measures, and associating any power with God whose unity is overwhelmingly stressed. Even the basic institutions of *Salat* (Prayers) and Zakat (Poor-Tax) were not fully formulated in this period. The implications of Zakat during the Meccan period were nothing more than merely spending one's money in helping the needy and the poor. The details about the amounts which should be given or the regulations regarding its disposal were given later in Medina where most of the legislation was evolved for a society which had settled down to peace.

In the case of prayers no details were worked out during the period of Mecca, for the number of times a Muslim has to pray was not laid down. Perhaps the most detailed Surah of the Quran in connection with religious teaching during this period is al-Anam. Legislation governing civil affairs like buying and selling, renting and hiring, and usury; criminal affairs like theft or murder; and personal affairs like marriage and divorce was promulgated after the Prophet had moved to Medina. The best example is the revelation of the two Medina Surahs, al-Baqara and al-Nisa' which deal in great detail with the subject of legislation in different fields. The fundamental principles of religion had to be emphasised over and over again during the period of the Prophet's stay in Mecca, for in the early phase the principles were more important than details of religious law which was later to be covered by legislation in Medina. The detailed laws could not be drawn up before the State came into existence. The Muslim State did not come into existence until after the Prophet's migration to Medina.

Holy Quran

There are not many mandatory verses in the Quran. In all the Quran comprises about 6000 verses of which not more than about 200 deal with the laying down of the law. In fact the jurists tend to exaggerate inasmuch as they include many verses and individual words in their sphere whereas strictly speaking they do not lend themselves to any derivation of rules where one has to read them in their proper context. Some jurists, for example, consider the word *Ashhad* as a form of legal oath-taking. This is not necessarily so as the word occurs in a number of different contexts at different places in the Quran. Take for example the following verses:

When the Hypocrites
Come to thee, they say,
"We bear witness that thou
Art indeed the Apostle
Of God." Yea, God
Knoweth that thou art
Indeed His Apostle,
And God beareth witness
That the Hypocrites are
Indeed liars.

*The following verses a*gain could not be included under those which lay down the law in a mandatory form and yet they have been included in that category by a large number of jurists. They deal with the flesh of horses, mules, and donkeys which, it is said, are meant for riding and not for eating:

And (He has created) horses,
Mules, and donkeys, for you
To ride and use for show;
And He has created (other) things
Of which ye have no knowledge.

In the following verse the virtues of prayer and sacrifices are stressed and no rules as such have been laid down. All the examples given belong to the Mecca period and to them could be added many more. Including such verses as the following among those which deal with the subject of legislation will be stretching the point a little too far:

To thee have We
Granted the Fount (Of Abundance).
Therefore to thy Lord
Turn in Prayer
And Sacrifice.

We have to contend with the fact that in the compilation of the Quran, neither the chronology of the revelation of a particular verse nor the unity of the subject it deals with has been considered as the guiding factors. We do not, for example, find verses on one subject at one place except very rarely as in the case of verses relating to inheritance and divorce. The most fundamental object of the Quran was clearly to establish the principles of Islam and as such stress was not laid on the details of law. The legislative purpose followed the establishment of the basic laws of morality which were stressed time and again. Even the few law-making verses that we come across during the period of Mecca do not seek so much to lay down the details of law as to emphasise the fundamental morality which Islam sought to commend to the pagan Arabs. The following verses revealed in Mecca are, we believe, an illustration of this point:

O ye who believe!
Intoxicants and gambling,
(Dedication of) stones,
And (divination by) arrows,
Are an abomination,—
Of Satan's handiwork:
Eschew such (abomination),
That ye may prosper.
Satan's plan is (but)
To excite enmity and hatred
Between you, with intoxicants
And gambling, and hinder you
From the remembrance
Of God and from prayer:
Will ye not then abstain?
Obey God, and obey the Apostle,
And beware (of evil):
If ye do turn back
Know ye that it is
Our Apostle's duty
To proclaim (the Message)
In the clearest manner.

The Quran was not revealed in its entirety at one time, if follows, therefore, that the law embodied in the Quran was not revealed on one particular occasion. On the contrary, the verses which lay down the law were revealed according to the problems confronting the community from time to time. Take the verses about the rights of orphans to their property. A definite case was referred to the Prophet who was asked for a ruling. A man from the tribe of Ghaftan had in his custody a huge property belonging to his nephew who had become an orphan. When the nephew came of age he claimed his property but the uncle refused to hand it over to him. This was the occasion for the revelation of the following verses which lay down the law on the subject:

To orphans restore their property
(When they reach their age),
Nor substitute (your) worthless things
For (their) good ones; and devour not
Their substance (by making it up)
With your own. For this is
Indeed a great sin.

Take another instance of a serious case being referred to the Prophet in respect of the rights of widows. The reader will recall the custom before and in the early days of Islam about the treatment meted out to widows. When a man died, leaving a widow, the son and successor of the deceased from another wife would throw his garment on the widow. This signified his right to marry her or give her in marriage to somebody else in lieu of a dowry for himself. The successor often used to force the widow to part with her inheritance in his favour; and he was always in a position to influence a course of action favourable to himself. If the widow offered any resistance he maltreated her and refused to confer freedom on her till she died when he automatically inherited property left by her.

One Abu Qays ibn al-Aslat al-Ansari died and left his wife Kubaysha a widow. His heir and son from another wife covered the step-mother with his garment in accordance with the prevailing tradition. He neither married her nor supported her nor freed her. The only course open to her, under these circumstances, was to part with whatever she had inherited in order to buy her freedom. She came to the Prophet and complained about the treatment meted out to her by her step-son. He advised her to wait till the word of God decided the case. The women of Medina were intimately interested and waited in a deputation on the Prophet urging him to come to the rescue of women who had been subjected so mercilessly to humiliating treatment. The following verses revealed in this particular case became the law on the subject:

O ye who believe!
Ye are forbidden to inherit
Women against their will.
Nor should ye treat them
With harshness, that ye may
Take away part of the dower
Ye have given them,—except
Where they have been guilty
Of open lewdness;
On the contrary live with them
On a footing of kindness and equity.

The incident of Kubaysha establishes that even during the period of Medina the Muslims used to follow the pre-Islamic tradition until such time as it was specifically changed or altered by Islam. We are told that some of the Muslims, during the period of Medina, preferred to take their cases, according to the pre-Islamic tradition, to diviners and sooth-sayers and not to the Prophet for they feared that a judgment given by the Prophet would rather seek a settlement away for him. Al-Tabari relates that Qays, a man from al-Ansar, had a quarrel with a Jew. Both of them went for a settlement of their case to a diviner in Medina and left the Prophet out of the picture in spite of the insistence of the Jew. The following verses revealed on this occasion lay down the law for such matters:

Hast thou not turned
Thy vision to those
Who declare that they believe
In the revelations
That have come to thee
And to those before thee?
Their (real) wish is
To restore together for judgment
(In their disputes)
To the Evil One,

Though they were ordered
To reject him.
But Satan's wish
Is to lead them astray
Far away (from the Right).
But no, by thy Lord,
They can have
No (real) Faith,
Until they make thee judge
In all disputes between them,
And find in their souls
No resistance against
Thy decisions, but accept
Them with the fullest conviction.

Growth of Legislation

The Quran has direct relevance to the growing needs of the people. We see a process of gradual evolution of laws if we follow the Quran according to the chronology of events. It begins with a peaceful invitation to Islam during the period of Mecca. It deals with the legality of war and the circumstances under which Jihad is permitted in the early days of Islam in Medina when the details of the law of war are laid down. The order of charity is fixed and the people who are entitled to it are described in detail. In the beginning friendliness to the Jews is advocated but when they turned against Islam and failed to appreciate all gestures of reconciliation and violated their treaties, a firmer attitude towards them was taken. In the early phase certain pre-Islamic institutions were accepted because there was no intention of suddenly bringing about a cleavage with the past. With the passage of time, however, when the spirit of Islam had come to permeate the minds of the Muslims the same institutions and practices which were tolerated in the first phase were clearly prohibited and outlawed. In the early phases of Islam, drinking, for example, which was extremely common, was suffered but later, with the growth of the moral conscience in society, this was prohibited. The law was promulgated only after the people had been prepared to accept it.

In this process of gradual evolution laws had to be modified and changed according to the requirements of the time. This process of amendment of laws is called *Naskh* in Arabic. It means that a lawful act is rendered unlawful and *vice versa*. The action which was once allowed is prohibited and the one which was once prohibited becomes permissible. This process of amendment of laws is necessary for any growing society. The Quran recognises the need of growth. In fact, the process of amendment of laws is started by the Quran itself. The period for which a widow had to wait in order to be able to remarry was originally fixed at one year but was later reduced to four months. The law in this regard was amended.

> *Those of you*
> *Who die and leave widows*
> *Should bequeath*
> *For their widows*
> *A year's maintenance*
> *And residence; . . .*
> *If any of you die*
> *And leave widows behind,*
> *They shall wait concerning themselves*
> *Four months and ten days.*

The Laws

The *Nask* or the principle of amendment of laws rarely, if at all, affected the revelation during the period of Mecca. The reason is simple. The Meccan revelation deals primarily with the principles of Islam. These fundamentals are not open to any amendment or alteration. The amendment comes in where details of law have been laid down. These rules and regulations belong to the period of Medina. The mandatory verses of the Quran or those dealing with the "Ahkam" cover all phases of human activity. It is a vast field comprising religious rites like prayers, fasting, charity, and pilgrimage; civil affairs like selling and buying and usury; criminal affairs like theft, murder, adultery, and highway robbery; personal affairs like marriage, divorce, and inheritance; international affairs like laws of war, relations of the Muslims with their enemies, treaties, and war booty. All this is, however, mentioned only in a general way and complete details are not laid down even for prayers.

The working out of details was left to the Prophet in all cases and he took care of them by explaining either by word of mouth or by his own personal example. In many respects of its legislation the Quran avoided a sudden break with the past. It sought to reform the pre-Islamic system which was, of course, subject to many changes which cannot be covered in this chapter. It ordered, for example, a reduction in the number of wives on which there was no limit, it bestowed a new freedom on women who were treated as mere chattle, it changed the pre-Islamic traditions of marriage and divorce, it laid down the law for inheritance which was radically different from the one existing before Islam. The pre-Islamic Arab did not concede the right of inheritance either to women or to minors. This right belonged only to the strong man who participated in wars and fought the enemies. Islam, however, bestowed the right of inheritance on women although this was not by any means a popular act and was resisted by the Arabs, who accepted it with great difficulty. Ibn ʻAbbas relates that the revelation about the right of inheritance to the male and female children was followed by vociferous protests by the people. "Why," they asked, "is a wife given a quarter and the one-eighth, the daughter a half, and so also the minor, while none of them would fight the enemy and bring in booty?" In its anxiety to ensure that the vested interests of man should not override the consideration regarding the rights of women the Quran has affirmed the right at more than one place.

Prophet's Life

Another field of legislation was covered by the Sunnah or the Prophet's tradition. The legislation laid down by the Sunnah differs from the one ordained by the Quran in its authenticity and in its binding force for the simple reason that while the one is ordained by God, the other is commended by the Prophet. Considering the status of the Prophet, however, judgments given by him in individual cases came to assume the authority of law. No human being could have better interpreted the spirit of the Quran than the person to whom it was revealed and his authority is, therefore, justifiably unquestioned on matters of Islamic law. A judgment passed by the Prophet is considered as valid a law as the one directly revealed in the Quran. The only trouble in the case of the Sunnah, however, is its genuine authenticity about which there can be considerable difference of opinion. We have covered this subject in our discussion on the Hadith separately and we do not, therefore, propose to go further into it at this stage.

Most jurists agree that the Prophet exercised his own individual judgment in cases in which no direct guidance was available in the revelation and that in doing so he sometimes made an error of judgment, like any other human being, as is proved by a very small number of cases in which his attention has been affectionately drawn by the

Quran. It is related that the Prophet said about Mecca, "its Vegetation should not be taken and its trees should not be cut." Al-Abbas interrupted, "except for the green grass." "Yes," agreed the Prophet,' "except for the green grass." We are also told that the Prophet during one of his campaigns decided to halt at a place.

The people of that place told him that they were all too willing to carry out his instructions if he was halting there in deference to Divine revelation but in case he had decided to do so on his own they ventured to suggest that the place was not suitable in accordance with the laws of strategy. The Prophet stated that he had used his own judgment in selecting the place and that he agreed with the suggestion and moved away. The important point is that the Prophet, while exercising his personal judgment, was capable of making human errors. He was at the same time all too willing to acknowledge his mistakes and quickly rectified them as soon as sufficient evidence was brought before him warranting a change in his decision. In view of this healthy attitude the precedents which he eventually set up were, therefore, acknowledged as authoritative law on which the Companions depended for deciding similar cases referred to them.

The Hadith contains a large number of legal verdicts covering all aspects of life briefly referred to by the law laid down in the Quran. The Sunnah, in addition to an explanation of the Quranic verses, both in general and in detail,also contains a number of verdicts on points which have not been covered by the Quran. The oldest work of Hadith which has been collected from the point of view of a jurist is the *Sahih* of al-Bukhari.

The Quran and the Sunnah are the two sources of legislation in Islam. There is no third source. It follows, therefore, that the basis of Islamic law is a Divine basis and that in theory the power of making laws rests with God and God alone. The Prophet merely explained, interpreted, and applied the law. Human discretion is used only in cases where a clear text is not available, in the Quran or indirectly in the Sunnah which is a commentary on the Quran in case it is authentic. The Islamic law, therefore, differs radically from the ordinary law in which the legislative authority is free to explain and comment on the law introduced by it which it can freely amend, cancel, or withdraw. This freedom does not exist in the case of the law laid down by the Quran. The jurists can only exercise their discretion, within the framework of the outlines laid down by the Quran, for the understanding of which they can draw freely on the Sunnah of the Prophet provided there is consensus of opinion that a given Hadith can be taken as genuine. The discretion can also be exercised in cases which are covered neither by the Quran nor by the firmly established Sunnah.

The Prophet died in Medina while Islam was still confined to the Arabian Peninsula. The revelation ended with his death but the Islamic Empire spread within a remarkably short time. In 14 A.H. Damascus was occupied; three years later the conquest of Syria and Iraq was completed; in 21 A.H. Persia was conquered; in 56 A.H. the Muslims reached as far as Samarkand. In the west, Egypt was conquered in 20 A.H. The process went further and Spain was taken in about 93 A.H. With this process of quick expansion the social life of the Bedouin naturally underwent a metamorphosis. They came to have luxuries of life which they could not have visualised in the wildest of their dreams. The conquered countries were not only rich in worldly wealth but also represented the highest that the contemporary civilisation had to offer.

The nomads came into touch with ancient civilisations of Persia and Rome, and adjustments, therefore, became essential. New problems arose in every sphere of life, and these problems needed new laws and fresh legislation which did not exist in the Arabian peninsula before or just after Islam. New irrigation systems had to be manned, complicated financial problems had to be tackled, the conquered nations had to be dealt with equitably not only in the sphere of taxes but in other fields covering international law, civil and criminal law in addition to the personal law which was very different from the code which existed in Arabia. The Muslims came across a personal code of marriage of which they were not aware, a judicial system of which they had no experience, a criminal code of which they could not have been aware in the simplicity of their primitive life. In short, they came across new issues in all conceivable spheres of life, both internal and external. Their legislators, therefore, clearly faced a problem of the first magnitude. No one had claimed at any stage that the Quran had laid down detail of every conceivable law. Recourse had, therefore, to be taken to the exercise of personal judgment which was later organised and called *al-Qiyas*. This was the only logical answer to the growing needs of a dynamic society which was developing fast and was soon to cater to the needs of a heterogeneous society. Many, of the Companions, therefore, did not falter and readily used their individual judgment in cases in which there was no clear text in the Quran nor was there an authentic tradition which could be used as a guiding principle. Historians, traditionists, and jurists have left to posterity an excellent collection of issues in which the Companions used their judgment.

The first issue with which the Companions were faced immediately at the death of the Prophet was the problem of succession. Who was to succeed the Prophet as the leader of the Muslim community? Was the community bound to elect a person from among the immigrants from Mecca or from among the Muslims who had helped the immigrants during the most crucial period of Islam? What were the qualities of the successor of the Prophet? Was it essential for him to belong to his family or could any Muslim be elected to the office? These were pertinent questions and there was no clear answer to them either in the Quran or in the Sunnah. The only answer was the exercise by the Companions of their own instructed judgment. They did not falter in the use of their judgment. The minutes of the meeting under there of *(Ijtima al-Thaqifa),* which have been recorded for us by the historians, throw a flood of light on the manner in which the Companions calmly studied the issue and took a decision in the larger interests of the community.

The man who was elected to succeed the Prophet (Abu Bakr) had hardly stepped into office when he was faced with the problem of apostasy. The tribes living near Medina marched on the capital of the Muslim State. Their messengers entered the city only ten days after the assumption of office by the first Caliph. They demanded exemption from the payment of Zakat. Abu Bakr consulted the Companions who advised the adoption of a mild policy. To this Abu Bakr replied indignantly: "Divine revelation has ceased, and our Faith has reached perfection. Now, should it be allowed to be mutilated during my life? I swear by Allah that if even so much as a piece of string is withheld (from Zakat) I shall order war against them." The whole fabric of Islamic society would have collapsed if the institution of Zakat had been eliminated, but how was the Caliph to deal with this new situation for which there was no precedent in the lifetime of the Prophet? Abu Bakr boldly took a decision on the basis of his own judgment and the result was that it was not necessary to wage a war against the Muslims who paid the Zakat and Islam was saved while it was still in its infancy.

One can quote extensively to show that the Companions appreciated the importance of exercising their own instructed judgment in cases where a clear text was not available either in the Quran or in the Sunnah. Take the all-important issue of collecting the revelation in the form of a book. There was no clear law on the subject in the Quran. The matter was freely discussed among the Companions and the suggestion about collecting the revelation in the form of a book, to which Abu Bakr was not initially agreeable, was finally accepted. One shudders to think of the confusion which would have been caused in the ranks of Islam if the Companions had shirked exercising their own judgment in this grave issue.

Individual Decision

It is established that the Companions used their own individual judgment in addition to their profound knowledge of the Quran and the Sunnah in interpreting and applying the Divine Law. 'Umar ibn Khattab was, perhaps, the most leading Companion in this respect. In. addition to his own intrinsic ability many opportunities came his way because it was during his tenure of office that the Muslim community required fresh legislation owing to the new issues it had to face. 'Umar's judgments in economic, political, military, and civil affairs have, therefore, assumed a great importance and have come to serve as the basis for jurisprudence. In fact, it appears that on occasions 'Umar went further than the mere use of common sense. Instead of following the letter of the law, as laid down in the Quran, he followed the spirit; keeping in view the context of events in which a certain law was promulgated by the Quran. For example, the Quran lays down as one of the objects of charity the winning over of those "whose hearts have been reconciled". One of the legitimate channels in which charity must flow is to win over the hearts of the new converts who may still be vacillating, but if economic aid continued for a considerable time their adherence to the new faith was cemented. We quote below the relevant verse from the Quran:

Alms are for the poor
And the needy, and those
Employed to administer (the funds):
For those whose hearts
Have been (recently) reconciled
(To Truth); . . .

It was in deference to this command that the Prophet gave considerable rewards during the fall of Mecca to those who had till then proved the most uncompromising enemies of Islam. Among others, he gave a hundred heads of camels each to Abu Sufyan, al-Aqra, Safwan ibn Umayyah, etc. Safwan it was who had said that "he [the Prophet] was the most hated man by me; but he gave me and continued giving me until he became the most loved man by me." This was the spirit in which part of Zakat was given to the new converts. The same person, i.e. Safwan, asked for a piece of land during the Caliphate of Abu Bakr. His request was granted. When 'Umar came to power, he cancelled the orders of Abu Bakr and said: "God has strengthened Islam. If you stick to it (then it is right), if you leave it the sword would be between us." It is clear from this example that the order for diverting a part of *Zakat* to those whose "hearts need to be reconciled" to Islam was not a permanent injunction but had to be carried out with due regard to certain circumstances. When these circumstances ceased to exist there was no point in drawing on public money and spending it on those who in any case belonged firmly to the Muslim society.

We are told that, contrary to the usual interpretation of the Quranic injunction, 'Umar did not cut the hand of a thief in a certain year which happened to be a year of famine. In another case he did not cut the hands of some slaves who had stolen a camel. Addressing the owners of the camel he said: "I would have cut their hands had I not known that you [the masters] give them hard work and then starve them. If anyone of them has eaten what God rendered unlawful it has become lawful (under the circumstances)." There was a clear tendency in the first century of Islam towards organising the use of personal judgment, through consultation, in matters in which there were no clear instructions, either in the Quran or in the Sunnah. Unfortunately, however, no definite rules were laid down to explain and fix the methods of consultation, the qualifications of those who deserved to be consulted, the validity attached to their judgment, etc. The Muslims in Spain took a step in this direction when they formed the consultative assembly, the members of which were appointed by the Caliph. But this is not the place to discuss this later growth.

Umar ibn al-Khattab was the leader of the school of thought which exercised individual judgment and personal discretion in matters in which no clear command existed in the Quran and for which there was no precedent in the Sunnah of the Prophet. To this school of thought belonged Companions like Abu Bakr, Zayd ibn Thabit, Ubayy ibn Kab, and Muad ibn Jabal, all of whom issued verdicts according to their own judgment in numerous cases. The most famous Companion who followed in the footsteps of 'Umar ibn al-Khattab was 'Abd Allah ibn Masud in Iraq. He was a great admirer of 'Umar; and he it was who said at his death that 'Umar had taken away with him nine-tenths of knowledge. He was, however, no blind follower of 'Umar and had his differences with him. Abd Allah ibn Masud was characteristically independent in his judgment in cases in which no clear text was available in the Quran or in the Sunnah. Abu 'Umar al-Shabani tells us that sometimes he passed a whole year with Ibn Masud without even hearing the Prophet being quoted on any matter. The 'Iraqi school of thought which later became famous for its advocacy of personal judgment and its contribution to the field of syllogism, owes much to him. This school developed during the first and second centuries and some scholars like Rabi at al-Ray added the word *Ray* to their name indicating that they belonged to this school of thought which advocated the use of *Ray* or opinion or personal judgment. The 'Iraqi school of thought which counted people like Hasan al-Basri among its adherents was later to has Imam Abu Hanifa as its outstanding exponent.

Significance of Iraqi School

The reason why this school was found so acceptable in Iraq was perhaps the lack of enough Hadith in this region. Most of the people who narrated from the Prophet lived in the Hijaz and 'Umar took care to warn his Governors and preachers that they should be scrupulously cautious in quoting from the Prophet and not indulge unnecessarily in relating traditions, the exuberance of which, he feared, might cloud the clarity of the Quran. Moreover, Iraq was in no advanced state of civilisation on account of the influences it had imbibed from Persia and Greece. This factor, coupled with the scarcity of Hadith, made the use of personal judgment more plausible in this region than in the Hijaz where people were obsessed with the traditions. In fact, so great was the enthusiasm for the use of personal judgment in Iraq that it was not confined to concrete cases but people started formulating principles in great detail for hypothetical cases. We have an interesting incident in *Al-Muwafaqat* which throws a flood of light on the attitude of the people towards this field of intellectual activity. We are told that Asad ibn al-Furat came to Imam Malik and started asking him questions about certain issues. Each time Imam Malik answered a question Ibn al-Furat put another one saying "and what would be the answer if such and such thing were to happen?" Imam Malik was calm and conciliatory till one day he got fed up and told Ibn al-Furat that he could not possibly answer an endless chain of hypothetical questions; and if he was keenly interested in this field he should go to Iraq!

The reason why the 'Iraqi scholars indulged in this speculative field was perhaps also due to the influence of Syriac logic which prevailed in Iraq long before the conquest by Islam. The 'Iraqis did not relate too much Hadith and they were a little too critical of tradition; for the acceptance of which they had laid down rigorous rules. In fact, the extremists went to the Extent of rejecting tradition altogether. It appeared that the influence of the section which was inclined forwards rejecting Hadith as doubtful was fairly strong, for in Imam Shafii's book *Al-Umm* we see a long chapter under the heading" The Chapter About Those Who Repudiate All the Stones." Imam Shafii in another chapter refers to the ideas of those who held that the Hadith should not be taken as genuine unless all narrators were agreed and in case of a difference of opinion the Hadith in question should be ignored and personal judgment and study *(Ijtihad* and *Qiyas)* should be resorted to.

Significance of Hijazi School

Opposed to this school was the school of Hadith. This school derived its, inspiration from Companions like Al-Abbas, al-Zubayr, 'Abd Allah ibn 'Umar ibn al-Khattab, and 'Abd Allah ibn 'Amr bin al-As. Al-Shabi who belonged to the second generation of Islam belonged to this school of thought. He said: "Take whatever these Companions of God's Apostle have given you but throw in the fire what they have created according to their judgment." If the leaders of this school of thought were asked about the solution of a problem they would look up the Quranic text or the Hadith and suggest an answer, but in case they failed to find anything in these sources they would not suggest any solution. We are told that a man asked Salim ibn Abd Allah ibn 'Umar a question. Salim said that he heard nothing about it, suggesting thereby that there was no answer either in the Quran or in the Hadith. The man asked for Salim's personal opinion. Salim replied: "How can I do that? An idea occurs to me while you are here but I change my mind while you leave. How can I find you then and tell you of my new solution when you have left?" This was a genuine difficulty confronting this school. Ahmad ibn Hanbal tells us that he asked his father, the celebrated Imam Hanbal, for his advice in matters in which there was no clear text either in the Quran or in the Sunnah; in such cases, he asked Imam Hanbal: Should one depend on the Hadith of whose accuracy one was not certain, or should one resort to one's own personal judgment? Imam Hanbal advised the former course because he thought that even a doubtful tradition was more dependable than one's individual judgment.

This school fourished in the Hijaz for exactly the same reason that the other nourished in Iraq. We have noticed the reluctance of this school in exercising its personal discretion as against complete dependence on the Hadith even though it may, in cases, happen to be doubtful. The standards set by this school for judging the accuracy of a tradition were much more lenient than those laid down by the opposite school of thought in Iraq. The school of Hadith was perhaps indirectly responsible for encouraging the movement of fabrication of traditions. Since it was reluctant to exercise personal judgment in the absence of a Hadith people started fabricating it in order to meet the requirements of a given situation which could not otherwise be met. 'Atiq al-Zubaydi has stated that Imam Malik included 10,000 traditions in *al-Muwatta*. He used to revise his collection every year and dropped a number of traditions until it became what we have today. Had he been alive he would have dropped all the traditions which he had included at first. Even Abu Hanifa who is known for his use of personal judgment depended a lot on the traditions of the Prophet or of the Companions in each chapter of his book. He was known, however, not to have much faith in traditions except in a few limited ones.

Adopting the Right Path

There were extremists in both schools of thought. Between the two extremes, however, arose a school which favoured the middle path. It did not ignore the use of personal judgment and at the same time accepted the Hadith. It drew up detailed circumstances in which the use of personal judgment was recognised. Among the leaders of this school were Imam Malik and Imam Al-Shafii. Thus the field of legislation expanded and benefited from a variety of schools.

During the days of the first three Caliphs, Medina was the centre of administration and, therefore, the centre of all legislative activity. We have already noticed that the first Caliph, Abu Bakr, used to consult the leading Companions in cases in which he could not find a clear Quranic text or a suitable precedent from the Hadith. He is, however, not known to have appointed any judge anywhere for the administration of justice. It is stated that with the increase in his work he entrusted judicial affairs to 'Umar. With the assumption of office of the Caliph by 'Umar an era of expansion began. This resulted in the appointment of judges for the first time in countries such as Egypt, Syria, and Iraq. With each judge was a group of Companions and Tabiin who were conversant with the traditions of the local inhabitants besides a sound knowledge of the Quranic sciences. These Companions were consulted in difficult cases by the judges; in fact, the Companions, by virtue of their knowledge and experience, became the leaders of legislative activity in their respective regions. Their judgments and rulings became the basis of the special tradition of the countries in which they worked and set up legal precedents which were followed in similar cases by other judges. Different regions came to attach importance to the verdicts of different jurists. The inhabitants of Medina, for example, were inclined to follow the verdicts of 'Abd Allah ibn 'Umar; the people of Mecca followed the rulings of Abd 'Allah ibn 'Abbas; the Kufis followed the judgments of 'Abd Allah ibn Masud, while the Egyptians preferred to take the lead from 'Abd Allah ibn 'Amr ibn al-As. The volume of these judgments and leading rulings grew with the passage of time as more and more cases were decided. A wealth of legal precedents was thus collected which was to prove useful to judges in different regions of the Muslim Empire in time to come.

With the assumption of office by 'Ali, the seat of the Caliphate shifted, for a time, from Medina to Kufa, and later with the assumption of power by the Umayyads the centre shifted to Damascus. This was the period in which alien influences found their way into the thought of Islam. We have dealt in some detail elsewhere with the impact of the Roman, Greek, and the Persian civilisations on Islam. Some Orientalists like Goldziher believe that Muslim jurisprudence in this era was influenced to a great extent by Roman law. It will be recalled that before the Muslim conquest, schools of Roman law existed in Syria, notably in Qaysariya and Beirut. Law-courts following the Roman code existed in Syria at the time of the Muslim conquest and they were allowed to continue for a considerable time after the conquest. It is claimed that the Syrians, after they entered the fold of Islam, adapted the existing law to the new circumstances. In support of this contention the Orientalists belonging to this school of thought quote articles which they claimed have been taken literally from the Roman law. They also suggest that the Arabic word *Fiqh* which means wisdom and knowledge has been taken from a Latin word which means the same thing. They put forward the plea that Islamic jurisprudence has, borrowed from the Roman law either directly or through Talmud which has in turn taken a lot from the Roman law.

It is difficult, however, to accept that the Muslim law has been borrowed from the Roman law only because of its superficial resemblance. All law, religious or secular, must be based on principles of justice. The Arabic word *Fiqh* in its original meaning denotes knowledge and understanding. Before the Arabs had an opportunity to mix with the Romans, the Quran used this word in this sense. Later the use of the expression was limited to the science of law-making because this branch of intellectual activity needed the knowledge of the religion, the Quran, and the traditions. Thus the meaning of the word came to be limited and it became a technical term. In the works available on Muslim law we have been unable to detect any noticeable dependence on Roman law. The first Muslim who is stated to have been influenced by Roman law was al-Awzai who lived in Beirut, the centre of the Roman school in Syria. He was the most important jurist of that region. Taking advantage of the loss of his work the Orientalists made bold to suggest that had his works been extant they would have provided evidence of incontrovertible influence of Roman law.

A good deal of al-Awzai's works can fortunately be found in the seventh volume of *Al-Umm*. Anybody who reads it carefully will come to the conclusion that al-Awzai was a protagonist of the school of Hadith and not of the school of personal judgment as Goldziher suggests. And the school of Hadith is the last to be affected, if any has at all been affected, by Roman law. It must be admitted, however, that Roman law proved useful to the Muslim jurists inasmuch as it helped them to study the different issues involved in a given case, but the final verdicts were always given in accordance with Muslim law. It must be understood that Islam set up precedents of tolerance and toleration. In the case of the administration of justice one can visualise the Muslim judges giving due consideration to the local customs and habits of the people and accepting them at times when they were not in conflict with the law laid down by Islam. In a supplement to *Qudat al-Misr* it is stated that Khair ibn Naim, who was appointed a judge in 120 A.H., used to listen to the Copts speaking in their own language. Not only that, he talked to them in their language, and listened to the witnesses in their language and passed his judgments accordingly. This, however, does not suggest that the presiding judge who was willing to show consideration to the local population inasmuch as he agreed to talk to them in their own language also accepted their own law in dealing with the cases before him.

The Umayyad dynasty, except for a few honourable exceptions like that of 'Umar ibn 'Abd al-Aziz, did little to further the ends of legislative activity in Islam. During this period we do not see a jurist of the eminence of Abu Yusuf who flourished during the Abbasid period. The Abbasid Caliphs conferred their patronage on eminent jurists whose verdicts were respected and who were held in high esteem by society. We do not find any such example during the Umayyad period except perhaps in the case of al-Zuhri who enjoyed the patronage of the Caliph. Moreover, during this era the four creeds of Islam had not yet emerged. Towards the end of the dynasty, however, the two creeds, namely, that of Abu Hanifa in Iraq and that of Malik ibn Anas in Medina, had emerged. Born of Persian decent in 80 A.H. in the days of Caliph 'Abd al-Malik ibn Marwan, Abu

Hanifa lived for eighteen years during the Abbasid dynasty. He studied jurisprudence from Jafar al-Sadiq, a member of the family of 'Ali, and from Ibrahim al-Nakhai, a leading jurist of his time. He learnt Hadith from Shabi al-Amas and Qatada. He had a special bent of mind for jurisprudence and his legal acumen won for him the fame of being the leader of the school of personal judgment during his lifetime. We have not received any of his legal works nor has it been proved that he wrote any book in which the principles of his creed could be studied at first hand. Two of his disciples Abu Yusuf and Muhammad have, however, recorded for posterity the achievements of Abu Hanifa.

The leader of the other school, Malik ibn Anas, was born in Medina where he lived, learnt, taught, and wrote, while Abu Hanifa was of Persian descent.

Malik ibn Anas came from an old Arab family. He became famous during his lifetime as an authority on Hadith and was considered the leader of the school of Hadith. He died in 179 A.H. His principal contribution is *Al-Muwatta'* which, although known as a book of Hadith, is in fact a book on jurisprudence. *Al-Muwatta'* is no mere collection of traditions which its author considered to be accurate, but it seeks to derive verdicts on principal issues from the Hadith collected in a volume which contains numerous personal opinions and views on a variety of matters.

We do not propose to enter into details of differences between the views of the two Imams nor do we propose to discuss the principles on which they based their arguments as this would be a fit subject to discuss while considering the contribution of the Abbasid regime which is outside the scope of our work.

Circumstances Leading to the Need of Recording Events : The religious movement was the most important single factor in ushering in a cultural era. The next movement which helped complement the work of the first was the historical movement. This movement should not be understood to mark the period of writing, compiling, or editing books on history. This was yet to come. Here we merely deal with the beginning of an awareness of history, of the need to record, not necessarily in writing, the events of early Islam starting with the life of the Prophet himself.

The need to understand and interpret the Quran was the fundamental factor in creating an interest in historiography. The pre-Islamic literature of the Arabs, both poetry and prose, the traditions and ways of living of the Arabs, both in Jahiliyya and in Islam, the leading historical events in the life of the Arabs during the Jahiliyya and Islam, the history of the Prophet's mission, the series of persecutions in Mecca, the conflicts with his adversaries and the subsequent migration to Medina, the campaigns launched by him to defend Islam from the City State of Medina, the laws promulgated by the Quran to weld the tribal Bedouins into a united community and brotherhood of Islam—all these and many more factors provided the historical data, an essential background to the verses in the Quran which dealt with various situations as they arose over a period of nearly twenty-three years.

The verses in the Quran referred briefly to incidents and did not provide the details. Those who read the references to certain historical events, therefore, sought further information. The story of the creation has been briefly given in the Quran but the curious student must look elsewhere for details. The Quran refers to many a prophet but does not give as much wealth of detail as one would want. The brief story of Moses in the Quran whets the curiosity of a reader who naturally looks about for more details. Who was the young man who was killed by Moses? Moses married one of the daughters of the Prophet Shuayb. Was she the younger or the elder of the two? What did she look like? What were the terms of the marriage contract? This information had, therefore, to be supplied. Some material could be had in the Tawrat and its commentaries and the marginal notes. Many Jews had embraced Islam and through them their stories came into the literature of Islam. The Arabs were mostly Bedouins and illiterate. If they happened to be eager to know something about the reasons of the creation, beginning of the world, or the secrets of being, they simply asked the People of the Book and made use of their knowledge. But the Jews and Christians among the Arabs themselves were as ignorant as the Muslims. Most of the *Tafsirs* or Commentaries, therefore, abound with what they brought to Islam. The commentators accepted this kind of knowledge emanating from the Jewish converts to Islam and readily included it in their works. Furthermore, with the territorial expansion of Islam the Caliphs became increasingly aware of the need to study the history of other nations.

The growing needs of the State—an efficient system of administration, taxation, the organisation of the army and civil services—could not be satisfied without a critical examination of contemporary systems which had run successfully for centuries. The Caliphs did not, therefore, hesitate in studying other systems and adapting their own to the changing requirements of an expanding State. Another factor helped the movement. People of different nationalities and religions embraced Islam. With them came the knowledge of their past. The Jews, for example, were responsible for spreading the stories of the Old Testament among the Muslims. In Tabari's "History" we come across one of the stories about the origin of the world. We are told that God started creating the world on a Sunday. By Monday He had created the earth, by Wednesday He created the heavens, and He finished His work at the last hour of Friday when He hurriedly created Adam. Resurrection, therefore, will come on Friday at this hour. Similar tales are told to elaborate the stories and parables in the Quran. Stories of the Old Prophets also became popular. The Persians had a rich legacy of legend and mythology which found its way to Muslim historical literature. The same is true of the Christians. The histories of the Arabs contributed to the growth of the historical movement.

The most important factor, however, was the Muslim zest for collecting the Hadith or the sayings of the Prophet. The word *hadith* means primarily a communication or narrative in general whether religious or profane, then it has the particular meaning of a record of actions or sayings of the Prophet and his Companions. Even before Islam it was considered a virtue to follow the Sunnah or the traditions of one's forefathers. With the rise of Islam, however, the Sunnah could no longer consist of following the customs and usage of heathen ancestors. The Muslim community had to hold up a new Sunnah. Every Muslim had now to take the conduct of the Prophet and his Companions as a model for himself in all the affairs of life, and every endeavour was, therefore, made to preserve information regarding it. Every tradition has the form of a personal statement. Every Hadith, for example, consists of two parts. The first contains the names of the persons who have handed on the substance of the tradition to one another; this part is called *Sanad,* i.e. the authority, for the trustworthiness of the statement. The second part is the text or the real substance of the statement.

This work, which was to distinguish the early Muslim historian, started early with the rise of Islam. The field covered almost all activities of the Prophet—his material utterances and speeches, prayers, religious rites, jurisprudence in both civil and criminal cases. An historical record was compiled of the life of the Prophet, the most elaborate details were recorded about his campaigns besides some acts of Abu Bakr and the conquests of 'Umar. This wealth of material, collected with the greatest care, formed the basis of all subsequent works on history and biography.

During the lifetime of the Prophet, the Hadith was not written. The Apostle employed scribes to write down the verses of the Quran as and when they were revealed to him, but he did not employ anyone to record his own sayings. On the contrary, a number of traditions forbid writing down of the sayings of the Prophet. Muslim, for example, quotes Said al-Khidri in his *Sahih* to the effect that the Holy Prophet stated: "Do not write what I say. Whoever has written anything from me other than the Quran, let him wipe it out. Whoever has deliberately attributed a false uttering to me, let him occupy his seat in Hell."

It cannot, however, be said for certain whether or not the Hadith was written during the lifetime of the Prophet. The very fact that he had to forbid people from writing it goes to show that people started writing the Hadith during his lifetime. Some scholars have tried to clear up this controversy by saying that the orders prohibiting the writing of the sayings of the Prophet were issued in order to ensure that the Quran was not mixed up with the Prophet's personal opinions expressed on different issues from time to time. While it is certain that the Quran was recorded and written in an authentic manner during the lifetime of the Prophet and was compiled soon after his death, it is known that the writing and compilation of the Hadith was not organised during his lifetime.

The Companions were extremely cautious and restrained themselves from unnecessarily quoting the Prophet. They exercised the utmost care in recalling and restating a sentence uttered by the Prophet for they were mortally afraid of being accused of falsely attributing a statement to him. They were fully conscious of the implications of such a tendency and did everything in their power to fight and control it.

It was an invariable custom with the Companions that whenever somebody quoted the Prophet to them they at once asked for an authority. A grandmother, for example, came to Abu Bakr and told him that she was entitled to part of the property of her grandson who had died. Abu Bakr told her that he did not know of any right accruing to her on this score, for he had come across no relevant passage either in the Quran or in the sayings of the Prophet that he could possibly recall. He, however, asked those who were present, and al-Mughira ibn Shuba testified that the Prophet had given a grandmother one-sixth of the property of her deceased grandson. Abu Bakr asked whether anybody else in that company had heard a similar statement from the Prophet. Muhammad ibn Maslama corroborated the statement of al-Mughira and Abu Bakr then accepted it as an authentic statement.

Notwithstanding all this care and caution on the part of the Companions one has to contend with the fact that the Hadith was not written in an organised manner and was not compiled during the early years of Islam. The inevitable result was, therefore, that people depended on their memory for the sayings of the Prophet during the twenty-three years of his life from the Relevation to his death. This was a wide field. The temptation to quote the Prophet was great. Not everybody could resist it. This soon led to deliberate forgery of traditions. Numerous traditions were put into circulation in which the Prophet was made to say or do something which was at that time considered the proper view. It seems that this kind of fabrication started within the lifetime of the Prophet who took an exception to it and forbade indulgence in such fabrication, the penalty for which was Hell. Such fabrication was even more difficult to control after his death. In the course of time the records of the Prophet's words increased in volume and copiousness. In the early centuries after the Prophet's death there was great difference of opinion in the Muslim community on many questions of the most diverse nature. Each party, therefore, endeavoured to support its views, as far as possible, with sayings and verdicts of the Prophet. He who could base his views on those of the Prophet was certainly right and thus arose the numerous contradictory traditions on the Sunnah of the Prophet.

Muslim quotes Ibn 'Abbas as saying: "We used to transmit the sayings of the Prophet when they could not be forged or fabricated. When people, however, started quoting without any scruples we stopped quoting from the Prophet." We are also told that Bashir al-Adawi once came to Ibn 'Abbas and started relating to him the sayings of the Holy Prophet. Ibn 'Abbas completely ignored him. He neither looked at him nor listened to him. When Ibn 'Abbas was asked why he was paying such scant regard to the sayings of the Prophet he turned round to answer: "Once when somebody used to say that the Apostle of God had uttered a certain word our eyes used to be fixed on his face and our ears were all anxiety to listen to him, but now when people have become unscrupulous in quoting from the Prophet we do not listen to them and do not believe them except in cases where we personally know that the Prophet made a certain statement."

This was the approach of the Companions towards the sayings of the Prophet. Their faith in him, however, could not be matched by the faith of the new entrants to Islam from far-flung countries like Persia, Egypt, Syria, etc. These people allowed themselves the liberty of freely quoting from the Prophet. Ibn 'Adiyy tells us that when one of these fabricators, 'Abd al-Karim ibn 'Abd al-Aja, was being taken to be beheaded for this crime he said, "I have fabricated four thousand traditions in which I rendered things lawful and things unlawful."

This 'Abd al-Karim was the uncle of Man ibn Zayda and was accused of being a follower of Mani. He used freely to fabricate the Hadith quoting distinguished names. Some of the traditions fabricated by him include fundamental deviations from the Muslim Law. The fabricated Hadith about the *Tafsir* or commentary on the Quran could be counted by thousands. Ahmad ibn Hanbal frankly stated that he believed in none of them. Al-Bukhari in his book of 7000 traditions, out of which 3000 are repeated, chose 4000 traditions from among 600,000 known in his day.

Not all the narrators fabricated the Hadith with a view to misrepresenting the Prophet. There were some honest people who transmitted what they heard; there were others, equally honest in purpose, who saw no harm in attributing to the Prophet what was otherwise morally correct. Khalid ibn Yazid has stated that he heard Muhammad ibn Said al-Dimashqi say: "If I found a correct thing I did not see any harm in attributing it to the Prophet." Again, we have it on the authority of Imam Muslim that Abi Jafar al-Hashimi al-Madani used to fabricate the Hadith, the text of which was not exceptionable although he was aware that it had not emanated from the Prophet. The idea was to invoke authority in order to inspire people into righteous action. Whatever the motive, the fact remains that the Hadith was fabricated on a large scale.

One of the reasons for this was the political conflict between 'Ah' and Abu Bakr, 'Ah' and Muawiyyah, 'Abd Allah ibn al-Zubayr and 'Abd al-Malik ibn Marwan, and finally between the Umayyads and the Abbasids. Ibn Abi al-Hadid, in his commentary on *Nahj al-Balagha* says: "The origin of the mis-statements in the Hadith about the virtues of different men can be traced to the Shia who started fabricating the Hadith in favour of their man ['Ali]. They were compelled to do so because of their enmity with the other party. When the followers of Abu Bakr saw the followers of 'Ali doing so they retorted by fabricating Hadith in order to lionise their own hero. This provided an incentive to the Shias to counter-attack. They forged many sayings of the Holy Prophet according to most of which leading Companions and their disciples were considered unbelievers and hypocrites. The partisans of Abu Bakr paid back the partisans of 'Ali in the same coin by attacking, through forged Hadith, 'Ali and his two sons. 'Ali was described as a weak statesman, a feeble-minded man in love with earthly pleasures. They could have, however, spared themselves all the trouble of defaming and praising the two men because virtues of both 'Ali and Abu Bakr were universally known and recognised, and they did not need to have partisans to win recognition for their great contribution in the field of Islam."

Another category of Hadith seeks to exaggerate the merits of one Arab tribe over the other. The Hadith was treated as a medium for achieving their individual needs and in fact was used to supplement the poetry of the Jahiliyya. One comes across many traditions praising the merits of the Quraish, al-Ansar, and other tribes. There are also traditions which seek to establish the superiority of the Arabs over the Persians and the Greeks. The non-Arab elements retorted by fabricating traditions to establish the superior merit of the Greeks, the Abyssinians, and the Turks. This was not the end of fabrication. Traditions were freely used to praise one city against the other. It satisfied local patriotism which received sanction from no less an authority than the Prophet.

With the passage of time the Hadith came to reflect religious and juridical ideas. Scholars of logic, for instance, differed from the Companions in their theories of fatalism and freewill. Some of them permitted themselves the liberty to back their theories by fabricating traditions in which they mentioned such details as made the Prophet a logician who examined these theories in the minutest details. They went as far as to mention opposing creeds and to make the Prophet curse them. The same attitude was adopted in jurisprudence. One hardly comes across any branch of Fiqh without a Hadith supporting it. Even Abu Hanifa who, it is stated, did not believe in more than seventeen traditions (according to Ibn Khaldun) has not escaped this influence.

The sycophancy of those who pretended to be scholars and wanted to flatter the ruling princes has made no mean contribution to the art of fabrication. We have an interesting instance of Ghiyath ibn Ibrahim who related a tradition to the contemporary Caliph, al-Mahdi, who was very fond of pigeons. Al-Ghiyath related a tradition from the Prophet: "There is no win (in a race) except by a horse's hoof, a camel, or by a wing." The Caliph bestowed a reward of 10,000 Dirhams on him but when Ghiyath was about to leave the court al-Mahdi said: "I am sure that your back is the back of a liar who forges things and attributes them to the Apostle of God who never said 'by a wing' but you said it in order to gain out favour."

It was not seldom that one came across traditions full of the virtues of people whom the Prophet had not even seen. Traditions were used to induce the people to read the Quran and it was freely stated in them that whoever read such and such Surah of the Quran would get such and such a favour from God. These traditions are mentioned after commentary on each Sura in the *Tafsir* of al-Baidawi.

Ubayy ibn Kab who was largely responsible for these innovations was asked about the source of such traditions and he simply stated: "When I saw the people getting busy with the *Fiqh* (jurisprudence) of Abu Hanifa and the stories of campaigns and wars written by Muhammad ibn Ishaq, I felt that the people were inclined to leave the study of the Quran. I, therefore, wrote this Hadith just for the sake of God."

This chaotic state of affairs in the field of Hadith led faithful Muslims to attend to the urgent need of rescuing the truth from unscrupulous scholars. An era of critical investigations was ushered in and detailed rules were framed to test the authenticity of a tradition. It is outside our province to go into the details of the rules prescribed for testing the accuracy of the Hadith. We would, however, like to point out that the bulk of these rules was directed at scrutinising the names of the narrators together with their antecedents, but proportionate attention was not given to the examination of the text of the Hadith itself. We seldom find, for example, a critic analysing the text of a Hadith with a view to finding discrepancies in it. A quotation from the Prophet could be examined from the point of view of fixed historical events. It might contain a contradiction. Again, the idiom and phraseology and the language employed might not be found to belong to the period of the Prophet. There might be a philosophical quotation in a tradition which might be alien to the surroundings of the Prophet. A tradition with a technically legal text might perhaps be traced to influences subsequent to the Prophet's period. The text of the Hadith was not examined from this point of view. Far too much attention was paid to the narrator than to the narration itself. One can find in the collection of even al-Bukhari, the greatest scholar in this field, inner contradictions in the text of the traditions which he had accepted and included in his collection.

No attempt was made in the first century of Islam to collect authentic traditions of the Prophet. No Caliph, for example, ever ordered any collection or even made an effort to ascertain the accuracy of the traditions which were known and were being circulated among the people during his period. Even though it occurred to some to collect all the available traditions in the form of one book, it was clearly not a practical proposition because we are told that at the death of the Prophet there were about 114,000 Companions who quoted from him. Each of them knew one or more traditions. All these had to be collected in the first instance and then their contents could not be reviewed except in consultation with the whole body of them. Most of them depended on memory and it was, therefore, apparently an extremely difficult task which remained unfulfilled.

In the first century of Islam traditions were neither recorded nor written. They were only told orally and were stored in the memory of the people. These who happened to write them down did so only for their own benefit and not for circulation among the people. During the second century, however, certain groups of scholars in different parts of the Muslim Empire started collecting traditions but not for the purpose of compiling an authentic copy of all available material. Each scholar tried to collect all the authentic traditions related to him. According to the *Sahih* of al-Bukhari who selected 7000 out of 600,000, the first to collect traditions were al-Rabi' ibn Sabi (died 160 A.H.) and Said ibn 'Uruba (died 156 A.H.) until the matter reached the leading scholars of the third generation when Imam Malik wrote *al-Muwatta'* in Medina, 'Abd al-Malik ibn Jari wrote in Mecca, al-Awzai in Syria, Sufyan al-Thawri in Kufa and Hammad ibn Salma ibn Dinar in Basrah.

The example of these scholars was later followed by others. Some collected traditions from the point of view of jurisprudence like *al-Muwatta'* of Malik and the two *Sahihs* of al-Bukhari and Muslim, others collected them according to the chain of narrators. In such collections all the traditions related by Abu Hurrayrah were collected apart from those quoted by others. These books came to be compiled much later than the period with which we are dealing and they do not therefore form part of our study.

The Study of Hadith as a Cultural Factor : The study of the Hadith, whether genuine or fabricated, went a long way in disseminating the culture of Islam. The mass of the Muslims were eager to learn about their religion. It is significant that the fame of all the scholars among the Companions and their successors is based primarily on the Hadith and *Tafsir*. Of these two Hadith took the place of precedence. It was not uncommon to see important scholars making long journeys through the length and breadth of the Muslim world in search of a Hadith. This activity not only brought together learned men from different parts of the Muslim world in person but touched off a cultural movement which was destined to exercise a deep influence on the growth of Islam.

The isolation of centuries was broken and ideas freely flowed between different parts of the Muslim world. So great was their devotion to the subject that scholars travelled hundred of miles in order to collect one tradition from the Prophet from some reliable source. We have it on the authority of Ahmad ibn Hanbal that Jabir ibn 'Abd Allah al-Ansar, on learning that a certain person in Syria,

'Abd Allah ibn 'Unayn al-Jahni, knew of a certain Hadith from the Prophet, immediately bought a camel and travelled for a whole month to collect the Hadith in question. And yet this is no extraordinary example of a scholar of traditions for in all biographies we will find that a major part of the life of scholars of Hadith was spent in travelling about collecting material. They travelled in addition to conduct a considerable correspondence with scholars in different parts of the Muslim world.

This is how the history of culture and in fact that of Islam started in its early phases. The stories of the campaigns and the virtues of men and nations narrated in the traditions constitute the first chapter of Muslim history. Early works on history like Ibn Hisham's *Sira,* Ibn Jarir's quotations from Ibn Ishaq, Baladhuri's *Futuh al-Buldan* were all written in the familiar pattern of the Hadith. The stories of the Prophets are mentioned briefly in the Quran, the Hadith fills up the gaps by supplying some details; more were added by various narrators and thus came about the art of story-telling. In due course, proverbs, rules of ethics, and philosophical thought from Greece, India, and Persia were added to the Hadith. All this was mixed indissolubly and the final result spread among the people as "religion" which affected them much more than any secular education. The Hadith, moreover, was the most important source of legislation in matters relating to religious rites, civil and criminal affairs. It was easily the most important influence on the cultural growth of Islam in the first century of its existence.

The Art of Story-telling as an Instrument of History : All sources agree on Tamim, a Christian from the Yemen, being the first story-teller in Islam. He embraced Islam in 9 A.H. He used to appear as an anchorite, a legacy from his Christian past. Tamim is supposed to have been the first man to light candles and lamps in the mosque of the Prophet—yet another practice inherited from the Christian tradition. The contents, the manner, and the method of his stories are not known. The general pattern is, however, familiar. The story-teller sat down in the mosque. The people gathered round him and he began a story with a seemingly historical setting which was inextricably mixed up with legend. The general trend was to tell stories of other nations with a view to moralise. The facts did not matter so much as the effect. The story-teller wove in interesting details and spoke in a manner which impressed the audience into voluntarily suspending their judgment and taking the story as literally a chapter from history.

The telling of a story for the high classes was organised as an art by Muawiyyah. He appointed qualified men who told a story after the morning prayers. A man would sit down and begin with the name of God, then invoke prayers for the Prophet, the Caliph, his family, servants and soldiers, and finally pray for the wrath of God to befall the enemies of the Caliph. After this ceremonial beginning, he would proceed with the story. This art became popular. With the growth of its popularity the facts of history yielded place to the fancy of fiction. Except for al-Hasan al-Basri, who was extremely careful with his facts, the story-tellers, as a class, degenerated into instruments of entertainment for the people. That is why 'Ali prohibited their entry in the mosque with the only honourable exception of Hasan al-Basri.

It appears that political capital was made out of an art which was undoubtedly popular. Stories served the purpose of the modern propaganda machine. The art of story-telling soon gained official recognition. In Kindi's *Quddat* we read of many judges who held appointments as story-tellers.

The stories introduced Christian and Jewish legends and opened a way for fabrications, half-truths and untruths into the Hadith. While the art of story-telling started as a movement of history it ended up by greatly distorting it. It made the work of a historian more difficult —the work of separating facts from fascinating fiction.

Involvement of the Elites

Beginning of Literacy : Before Islam illiteracy was the rule rather than the exception. The Quraish, the most important tribe in Arabia, could boast of no more than seventeen men who could write. The tribes of Aws and Khazraj did not have more than eleven literate persons. So rare indeed were men of culture that a person who knew writing, swimming, and shooting was called a perfect man.

With the rise of Islam, the Prophet, himself an unlettered man, needed the services of those who knew how to write in order to record the Revelation. The first among the Quraish to have this honour was 'Abd Allah ibn Sad ibn Sarh. The scribes employed by the Prophet used to write on sheets of skin, ribs of bone, palm leaves, and stones.

Islam thus provided an incentive to literacy. The Revelation had to be written and once it was recorded the Quran had to be read out to the mass of men who were illiterate. While it was necessary, on the one hand, to have people who could correctly take down the Quran, it was equaly essential, on the other, to have a team which could accurately read it out to the people. The Prophet, therefore, encouraged the arts of reading and writing. In the Battle of Badr the literate captives were promised their freedom after each had taught writing to ten boys of Medina. The Prophet not only encouraged the reading and writing of Arabic but he also exhorted people to learn other languages. Zayd ibn Thabit, who used to write for the Prophet, learnt to write the Jewish language at his bidding. He is also said to have learnt the Syriac language because the Prophet asked him to do so.

With the gradual spread of Islam reading and writing became necessary, not only for the limited team which worked for the Prophet but also for the expanding circle of the Muslims who could not master their religion without the aid of literacy. Moreover, the non-Arabs who embraced Islam had to learn Arabic, not only for purposes of religious instruction but also for material benefits which accrued from the knowledge of the language.

The Quran was instrumental in creating an interest in education at large. To the Arabs were related beautifully the stories of Adam, Noah, Abraham, Joseph, Moses, David, Solomon, and other prophets. These stories were, however, not related for the sake of a story. The idea was not to tell the whole tale but to briefly refer to it with a view to driving home a certain point. The curious had to fill in the blanks for much was left to the imagination of the reader. This created a taste for more knowledge and the Arabs began to look round with avid interest for the history of other nations, particularly the Jews and the Christians. The Prophet placed such a high premium on learning that he went to the extent of treating the ink of a scholar as being like or equal to the blood of a martyr. He exhorted his people to go unto China for the sake of learning. The Quran is replete with passages inviting the reader to study the phenomena of nature around him, for in the smallest and what may appear to the eye the most insignificant act lies a challenge to human thought. The ant and the bee are much too trivial to merit the attention of a casual man but they offer a world of wisdom to those who care to pause and ponder. The Quran lays great stress on the value of knowing the nature of things for it is the knowledge of creation which will lead man to the knowledge of the Creator.

The word knowledge *(ilm)* is used in a general sense and does not denote the knowledge of any particular branch of life. It covers both the spiritual and material aspects of life, not only of man but of the entire creation. This spirit awakened a new impulse for knowledge with the coming of Islam. Medina became a centre of attraction for scholars from abroad. Here flocked the Persians, the Greeks, the Syrians, the Iraqis, the Africans; men of diverse nationalities came from all directions to seek light from the Master who preached: "Acquire knowledge, because he who acquires it in the way of the Lord performs an act of piety; who speaks of it, praises the Lord; who seeks it, adores God; who dispenses instruction in it, bestows alms; and who imparts it to its fitting objects, performs an act of devotion to God. Knowledge enables its professor to distinguish what is forbidden from what is not; it lights the way to Heaven; it is our friend in the desert, our society in solitude, our companion when bereft of friends; it guides us to happiness; it sustains us in misery; it is our ornament in the company of friends; it serves as an armour against our enemies. With knowledge, the servant of God rises to the heights of goodness and to a noble position, associates with sovereigns in this world, and attains to the perfection of happiness in the next."

The cultural movement in the first century of Islam followed four courses: religious, historical, juridical, and philosophical. The first was the most important and started in the lifetime of the Prophet. It was based entirely on the need to read and understand the Quran. Knowledge was, therefore, definitive knowledge, as pointed out by Ghazali, and had an intimate relationship with the obligations of a Muslim to discharge his duties in accordance with the commands of the Quran. It is in this sense that the seeking of knowledge is an ordinance obligatory upon every Muslim.

The Quran was revealed to the Prophet over a period of about twenty-three years. All the verses were written during his lifetime. They were recorded by different scribes. Besides the written record the Quran was committed to memory by a large number of contemporary Muslims. The first Caliph, Abu Bakr, ordered the collection of all the written record. He also caused portions which had been committed to memory by different people to be reduced to writing. All these manuscripts were collected under the supervision of Zayd ibn Thabit, the chief scribe of the Prophet. This record was kept in the personal custody of Abu Bakr. With his death the manuscripts passed to his successor, 'Umar ibn al-Khattab, and after him the records were found with Hafsa, the daughter of 'Umar. The third Caliph, 'Uthman, appointed a board of editors which included famous companions like Zayd ibn Thabit, 'Abd Allah ibn Zubayr, and Said ibn al-As. This board undertook to collect all the material which had not till then been compiled in a single volume. Many copies were made and distributed to different parts of the Empire. With the final preparation of the authentic version of the Quran all other versions in the custody of individuals were destroyed.

The Quran was revealed in Arabic. "Had We sent this as a Quran in a language other than Arabic, they would have said: Why are not its verses explained in detail? A book not in Arabic and a messenger in Arabia?" Even though the Book was in Arabic all that it contained was not understood by the Arabs. The understanding of a book requires more than mere proficiency in speaking the language. There are instances on record when Companions with a high reputation for learning and scholarship failed, on occasions, to understand the meanings of some words in the Quran and referred them to the Prophet for guidance. The Quran itself supports the view that the mere knowledge of the Arabic language is not enough for the reader to grasp its full significance:

> *"He it is who has sent down*
> *To thee the Book:*
> *In it are verses*
> *Basic or Fundamental*
> *(Of established meaning);*
> *They are the foundation*
> *Of the Book; others*
> *Are allegorical. But those*
> *In whose hearts is perversity follow*
> *The part thereof that is allegorical,*
> *Seeking discord and searching*
> *For its hidden meanings,*
> *But no one knows*
> *Its hidden meanings except God*
> *And those who are firmly grounded in knowledge".*

The major part of the Quran consists of clear and unambiguous verses with an established meaning. These verses relate to the fundamentals of religion and were understood by the majority of the people, specially those of an Arab origin. The allegorical verses were, however, understood by the few gifted and learned readers, "those who were firmly grounded in knowledge". The Companions were at the top of this class. Even so their understanding varied with their knowledge and ability. Some of them were more well versed in the literature of the Jahiliyya, others had the good fortune to spend much time in the company of the Prophet and personally witnessed the events which led to the revelation of certain verses. To give an example: 'Umar ibn al-Khattab had appointed Qudama ibn Madhun as his viceroy in Bahrain. Before the appointment could materialise an allegation was levelled against the viceroy-designate that he had taken wine and had been found drunk. A man as eminent as Abu Hurrayrah was cited as a witness. The viceroy-designate was summoned to the presence of the Caliph who announced his decision to flog him in conformity with the law of the Quran. "By God," said Qudama, "even if I drank, as is alleged, you have no right to flog me." The Caliph asked him to cite his defence at which Qudama recited the following verses from the Quran:

"On those who believe
And do deeds of righteousness
There is no blame
For what they ate.
When they guard themselves
From evil and believe,
And do deeds of righteousness,—
(Or) again guard themselves
From evil and do good".

Qudama stated that he was one of those who believed and did deeds of righteousness. He claimed that he could cite witnesses to prove that he had participated in the Battles of Badr and Uhud and Khandaq. 'Umar asked for a reply from the prosecution. Ibn 'Abbas advanced the plea that the cited verses were revealed in order to pardon and condone the conduct of those in the past before accepting Islam, but to guard against those who would come in the furure, the Quran had stated:

O ye who believe
Intoxicants and gambling,
(Dedication of) stones,
And (divination by) arrows,
Are an abomination,—
Of Satan's handiwork.

The Caliph accepted this plea and punished the viceroy-designate.

The interpretation of the Quran began almost simultaneously with the revelation of the Quran. This was inevitable because not everyone who heard or read it was equipped with the same measure of understanding.

Holy Quran : Interpretation

A commentary on the Quran emanating from the Prophet and heard or related by someone is called *al-manqul,* i.e. heard. It is held, for example, that the Prophet explaining the expression *al-salat al-wusta* occurring in the Quran stated that it denoted the afternoon or Zuhr prayers. This then is a commentary on the Quran heard from the Prophet and, therefore, accepted universally by the Muslims and is open to no further interpretation. We can find numerous examples of this category of commentary on the Quran in the six volumes of *Sahih* of al-Bukhari.

All that has been allegedly quoted from the Prophet, however, is not universally accepted by all scholars of Islam. The sources quoting such commentaries are subjected to the severest scrutiny; and unless it is proved that the source was wholly authentic, the tendency is to reject these quotations. If one were to accept all of them one would be confronted with a series of contradictions. These contradictions could not have come from the Prophet for he could not have possibly interpreted the same verse in different ways at the same time. In view of this difficulty certain scholars have gone to the extreme position of completely repudiating all commentaries on the Quran alleged to have emanated from the Prophet. Imam Ahmad ibn Hanbal believed that there was no basis in epics, stories of campaigns and *Tafsir.*

The early commentators were not always certain of the material they received and it was riot seldom that they used their own judgment in supplementing it. The wealth of commentary increased with the passage of time. All works in the early years of Islam were limited to the commentary which was supposed to have been quoted from the Prophet.

Another source of *Tafsir* or commentary was personal judgment and study of the Quran and the allied subjects. The scholars, for example, who had a command of the language of the Arabs, both in Jahiliyya and in Islam, and who had studied the background and the circumstances leading to the revelation of a verse, and felt competent in applying their knowledge in interpreting or explaining a given verse, could do so without having to quote a commentary from the Prophet. Companions like Ibn ‘Abbas and Ibn Masud followed this method. There could be a difference in individual study and judgment, there could be a difference in the meaning of words and verses. These scholars did not believe that any meaning or interpretation could be declared final for all time to come by attributing it to the Prophet.

There were, however, two categories both among the Companions and the generation following them. Some of them believed in complete reserve in pronouncing their judgment and were most reluctant to offer any commentary on the Quran. Said ibn al-Musayyib, for example, would not offer any commentary. Hisham ibn 'Urwa ibn al-Zubayr would say that he had not heard his father interpret any words of God's revelation. As against this attitude of a set of Companions there was another category which believed that by maintaining reserve they would be depriving people of the benefit of their knowledge. This group was in a majority and among them were Companions like Ibn Masud, Ibn 'Abbas, 'Ikrima and others.

They were willing to explain the meaning of the Quran. They would not suffer a person who did not command mastery over the language or who had not thoroughly studied the Quran to attempt a commentary. They were also averse to partisan interpretation by followers of religious creeds like the Mutazila or the Shiis, etc. To try to interpret the Quran according to the preconceived prejudice of a sect is to wilfully damage the spirit of the Book. This amounted to re-casting the Quran according to one's own belief—an attitude which would be abhorrent to any student approaching a book with the sole lawful purpose of making an attempt at an objective understanding. The Companions of the Prophet did not, as a rule, interest themselves in a commentary or *Tafsir* of the Quran. Most of the commentary which is alleged to have emanated from the Companions belongs to the period after 'Ali ibn Abi Talib, 'Abd Allah ibn Masud, 'Abd Allah ibn 'Abbas and Ubayy ibn Kab. Some commentary is also attributed to Zayd ibn Thabit, Abu Musa al-Ashari and 'Abd Allah ibn Zubayr. To the first four is, however, attributed most of the commentary.

They were eminently fit to comment on the Quran in view of their command of the Arabic language, their long association with the Prophet, and their intimate knowledge of the circumstances in which various verses of the Quran were revealed. They were not reluctant to express their personal opinion and were willing to exercise their instructed judgment. In the order of merit, so far as the commentary on the Quran is concerned, these Companions are ranked as follows: (i) Abd Allah ibn Abbas, (ii) Abd Allah ibn Masud, (iii) Ali ibn Abi Talib, and (iv) Ubayy ibn Kab.

To Ali ibn Abi Talib and Abd Allah ibn Abbas a lot more has been attributed than to the other two. The reason is simple. 'Ali ibn Abi

Talib and 'Abd Allah ibn 'Abbas were members of the Prophet's family and anything which is attributed to them becomes doubly more credible in the eyes of the layman who looks upon the great Companions with reverence and respect on account of their long and intimate association with the Prophet.

Commentary in the Generation following the Companions of the Prophet.

Scholars in the generation following the Companions continued their work on the commentary of the Quran. This activity was, however, confined to quoting from the outstanding Companions already mentioned. Those who quoted most from these sources and particularly from Ibn 'Abbas were Mujahid, 'Ata' ibn Abi Raba, 'Ikrima, the Mawala of Ibn 'Abbas, and Said ibn Jubayr. Mujahid being the least voluminous in his quotations from Ibn 'Abbas is the most authoritative. Al-Shafii and al-Bukhari depend upon his quotations while others do not place as much reliance on the commentary of Mujahid. Ibn Sad in his *Al-Tabaqat al-Kubra* states that al-Amas, on being asked why Mujahid's *Tafsir* was not taken as authentic, replied that he depended for most of his knowledge on the people of the book.

While Scholars may differ in their interpretation of Mujahid, he is not accused of being untruthful in his quotations from Ibn Abbas. The same is true of 'Ata' ibn Abi Raba and Said ibn Jubayr. As for 'Ikrima, he quoted most profusely from Ibn 'Abbas whose slave he was. He was from a Berber tribe from North Africa and critics differ in their judgment of his authenticity as a narrator of commentary from Ibn 'Abbas. Some of them doubt the veracity of his statements while others like al-Bukhari use his quotations. A section of critics looks upon him as an arrogant source because he is alleged to have claimed to have known everything about the Quran.

In the era when the disciples of the Companions held sway, *Tafsir* tended increasingly to depend on Christian and Jewish traditions which grew in volume owing to the large number of Jews and Christians who embraced Islam. The reason for the growth of these traditions was perhaps the anxiety of the people to pursue the references in the Quran to Judaism and Christianity. In their anxiety to do this the Muslims seemed to accept all kinds of traditions emanating from Jewish and Christian sources without making an attempt at subjecting them to a careful scrutiny.

In the *Tafsir* of al-Tabari for example, many a verse about the people of Israel has been commented upon and the source, which is quoted on the subject is hardly known to be authentic. This particular source is Wahhab ibn Munabbih. He was a Jew from the Yemen who embraced Islam. He is known to have spread knowledge about Jewish books and stories without any deep and careful study of the subject. Again, most of what al-Tabari relates about Christian subjects is related from Ibn Jari, who was of a Roman origin. According to some scholars, he it was who fabricated the Hadith and married ninety wives, all of them temporarily, according to the Shii custom of Muta. He is said to have been the first man ever to write a book on Islam.

No books of *Tafsir* were written during the days of the Companions and their successors. Scholars started writing them after the second generation. The early books on *Tafsir* are not extant. The commentary on the Quran was influenced in each generation by the contemporary cultural milieu. This is true of all commentaries from the days of Ibn 'Abbas to the days of Shaykh Muhammad 'Abduh in the nineteenth century and Mawlana Abu al-Kalam Azad in the twentieth century. In the days of the Companions the tendency was to explain the literal meanings of each verse. Sometimes the circumstances leading to the revelation of a verse were dilated upon, but never did the Companions indulge in hair-splitting as was the case in succeeding generations. Those who came after the Companions added to their work by way of supplementing the literature on the subject with Jewish and Christian stories.

In both cases there was little effort at a detailed explanation or at a personal stand in interpretation. Neither the Companions nor their successors showed any particular inclination towards any religious creed and they did not, therefore, interpret the Quran from any fixed point of view. Later, however, certain theories like fatalism and self-determination came into existence. These theories had their impact on contemporary commentary of the Quran. With the passage of time we find jurisprudence evolving a system of laws from the verses of the Quran. In brief, the scope of the commentaries enlarged with the growing needs of the people.

What is the cultural background of a handful of men who were considered the leading commentators of the Quran? Take 'Umar for example. He was by no means a scholar. He was neither a collector of Hadith nor a commentator of the Quran. He was, however, a keen judge of men and matters and was easily the best administrator produced by Islam. He was frank, sincere, outspoken, and almost invariably correct in his judgment. He had an incisive legal mind and helped solve many an issue in the lifetime of the Prophet. Without holding any official position 'Umar made a significant contribution to the strength and stability of the infant State of Medina during the days of the Prophet. He is known for a number of decisions which had a far-reaching effect on the consequent growth of Islam. His judgment of men was unerring. It is mentioned in *Al-Iqd al-Farid* that among all the Companions 'Umar liked 'Abd Allah ibn 'Abbas most. Although 'Umar greatly valued and respected him, he did not appoint Ibn 'Abbas as a governor because he feared that his holy friend might distribute the revenues accruing from State taxes by misinterpreting the following verses from the Quran:

And know that out of
All the booty that ye
May acquire (in war),
A fifth share is assigned
To God—and to the Apostle,
And to near relatives.

'Umar was apprehensive that Ibn 'Abbas would extend the definition of booty to cover the State taxes. His worst fears came true when Ibn 'Abbas was appointed Governor of Basrah during the reign of 'Ali faced with many a new problem which did not exist either in the time of the Prophet or the first Caliph. 'Umar resolved them to the satisfaction of the people in conformity with the principles of the Quran.

A creative effort at an original interpretation and successful application of the law to changing circumstances could have come alone from a dynamic mind well versed in the intricacies of religion and law. The regulations for his non-Muslim subjects, the institution of a register of those having the right to military pensions, the founding of military centres out of which were to grow the future great cities of Islam, the creation of the office of Qadi were all his work. It is to him that we owe a series of ordinances religious as well as civil and penal. *Ibn 'Umar.* 'Umar's son, 'Abd Allah, who by common consent is acclaimed as a man in the first grade of learning in Islam, was wholly different from his father.

His cultural pattern is that of a traditionalist searching assiduously for the traditions of the Prophet—a pursuit which commanded his whole lifetime and took him to remote corners to people who had come in contact with the Master. Honest, humble, and God-fearing, 'Abd Allah refused to be dragged into discussions. He avoided lending his name to religious verdicts for he dreaded being involved in contemporary controversies. It was his conscientious objection to differences and disunity that led him to withdraw his claim to the Caliphate although the Syrians made clear their inclination to elect him. He did not lend his support to any party in the disputes between the Muslims and refrained from taking part in any of the wars waged by 'Ali. 'Abd Allah was an acknowledged authority on the history of early Islam for he had the privilege of having had direct contact with the Prophet and all the four Caliphs after him.

He was extremely careful in the narration of his facts. He was essentially the genius of an editor and research scholar and not that of a legislator or a lawgiver capable of a dynamic interpretation of law. Strictly neutral in domestic politics, 'Abd Allah was held in high esteem for noble and unselfish character. His traditions were handed down by his sons and disciples.

Abd Allah Ibn Al-Abbas : A cousin of the Prophet, 'Abd Allah owes his fame to his greatly admired knowledge of tradition, of jurisprudence, and exegesis of the Quran. He is celebrated as the Doctor of the community. He was a versatile scholar who devoted a whole lifetime to learning. Except for a brief interval when 'Ali appointed him Governor of Basrah, 'Abd Allah took no interest in politics, a field which was alien to his training and temperament. He was essentially a scholar. In Medina it was not seldom that he called on the people to collect the traditions of the Prophet. If he found them asleep, he would wait for hours in the scorching sun and would not return till he had verified the point he had in mind.

Ali Bin Abi Talib : Soldier, statesman, saint, and scholar, 'Ali was a cousin and son-in-law of the Prophet. No other companion is the subject of so much controversy as 'Ali. Legends have grown round his name, and his admirers have gone to the extent of bestowing divinity on him. 'Ali is said to have transmitted 586 traditions, twenty of which were accepted unanimously by Bukhari and Muslim; nine others were acknowledged by Bukhari alone; and fifteen by Muslim only.

A collection of poems has been attributed to 'Ali. The *Nahj al-Balagha* has also been attributed to him. It is a collection of his sayings and speeches. The old critics like al-Safadi and the modern ones like Huart doubt the authenticity of this work. The artificial rhyming and the phraseological art, so richly employed in the *Nahj al-Balagha* were not known in the days of 'Ali. A number of expressions which occur in the book were not known to the contemporary Arab till after his introduction to Greek philosophy; certain subtle uses of symbolism like that of the peacock, employed in the book, were introduced in the Abbasid era. It is difficult, therefore, to trace with full authority the origins of 'Ali's authorship of the books. A fantastic book attributed to him records all the events which would take place till the end of the world.

Breaking through the cobweb of legends woven round the personality of 'Ali, it is possible to have a glimpse of the scholar. There is no doubt whatever about his piety and knowledge. At Medina, his opinions had authority. He was consulted about difficult questions. Marked by a judicial bent of mind, he was entrusted by the Prophet with the administration of justice in the Yemen. He had definite ideas on many legal issues. He had the reputation of being one of the most able men in judicial affairs in Medina. He took deep interest in the study of the Quran and was considered an authority on the complicated and difficult passages. He was the tutor of 'Abd Allah ibn 'Abbas, an outstanding scholar of the age. It is related that Abu al-Bakhtari once came to 'Ali with a view to consulting him about the intellectual attainments of the Companions. Asked about 'Abd Allah ibn Masud, 'Ali remarked that he had mastered the knowledge of the Quran and the Sunnah.

About Abu Musa, 'Ali said that he was merely dyed with knowledge and that was all. 'Ammar ibn Yasir was a believer, in his opinion, who had forgotten and remembered only when he was reminded. He considered Hudhayfa as the most well acquainted, among the Companions, with the affairs of the hypocrites. Abu Dharr, he thought, had acquired some knowledge but had failed to use it. 'Ah' was, however, enthusiastic about Salman Farisi who, according to him, had mastered the knowledge of the old and the new and was like a deep sea whose bed could not be reached. When asked about an appreciation of his own talents, 'Ali acclaimed in obvious embarrassment: "This is what you are after!" He then said, "When I used to ask the Prophet (a question) he answered me, and when I did not, the Prophet used to ask me in order to increase my knowledge." This is saying a great deal and, even though 'Ali was being modest, he displayed profound knowledge and wisdom, qualities which, by universal consent, belonged to him in an ample measure.

Abd Allah Ibn Salam : Abd Allah was a Jew. He embraced Islam after the migration of the Prophet to Medina. He accompanied 'Umar to Syria, spoke publicly in defence of 'Uthman against the rebels and died in about 40 A.H. 'Abd Allah had a reputation for knowledge, particularly that of the Tawrat. Many Israelites gathered round him and he is stated to have been a source of a number of traditions. Al-Tabari has attributed many sayings to him on historical and religious issues. It is quite obvious that he was the representative of Jewish culture. It was through him that some passages of the Tawrat entered the sayings of the Muslims and found their way later to the exegesis of the Quran.

Salman al-Farisi : According to one tradition, Salman was the son of a villager in old Isfahan. Attracted by Christianity, while still a boy, he left his father's house to fellow a Christian monk, and having changed his teachers several times arrived in Syria; from there he went right down to the Wadi al-Kara in Central Arabia seeking the Prophet who was said to have restored the religion of Abraham, the imminence of whose coming had been predicted to him by his last teacher on his death-bed. Betrayed by Kalbi Bedouins, who were acting as his guides through the desert and sold him as a slave to a Jew, he had occasion to go to Yathrib where soon after his arrival the migration of Muhammad took place. Recognising in the latter the marks of the Prophet which the monk had described to him, Salman became a Muslim and purchased his liberty from his Jewish master, after being miraculously aided by the Prophet himself to raise the sum necessary to pay his ransom.

The name of Salman is associated with the siege of Medina by the Meccans, for it was he who on this occasion advised the digging of the ditch. Salman became the national hero of Muslim Persia, just as Bilal became a hero of Abyssinian Muslims and Suhayl of the Greeks. Salman is one of the favourite personages of the Shuubiyya (anti-Arabs) and figures most prominently in the traditions of the Persian Shii. He also appears as one of the founders of Sufism and is considered one of the principal links in the mystic chain. He has risen to a still higher rank in the gnostic speculations of the extreme Shii. His historic figure is lost in the divine emanation which his admirers make him represent on earth in an exaggerated fit of enthusiasm. He led a devoted religious life and died in Madain, near Baghdad, in the days of 'Uthman. 'Ali's estimate of his talents, quoted earlier, shows his greatness as a saintly scholar who was in the vanguard of the cultural movement in Islam.

These and other Companions acted as a spearhead of the cultural movement of Islam, and fanned in different directions to carry the torch of knowledge to the remotest corner of the Muslim dominions. The Prophet assigned different men to various cities of Arabia. He also sent learned men to the Yemen and Bahrayn.'Umar followed the lead and sent various men of learning to various countries which came under the sway of Islam during his time. Zayd ibn Thabit was one of them. Muad ibn Jabal went to Syria during Abu Bakr's tenure of office. 'Umar sent 'Abd Allah ibn Masud to Kufa as a teacher and a minister. In doing so he preferred the needs of the people of Kufa to his own, for the assignment of Ibn Masud abroad was a serious loss to Medina where he was deeply respected for his knowledge and piety. These Companions carried the torch of learning wherever they went. They taught thousands of people and came to found schools of thought which made their influence felt on the growth of Islam.

The Muslim Empire comprised two elements, the Arabs and the non-Arabs. Most of the Companions were Arabs and they, therefore, formed the vanguard of the cultural movement. While they embarked on their career of cultural conquest they embraced both Arab and non-Arab and made no distinction between the two. He who was most keen to learn was most welcome. The circle went on expanding till in the days of the disciples of the Companions (Tabiin) the majority of the men of learning came from the class known as Mawali. Ibn Khaldun explaining this phenomenon remarks that the Arabs, owing to their primitive Bedouin life, had originally no knowledge. With the dawn of Islam they learnt the commands of the Quran by heart.

Their knowledge of Islam was based on whatever they had heard of the Quran coupled with the precepts of the Prophet and his Companions. They did not, therefore, know much of teaching, writing, or editing as they did not need to know all this. This condition prevailed till the time of the Companions and their disciples, the Tabiin. They were called the Specialists (*Mukhtassin)* or those that were not illiterate. Illiteracy was common among the Companions. Whoever could read the Quran was called a Qari (Reader). With the passage of time the knowledge of Islam became a specialised subject and needed men of calibre and talent to expound it. Civilisation is not a characteristic of rural people. The knowledge of Islam, therefore, became the preserve of the urban people. The majority of urban Muslims were Persians and Mawali, and the torch of knowledge eventually reached them.

Ibn Khaldun is harsh on the Arabs and is certainly not correct when he wholly excludes them from any share in the cultural movement of Islam. There is no doubt that the majority of men of learning in the Umayyad dynasty were Mawali and non-Arabs, but we cannot possibly ignore famous Arab scholars like Said ibn al-Musayyib, 'Alqama, Shuray, Masruq, al-Nakhai, and others. In Medina, there was Sulaiman ibn Yasar, a recognised authority on jurisprudence. His father was the freed slave (Mawla) of the Prophet's wife, Maymuna. Then there was Nafi', the Mawla of 'Abd Allah ibn 'Umar, who narrated Hadith from his master. He hailed from Daylam. Again in Medina lived Rabitat al-Ray, the teacher of Imam Malik. His father, Farrukh was a Mawla.

In Mecca, there were Mujahid ibn Jubayr, a Mawla of the tribe of Banu Makhzum; 'Ikrima, the Mawla of Ibn 'Abbas; 'Ata' ibn Raba, the Mawla of Banu Fihr—a black slave from al-Jand in the Yemen, Abu al-Zuhayr Muhammad ibn Musim Tadrus, the Mawla of Hakim ibn Hizam—a reliable narrator of the Hadith. Among scholars in Kufa was Said ibn Jubayr, a black Mawla of Banu Waliba. In Basrah there were al-Hasan ibn Yasar, the Mawla of Zayd ibn Thabit; Muhammad ibn Sirin —his mother was Safiyya, the Mawlat (female slave) of Abu Bakr; and last but certainly not the least there was the distinguished personality of al-Hasan al-Basri. In Syria one came across Makhul ibn Abd Allah; his father was from Herat while his mother was a daughter of a king of Kabul. In Egypt lived the famous scholar Yazid ibn Habib, the Mawla of the tribe of al-Azd—he was the Mufti of Egypt and came from Berbers. There were many others with a mixed parentage. Some of the outstanding cases in this category are Salim, al-Qasim and Zayn al-Abidin, the grandsons of 'Umar, Abu Bakr and 'Ali, respectively. Their mothers are stated to have been daughters of the Persian King Yazdigird. Al-Shabi had an Arab father and a Persian mother who was one of the captives of Jalula. It is difficult to deal with individual scholars of this era but even a casual study of their lineage proves that most of them were from the Mawali.

There is an interesting story nerrated by Ibn Abi Layla in *al-Iqd al-Farid* about the predominance of Mawali scholars. We are tempted to quote it at some length for it gives a vivid idea of the hegemony of non-Arab scholarship. This is how the story runs: " 'Isa ibn Musa, who was a confirmed protagonist of the Arabs, asked me about the jurists of Basra. I told him their names in the order of their merit. Who are they? he asked. I stated that they were Mawali. Then who are the jurists of Mecca? he asked. I repeated their names— 'Ata' ibn Abi Raba, Mujahid, Said ibn Jubayr and Sulaiman ibn Yasar. Who are they? he repeated his question. From the Mawali! I answered. What about the jurists of Medina? he inquired. I counted them by name—Zayd ibn Aslam, Muhammad ibn al-Munkadir and Nafi ibn Abi Najih—and as I added that they were also from the Mawali I could see the colour of ibn Musa's face change.

He then asked about the jurists of Quba. As I named them and told him that they were all from the Mawali I saw his face turning red with rage. Then he asked me about the men of learning in the Yemen. I named Tawus, his son, and Ibn Mumbi, and told him that they too were from the Mawali. At this he jumped from his seat in fury and asked about the jurists of Khurasan. I named 'Ata' ibn 'Abd Allah al-Khurasani who was also from the Mawali.

At this his face blackened and his eyes turned red with anger. But he did not give up his questions and asked me about the leaders of learning in Syria. When I told him it was Makhul, a Mawla, he took such a deep breath that one felt his soul was leaving the body. He persisted in his searching inquiry and asked about the jurists of Kufa. By God, had I not been frightened to death by his visible rage I would have named al-Hatim ibn 'Utba and 'Ammar ibn Abi Sulaiman who were also from the Mawali, but I named Ibrahim al-Makhi and Al-Shabi instead. Who are they? he thundered like a desperate lion. I told him they were Arabs. Allah Akbar! he exclaimed and heaved a deep sigh of relief."

There are many stories of this kind which have an obvious anti-Arab touch. Although such stories tend to exaggerate the paucity of Arab talent in this era, they are essentially correct inasmuch as the majority of men of learning were Mawali and not Arabs. One of the reasons for their leadership in this field towards the end of the first century of Islam was the fact that towards the beginning of the Islamic era, the Mawali and not the Arabs became the devoted disciples and students of the Companions of the Prophet. If a Companion was a tradesman his lieutenant who helped him in his profession was from the Mawali. If he was a teacher or a man of learning, the majority of his students and disciples comprised the Mawali. They were thus in constant touch with their masters and naturally excelled those who were but part-time students and had other preoccupations more pressing to attend to.

Chapter 3

Muslim Sects and their Development

In our scheme of cultural reconstruction, personal character and individual qualities are related to the essential nature of man. They all depend on the concept of the essential nature. The measure of character is determined by this concept.

In Western Culture the Measure of Character is Worldly Gain : In western culture the essential nature of man is regarded as animalistic and therefore the nature of character is determined in terms of material power and worldly gain. Only those qualities are valuable which have a direct bearing on worldly gain and material power. For example in business, honesty, forthrightness, keeping up promise, industry, dutifulness, punctuality, patriotism, social sense, national interest etc. are the criteria. The qualities which do not have a bearing on worldly gain are not valued. On the other hand violation of these qualities is considered as a merit. But qualities like modesty, chastity, affection and regard, mutual friendship and love, caring for the family, generosity of heart, soft-heartedness, sincerity, humanity and considerateness for the rights of others are of no value.

In the Scheme of Cultural Reconstruction Divine Attributes are the Measure of Character : In our scheme of cultural reconstruction the essential nature of man is numinous. For this reason, the measure of character is Divine Attributes, and only those qualities are considered valuable which are a direct reflection of Divine Attributes. The qualities that do not reflect them are discarded.

Two Dimensions of Divine Attributes : Divine Attributes have two dimensions: (1) Through them gnosis of the Essence of God is achieved; and (2) through them the measure of human character is determined.

According to the first dimension. Divine Attributes can be divided into three categories: (1) those related to Eternal Beauty; (2) those related to Eternal Power and Glory; and (3) those related to Eternal Perfection. From the first kind of Attributes emanate mercy, compassion and forgiveness, love and affection. From the second kind emanate Greatness, Power and Kingship of God. From the third emanate Good, Uniqueness, perfection etc.

Four Categories of Attributes According to Second Dimension : According to the second dimension of Divine Attributes, they can be divided into four categories: (1) Essential, (2) Distinctive, (3) Constructive and (4) Complementary. The first category includes the qualities which go to inculcate the realization of self and the realization of God. Under the second category come those qualities which distinguished man's nature from that of the animal. The third category comprises the qualities which go to manifest man's nature and dignity and his superiority and power and kingship. The fourth category includes the qualities which distinguish the nature of man from that of the angels.

It need not be told that for the determination of the measure of character it is sufficient to have a cumulative image or reflection of the Divine Attributes; it is not necessary for every Attribute to be imaged in its full form. Similarly, having the image of God in man does not imply having a partner to God, nor does it imply the dissolution of the human individuality. The Divine Attributes according to the second dimension are discussed as follows:

Under the category of essential attributes those qualities are manifested which are exclusive to the Essence of God. For example *Al-Ahad:* the One and Only; *Al-Wahid:* One; *Al-Samad* Eternally and Absolutely Independent of Everything; Al-Quddoos; Absolutely Holy; *Al-Hai:* Eternally Living; *Al-Qadeem:* That Which Has Always Existed; *Al-Daim:* Ever Lasting; *Al-Awwal:* The Absolutely First; *Al-Akhir:* The Last Which Endures After Everything Else Perishes; *Al-witr:* The Odd, Which Has No Match, etc.

Specific Qualities

Under the category of distinctive attributes are manifested those qualities which are related to beauty. For example *Al-Raheem, Al-Aleem:* the Merciful, the Knower; *Al-Wahhab, Al-Ghaffar:* The Bestower of Infinite Bountees, Most Forgiving: *Al-Salam, Al-Momin:* The Source of Peace (and Perfection), The Guardian of Faith; *Al-Bari, Al-Mussawwir: The Evolver, The Bestower of Forms, Al-Razzaq, Al-Fattah:* Sustainer, The Resolver; *Al-Basit, Al-Rafe'* The Expander, The Exalter; *Al-Lateef, Al-Khabeer,* One Who understands the Finest Mysteries, The All-acquainted; *Al-Moiz, Al-Hafeez:* Giver of Power and Honour, Giver of Protection; *Al-Wajid, Al-Moqeet:* One Who Receives, One Who Provides Sustenance; *Al-Haseeb, Al-Moqsit;* One Who Calls to Account, One Who Dispenses Justice; *Al-Haleem, Al-Kareem :* The Meek One, The Generous One; *Al-Wakeel, Al-Hameed:* The Best Dispenser of Affairs, The Most Worthy of Praise; *Al-Mudda, Al-Moeed:* One Who Brings things Into Existence, One Who Causes things to Return; *Al-Mohi, Al-Momeet:* Giver Of Life, Sender of Death; *Al-Munim, Al-Mohib-* One Who Gives Rewards, One Who Loves; *Al-Raoof, Al-Bar, Al-jameel*: Most Kind, Most Good, Most Beautiful; *Al-Mughni, Al-Moti*: Who Frees from Need, Who Bestows; *Al-Nafe', Al-Hadi:* Giver of Benefits, Giver of Guidance; *Al-Badi', Al-Rasheed:* One Who Devises, One Who Moves along the Straight Path, *AMojeeb, Al-Kafeel:* One Who accepts, One Who Provides For; *Al-Hannan, Al-Mannan:* Most Affectionate, The Greatest Doer of Good; *Al-Kamil-Al-Jawwad:* The Absolutely Perfect, The Most Generous; *Al-Kafi, Al-Shafi:* One Who is All Sufficient, One Who Heals; *Al-Wadood, Al-Shakoor:* The Greatest Lover, The Greatest Acknowledger; *Al-Wali, Al-Tawwab:* The Greatest Friend, Approver of Repentance; *Al-Naseer, Al-Mughees; Al-Mujeer:* The Greatest Helper, One who Listens to Cries of Help, One Who Gives Shelter, Zul-Taul Zul-Fazl: One Who Has Long Reach, Bounteous.

Amongst constructive Attributes those qualities are imaged which belong to *Al-Qabiz, Al-Khafis:* One Who Covers, One Who Spreads; *Al-Wase', Al-Mumeet, Al-Mueed:* One Who Spreads Infinitely, One Who Sends Death, One Who Causes Things to Return; *Al-Mozil, Al-Raqeeb:* One Who Lays Low, One Who keeps Watch; *Al-Qavi, Al-Mateen; Al-Shaheed:* The Powerful, The Firm, The All-Acquainted; *Al-Muntaqim, ZulJalal Wal Ikram;* The Avenger of Wrongs, The Possessor of Glory and Power and Greatness; *Al-Mane', Al-Dhar;* One Who Prevents, One Who Dispenses Losses and Adversity; *Al-Suboor, Al-Baseer:* The Most Patient, The Greatest Seer; *Al-Moazzib, Al-Dayyan:* Dispenser of Punishments, The Judge *ZulBatsh Shadeedul Iqab:* The Most Powerful in Catching and The Giver of the Greatest Punishment.

Supportive Aspects

Among complementary attributes the qualities related to Divine Perfection are reflected. For Example *Al-Rab, Al-Rahman;* The Lord and Sustainer, The Beneficent, *Al-Khaliq, Al-Adil, Al-Hakim;* The Creator, the Justicer the Wise; *Al-Samee', Al-Baseer, Al-Qayyum:* One Who Listens, One Who Sees, One Who Holds Up; *Al-Tahir, WalBatin,* The Manifest, and The Hidden; *Al-Majid, Al-Jame', Al-Bais:* The Glorious One, The Greatest Gatherer, One Who Causes everything; *Al-Muheet, Al-Mureed, Al-Qareeb:* The All-Encompassing, One Who Wills Absolutely, One Who is Absolutely Close; *Al-Ali, Al-Rafi, Al-Jalil, Al-Kaleem;* The Exalted, The High, The Glorious, The Noble; *Al-Modabbir, Al-Motakallim:* One Who Plans, One Who Speaks; *Malikal Mulk:* The Sovereign of All the Worlds; *Allamul Ghuyub:* The Knower of Secret Things; *Aleemum Bizzatis Sudoor:* The Knower of the Secrets of the Hearts; *Laisa Kamislehi Shaiun:* There Is None Like Him.

Among the above Divine Attributes there are some which overlap one another; but it makes no difference in respect of their reflection or imaging in man.

Virtues Emanating from Essential Attributes : The following virtues emanate from the Essential Attributes of God:

Owing to self-respect man is able to rise above objection and lowliness. Once he is lifted to the state of self-respect, he does not bow before any worldly power or greatness. He believes that the greatest agents of power and the greatest dispensers of profit and loss themselves depend on Almighty God. The Quran says.

... that to God
Belongs all power (II-165)
... the Command
Rests with none but God (VI-57)
Verily those whom ye
Call upon besides God
Are servants like unto you (VII-194)
No aid can they give them,
Nor can they aid themselves! (VII-192)
There is no help
Except from God,
The Exalted, the Wise (III – 126)
To Him belongs the Keys
Of the heavens and the earth (XLII-12)
If God do touch thee

With hurt there is none
Can remove it but He:
If He had designed some benefit
For thee, there is none
Can keep back His favour: (X-107)

Broad Vision

From the Essential Attributes is derived a comprehensive outlook. By virtue of this outlook man is able to transcendend personal, communal and national limitations so as to have his being spread over the whole universe. In all his attitudes, in his friendship and animity, his love and hatred, his regard and disregard, he achieves a universal standard. Everything in the universe belongs to him simply because it belongs to his God.

The Quran says:
... While all creatures
In the heavens and on earth
Have, willing or unwilling
Bowed to His Will
(Accepted Islam),
And to Him shall they
All be brought back. (III-83)
O mankind, we created
You from a single (pair)
Of a male and a female,
And made you into
Nations and tribes, that
Ye may know each other
(not that ye may despise
Each other). Verily
The most honoured of you
In the sight of God
Is (he who is) the most
Righteous of you.
And God has full knowledge
And is well aquainted
(with all things) (XLIX-13)

It is He Who hath created for you
All things that are on earth: (II-29)

Mohammad (peace be upon him) said:

All human beings are brothers to one another.
(Muslim, Abu Daud).

At another place he said:

Undoubtedly the earth belongs to God and human beings are servants of God.
(Abu Daud, Nasbul Raya).

On one occasion Ali said:

Their goods (the goods of other human beings) are like our goods and their lives are like our lives. (Nasbul Raya, Vol. III, Kitabul Sair)

Another virtue is peace of heart. Owing to this virtue a man does not give way to despair, even if circumstances go against him. God is always with him.

This is such an invaluable virtue that all efforts of intellect and philosophy fail to achieve it. All the advancement of western civilization and all its material equipment cannot equal it in value. The Quran says:

When My servants
Ask thee concerning Me,
I am Indeed
Close (to them): I listen
To the prayer of every
Suppliant when he calleth on Me:
Let them also, with a will,
Listen to My call,
and believe in Me:
That they may walk
In the right way (XXXIX-53)
... and never
Give up hope of God's
Soothing Mercy: Truly
None despair of God's
Soothing Mercy, Except
Those who have no faith (XII-87)

Tolerance and Strength

Through this virtue, a man's heart becomes strong and he sees the power of God with him. He learns to bear afflictions. The Quran says:

Nay seek (God's) help
With patient perseverance
And prayer: *(II-45)*
...For God is with those
Who patiently persevere *(II-153)*
And We appointed, from among
They, leaders,
Under Our command, so long
As they persevere with patient. *(XXXII-24)*

On one occasion, the Holy Prophet said: Patient perseverance is the commander of his (somebody's) army. Ali has brought out the psychological aspect of patience as follows:

> *Patience has the same relation to(the body of faith as the head to the human body. Just as on severing the head the body becomes useless and dead, in the same way the man who has lost patience cannot attain the faith.*
>
> *(Ibn-i-Abi Shaibah,* Musannaf; Baihaqi)

Owing to this virtue base emotions like lust and greed and jealousy are got rid of. For achieving benefit and avoiding harm a man abstains from adopting a method which may injure self-dignity and self-respect, for he knows that the ends of all things are in the hands of God. The Quran says:

... All bounties
Are in the hand of God.
He granteth them
To whom he pleaseth:
And God careth for all,
And He knoweth all things *(III-73)*
For the earth is God's
To give as a heritage
To such of His servants
As He pleaseth: *(VII-128)*

Thou enduest with honour
Whom Thou pleasest:
And Thou bringest Low
Whom Thou Pleasest:
In Thy hand is all Good.
Verily, over all things
Thou hast power. (III-26)

Simplicity

Owing to the virtue of humility self-respect is created, and the self-respect so created does not lead to any pride. On the other hand, a man always feels himself humble and low before the power of the Almighty. The Quran says:

He is the Irrestible, (watching)
From above over his worshippers *(VI-61)*
But God is free of all warts
And it is ye that are needy. *(XLVII-38)*
And the servants of (God)
Most Gracious are those
Who walk on the earth
In humility, and when the ignorant
Addressed them, they say,
"Peace!" *(XXV-63)*

Through this virtue, a man does not continue to have real trust in material means. His trust is established only in God. The Quran says:

The parable of those who
Take protectors other than God
Is that of the Spider,
Who builds (to itself)
A house: but truly
The flimsiest of houses
Is the Spider's house:— *(XXIX-41)*
If God hellps you,
None can overcome you: *(III-160)*
...whoever

Rejects evil and believes
In God hath grasped
The most trustworthy
Underhold, that never breaks. (II-256)

Doubtful Mind

Through these virtues man becomes fearless and independent of everything except God. Only with God he establishes a relation of hope and fear. In this way, his life acquires a centrality and his conviction acquires a force. This attitude makes for success and well-being. We can quote the following Verses from the Quran:

(God) who begets no son
And has no partner
In (His) dominion: (XVII-111)
Who is there can intercede
In His presence except
As He permitteth? (II-255)
God forgiveth not
(The sin of) joining other gods
With Him: but He forgiveth
Whom He pleaseth other sins
Than this. (IV-116)
Do no mischief on the earth,
After it hath been
Set in order, but call
On Him with fear
And longing (in your hearts). (VII-56)

It is a strange fact in history that when the intellectuals of Greece wanted to break the yoke of their tyrinnical rulers they encouraged polytheism. They came forward with the idea that just as the universe is not ruled by one God, in the same way government on earth should not be the sole monopoly of one person. The idea worked with the Greeks; they were able to dethrone their ruler from his position of autocracy.

Similarly the philosophy of history ascribes the real greatness of the Romans to two things:

(1) Limited resources for the needs of life and

(2) The force of Conviction, because of which an individual sacrifices his life, property, family and everything for the sake of some conviction.

This virtue inculcates realistic outlook and self-confidence in a man. He stops relying on false trust and hope and does not hesitate in making the greatest sacrifice for the sake of achieving his goal or ideal.

The following Verses of the Quran throw light on the subject:

That man can have nothing
But what he strives for: (LIII-39)
And say: "work (righteouseness):
Soon will god observe your work,
And His Apostle, and the Believers" (IX-105)
That (the fruit of) his striving
Will soon come in sight;
Then will he be rewarded
With a reward; (LIII-40-1)
God hath purchased of the Believers
Their persons and their goods;
For theirs (in return)
Is the garden (of Paradise):
They fight in His Cause,
And slay and are slain: (IX-111)

Virtues Emanating from Distinctive Attributes : The virtues that emanate from Distinctive Attributes are of two kinds: (1) Those that are related to the goodness and nobility of personal character; and (2) Those that are related to the well-being of other human beings. The first kind has the following implications.

Honesty

The greatest virtue emanating from Distinctive Attributes are truth and sincerity. The Quran says:

And whose word can be
truer than God's? (IV-87)
God's promise is the truth. (IV-122)

Truth is of many kinds: the truth of the tongue, the truth of the heart and the truth of action. The truth of the tongue means that falsehood should not be spoken. The truth of the heart means that what the tongue speaks should be supported by a conviction from the heart. The truth of action means that what is expressed through the tongue and the heart should correspond to action. This last is the perfect form of truth. It is called sincerity. The Quran says:

Only those are Believers
Who have believed in God and His Apostle,
And have never things doubted, but
Have striven with their
Belongings and their persons
In the cause of God:
Such are the sincere ones. *(XLIX-15)*

Falsehood And Hypocrisy are the Opposites of Truth And Sincerity : Falsehood is the opposite of truth. Falsehood too is of many kinds. There is the falsehood of the tongue, which means speaking lies so that the heart does not go with what is spoken by the tongue. It may even go contrary to it and what is spoken may not be translated into action, rather the action may be contrary to what is spoken.

This is called hypocrisy:

And invoke the curse
Of God on those who lie! *(III-61)*
... they solemnly
Invoke the curse of God
On themselves if they
Tell a lie. *(XXIV-7)*

To say one thing and to have another thing in the heart is hypocrisy: and it is worse than a lie.

For this reason, the Quran harshly condemns hypocrites:

And God beareth witness
That the Hypocraites are
Indeed liers *(LXIII-1)*

The hypocrites say one thing and have another thing in their hearts:

Saying with their lips
What was not in their hearts *(III-167)*

The hypocrites say something and do something else:

... because

They broke their Covenant
With God, and because they
Lied (again and again). *(I-77)*

Once, the Holy Prophet was asked if a Believer can be a coward. He said: 'Yes'. Then he was asked if a believer can be a miser. He said: 'Yes' and then he was asked if a believer can be a lier. He said: 'No' (Moatta Iman Malik)

There are other forms of falsehood. For example: simulation; speaking falsehood for the sake of amusement; propagating mere hearsay.

The Quran says:

And pursue not that
Of which thou hast no knowledge;
For every act of hearing
Or of seeing
Or of (feeling in) the heart
Will be enquired into
(On the Day of Reckoning). *(XVII-36)*

The Holy Prophet once said:

This is enough of a lie for a man if he goes reporting what he has merely heard.
(Mishkat; Muslim; Preface)

Charity or generosity means doing the utmost good to others. It has many forms. For example:

(1) Foregoing one's right;
(2) Giving priority to the needs of others over one's own needs;
(3) Deploying one's goods, energy and intellect for the well being of others;
(4) Undergoing loss for the sake of the benefit of others;
(5) Sacrificing one's self interest for the sake of the survival of others.

Without charity there can be neither sympathy nor love, which are the very essence of humanity. Nor can there be any perfection of virtue, which is the embellishment of humanity. This is why the Quran incites on spending out of what one has in the way of God:

O ye who believe!
Spend out of (the bounties)
We have provided for you,
before the day comes
When no bargaining
(Will avail), nor friendship
Nor intercession
Those who reject faith— they
Are the wrong doers. (II-254)
By no means shall ye
Attain righteousness unless
Ye give (freely) all that
Which ye love. (III-92)

Owing to charity a man gets rid of inordinate love for material wealth, which is the root cause of many evils:

The Evil One Threatens
You with poverty
And bids you to conduct
Unseemly. God permitteth
You His forgiveness
And bounties.
And God careth for all
And He knoweth all things. (II-268)

By virtue of charity a man acquires wisdom. Hence the next Verse in the Quran:

He granteth wisdom
To whom He pleaseth:
And He to whom wisdom
Is granted receiveth
Indeed a benefit overflowing. (II-269)

Wisdom is such an invaluable gift of God that it has been mentioned with reference to almost all the Prophets. Defining wisdom Imam Raghib Asfahani says: 'To reach the truth through knowledge and intellect is wisdom.' In Lisanul Arab we have the following definition: "To attain knowledge of higher values through higher sciences is wisdom." Ibne Maskoya lists the following features of the wisdom:

"Sharpness of mind; power of understanding; clear headedness; intellectual acumen; aptitude for learning etc. He says: 'Through these qualities the power capacity for wisdom is constituted'. Exegetes have given various interpretations of wisdom which can be summarised as follows:

> *Wisdom is a kind of power through which the knowledge of realities is attained, as also the ability to order experience. Furthermore after attaining wisdom a man's attention is focussed on the cultivation of moral sense and he directs his attitude towards this Holy task.*

The Quran states an extremely high standard of charity. For example, it prescribes that (1) no useless thing should be given to the other person, none that the giver would not like to have for himself; (2) that after giving something no benefit should be obtained in return; (3) that the receiver of obligation should not be put to any uneasiness or trouble; (4) the receiver should not be taunted with the mentioning of obligation; (5) the receiver should not be made small by the reminders of obligation; (6) recompense should not be expected:

O ye who believe!
Give of the good things
Which ye have (honourably) earned
And of the fruits of the earth
Which We have produced
For you, and do not even aim
At getting anything
Which is bad, in order that
Out of it ye may give away
Something when ye yourselves
Would not receive it
Except with closed eyes. (II-267)
O ye who believe!
Cancel not your charity
By reminders of your genoriosity
Or by injury. (II-264)
Those who spend
Their substance in the cause
Of God, and follow not up

Their gifts with reminders
Of their gernorisity
Or with injury, — for them
Their reward is with their Lord: (II-262)

Usually there are two considerations which hinder charity or generosity: (1) Why should one give away one's things to others? (2) By giving away things to others one would suffer from scarcity and therefore it would cause trouble.

The Quran repudiates the first consideration by proclaiming that Allah is the owner of everything. Man is only a trustee and the trustee is bound to the wishes of the owner in making use of the trusted goods. The second consideration is repudiated by the idea that scarcity and bounty, comfort and discomfort, are all in the power of Allah. His servant depends on him in every conditions:

And what cause have ye
Why ye should not spend
In the cause of God?
For to God belongs
The Heritage of the heavens and the earth. (LVII—10)

And spend (in charity) out of the (substance)
Whereof He has made you
Heirs. (LVII—7)

To him belong the keys
Of the heavens and the earth:
He enlarges and restricts
The Substance to whom
He will: for He knows
Full well all things. (XLII-12)

The Opposite of Charity or Generosity is Miserliness : The Opposite of charity or generosity is miserliness which is the source of many evils and discourtesies. For example, greed, lust, dishonesty, ingratitude, cruelty, hard-heartedness, narrow mindedness, timidity, unfair dealings, selfishness etc. This is why, the Quran condemns it harshly and dwells on its evils:

and there are those
Who bury gold and silver

And spend it not in the Way
Of God: announce unto them
A most grievous penalty—
On the Day when heat
Will be produced out of
That (wealth) in the fire
Of Hell, and with it will be
Branded their foreheads,
Their flanks, and their backs,
— "This is the (treasures) which ye
Buried for yourselves: taste ye
Then, (treasures) ye buried!" *(IX—34-5)*
By no means! for it would be
The fire of hell!—
Plucking out (his being)
Right to the skull!—
Inviting (all) such
As turn their backs
And turn away their faces
(From the Right) *(LXX—15-18)*
Seest thou one
Who denies the Judgement
(To come)?
Then such is the (man)
Who repulses the orphan
(With harshness), and encourages not
The feeding of the indigent. *(CVII—1-3)*
Who pileth up wealth
And layeth it by
Thinking that his wealth
Would make him last
For ever!
By no means! he will
Be sure to be thrown into
That which Breaks the Pieces. *(CIV—1-4)*

Nay Nay! but ye
Honour not the orphan!
Nor do ye encourage
One another
To feed the poor!—
And ye devour inheritance—
All will greed,
And ye love wealth
with inordinate love! (LXXX IX—17-20)
For God loveth not
The arrogant, the vainglorious,
(Nor) those who are niggardly
Or enjoin niggardliness on others,
Or hide the bounties
Which God bestowed
On them, (IV—36-7)

The harm of miserliness or niggardliness is not restricted to an individual or a few individuals only; it encompasses the whole society. For this reason, very often it happens that the increase of miserliness destroys faith and degrades the whole society:

Behold, ye are those
Invited to spend
(Or your substance)
In the Way of God:
But among you are some
That are niggardly. But any
Who are niggardly are so
At the expense of
Their own souls.
But God is free
Of all wants,
And it is ye that are needy
If ye turn back
(From the Path) He will
Substitute in your stead

Another people; then they
Would not be like you! (XLVII-38)

According to one of the Quranic Verses, the consequence of niggardliness is hypocrisy which destroys faith:

So He hath put as a consequence
Hypocrisy into their hearts,
(To last) till the Day Whereon
They shall meet Him: (IX-77)
And spend of your substance
In the course of God,
And make not your own hands
Contribute to (your) destruction; (II-195)

For all these reasons, Mohammad (peace be upon him) has always prayed for refuge against niggardliness. He says: "I seek refuge with God against niggardliness." It would not be irrelevant to mention that niggardliness is not found only in matters of wealth or goods; it applies to knowledge and power as well as to material wealth. Whatever God has bestowed upon man is meant for giving away to others, and the question of niggardliness arises in relation to every gift of God. One who is niggardly of knowledge and power also deserves punishment from God.

Purity

Chastity is the soul of all virture and the very essence of humanity. It enlightens one's life and makes for the distinction between man and animal. In Western civilization, the measure of character is worldly benefit and therefore chastity is not very much valued, nor does anybody bother to protect it and keep it up. But in the Islamic scheme of cultural reconstruction, the measure of character is Divine Attributes. So the virture of charity aquires a great salience and special attention is given to its protection and maintenance. Chastity is the integral part of Prophethood. It is the distinctive characteristic of the family of the Holy Prophet and of the saints and the godly. In the Quranic Verse, there is the evidence of the wife of the Governor of Egypt in favour of Joseph:

I did seek to seduce him
From his (true) self but he did
Firmly save himself
Guiltiness!... (XII-32)

Earlier it has been said of Joseph:

... thus
(Did We order) that We
Might turn away from him
All evil and shameful deeds:
For he was one of Our servants,
Sincere and purified. (XII-24)

Regarding Yahya the Quran say:

... and (s/c
Besides) noble, chaste,
And a Prophet,—
Of the (godly) company
And the righteous (III-39)

After mentioning the stories of many other Prophets. The Quran says:

They were, in Our sight,
Truly, of the company
Of the Elect and the Good. (XXXVII-47)

Regarding the members of the family of the Holy Prophet, the Quran observes:

These are not affected
By what people say (XXIV-26)

Regarding the Saints and the godly, the Quran says:

Those who invoke not,
With God, any other god,
Nor slay such life as God
Has made sacred, except
For just cause, nor commit
Fornication; (XXV-68)

There is very strict punishment for one who falsely accuses somebody of fornication, which implies the special importance of chastity:

And those who launch
A charge against the chaste women,
And produce not four witnesses

(To support their allegation),—
Flog them with eighty stripes;
And reject their evidence
Ever after: for such men
Are wicked transgressors;— *(XX IV-4)*

Lewdness is the Opposite of Chastity : Although the word 'lewdness' covers all kinds of evils, but it is mostly used for shamelessness and promiscuity (or adultery)—the Quran says:

If any of your women
Are guilty of lewdness, *(IV-15)*
... except
Where they have been guilty
Of open lewdness: *(IV-19)*

Encouragement of Lewdness in Western Civilization : Western Civilization has a paraphernalia which serves to deprive man of chastity and to encourage in him lewdness both on the level of thought and action. On the level of thought there are "isms" which condemn the suppression or concealment of sex desires. Then there is a hedonistic philosophy which says that man is as free to gratify his desires of sex as he is to gratify his desire for water; any interference in this matter is deemed as an interference in personal or private matters.

On the level of action, there are nude pictures of women, parties of dance and music, free mix up of sex, night clubs, blue films, dresses exposing or involving nakedness, exhibition of beauty and even beauty contests, dances charged with sexuality, sexy music and art, different types of female friends, for example, girl friend, call girl, company girl, party girl etc.

Encouragement of Chastity in the Scheme of Cultural Reconstruction : In our scheme of cultural reconstruction arrangements are made to prevent lewdness and to encourage chastity. Hence all things that directly or indirectly lead to lewdness have been rejected and disapproved of. For example, the human eye takes precedence in conveying messages of lewdness and therefore a check is put on the aberration of the eyes.

The Quran says:

Say to the believing men
That they should lower

Their gaze and guard
Their modesty: that will make
For greater purity for them:
And God is well aquainted
With all that they do. *(XXIV-30)*

The slight carelessness and forwardness on the part of women may create misunderstanding in a man and may encourage them to take liberties with them. For this reason, special checks are put on women.

The Quran says:

And say to the believing women
that they should lower
Their gaze and guard
Their modesty: that they
should not display their
beauty and ornaments except
What (must ordinarily) appear
Thereof; and they should
Draw their veils over
Their bosoms ... *(XXIV-31)*

O Prophet! tell
Thy wives and daughters,
And the believing women,
That they should cast
Their outer garment over
Their persons (when abroad):
That is most convenient,
That they should be known
(as such) and not molested. *(XXXIII-51)*

In the Traditions, there are various instructions regarding keeping away from lewdness and maintaining chastity. Once the daughter of Abu Bakr, Asma, came into the presence of the Holy Prophet wearing a very thin piece of clothing. The Holy Prophet said:

> *Asma, when a girl attains puberty, it is not decent to look at any part of her body except her face and palms.* (Abu Daud, Mishkat: Kitabul Libas)

As regards looking at women, the Holy Prophet said:

> *After the first glance, which is accidental, do not cast another glance. The first glance is alright for you but the second glance is not so.*
> (Tirmidhi, *Kitabul Istizan, Bab 'Maja-afi Nazratil Fuja-ah)*

It means that if one happens to cast a glance on a woman, he must not cast the glance the second time. Jarir b. Abdullah said: 'I asked the Holy Prophet regarding the casting of accidental glance. He instructed that one should turn away one's glance'.

Extreme Care Commanded : Besides this, there is prohibition against all those things that interfere with the maintenance of chastity—improper dresses and manners, immodesty of behaviour, use of perfumes, exhibition of body or dress or ornaments.

In Western Culture there are No Strict Laws Against Lewdness : One way of depriving man from chastity and encouraging lewdness in him is to have leniency in laws and punishment regarding lewdness. In Western culture lewdness is divided into "with consent" and "without consent" and thus rape is regarded as a form of amusement. But even in the case of the evidence of an assault on woman there is no very severe punishment, such as may set an example for the society and bring correction in it. At first the freedom of the West in these matters looked very commandable, particularly when it was seen as non-interference in personal matters. But when things went too far and the violation of chastity became common and open proposals like the following came up:

> *"The habitual sex criminals, should be castrated through surgery instead of being kept in prison for years and years."* (London, *14 April, quoted by* Sidq-e-Jadid, *30 April 1965). In 1965 Mary Stock, an eminent British Gynaecologist, proposed that such a law should be promulgated. It exists in Denmark where sex crimes have very much decreased, she said.*

Severe Punishment in the Scheme of Cultural Reconstruction : In the scheme of cultural reconstruction the crime of lewdness is punished very severely and there are very strict laws against it. Thus, on the one hand, criminals get their due and on the other the whole society learns a lesson. For example, for women with whom adultery is a first offence the following punishment has been prescribed:

> *If any of your women*
> *Are guilty of lewdness,*

Take the evidence of four
(Reliable) witnesses from amongst you
Against them; and if they testify,
Confine them to houses until
Death do claim them,
Or God ordain for them
Some (other) way. *(IV-15)*

This commandment applies to the situation of first offence. The last phrase of the Verse has the same implication otherwise strictures against this crime would have been mentioned at one place. For men the punishment is prescribed as follows:

If two men among you
Are guilty of lewdness,
Punish them both.
If they repent and amend,
Leave them alone; *(IV-16)*

Corporeal Punishment for men and imprisonment for women are prescribed probably in view of the physical weakness of the latter. Another reason for the punishment of imprisonment in the case of women is that their immodesty creates greater mischief and therefore by shutting them up this mischief can be prevented. These punishments cover all forms of lewdness and promiscuity, be they heterosexual or homosexual. Regarding the next phase of the crime of lewdness, which is one of hardened criminality, the following punishment is prescribed for both the man and the woman guilty of lewdness:

The woman and the man
Guilty of adultery or fornication,—
Flog each of them
With a hundred stripes:
Let not compassion move you
In their case, in a matter
Prescribed by God, if ye believe
In God and the Last Day:
And let a party
Of the Believers
Witness their punishment. *(XX IV-2)*

Dishonesty in Married Life

The above punishment was meant for unmarried persons. For married persons guilty of lewdness, the Holy Prophet has ordained stoning to death. Thus a Tradition says:

> *A man called Maiz came to the Holy Prophet and confessed his adultery four times. The Holy Prophet gave orders for the stoning of the man to death (Abu Daud;* Mishkat). *The punishment for lewdness is very severe. This is why, there are very strict conditions laid down for the establishment of the crime. These details are found in books of Islamic Jurisprudence.*

To modern civilised man, these punishments appear not only severe but savage. It is because he is not very much aware of the value of chastity and the bad influences of lewdness on society, when in his society he sees lewdness being encouraged. The culture having this awareness would make severeness of punishment in such matters inevitable. In that case, severeness of punishment would be considered like some bitter medicine necessary for the health of the society.

Western Culture Not Aware of the Monstrosity of Lewdness *:* In fact, Western culture lacks the awareness of the monstrosity of the offence of lewdness. It is for this reason that it does not feel need of having strict laws against it, laws that may prescribe very severe punishments.

If the awareness had been there, western society would not have hesitated in prescribing such punishments against this offence, punishments similar to those it prescribes for offences like treason or spying—in which case the victim is subjected to death by various kinds of torture, electirc shocks and all. If the occurrence of sex crimes continues as such and if chastity is commonly violated in western culture, the day is not far off when western society would take recourse to very severe punishment for habitual criminals.

Monstrosity of Lewdness Realised in the Scheme of Cultural Reconstruction : In our scheme of cultural reconstruction, the monstrosity of lewdness is realised fully. This is testified by the following Traditions of the Holy Prophet:

> *Nobody commits the act of lewdness in the state of faith.*
>
> *(Mishkat).*

It means that purity and nobility of faith and the monstrosity and corruption of lewdness are incompatible. On one occasion, the Holy Prophet listed the activities of certain organs as lewdness, for these organs act as instruments of this crime:

The lewdness of both the eyes is looking at private or forbidden parts. The lewdness of the ear is listening to forbidden voices. The lewdness of the tongue is uttering forbidden discourse. The lewdness of the hand is to make use of the hands for forbidden actions. The lewdness of the feet is walking in forbidden ways. (Mishkat, *Babul Qadr).*

This gives an idea of the awareness of the monstrosity of lewdness in Islamic culture. Thus, even 'going near this deed' has been forbidden:

Nor come nigh to Adultery,
For it is a shameful (deed)
And evil... *(XVII-32)*

Once the Holy Prophet was asked: 'Which sin is the greatest?' He replied: Regarding somebody as equal to God, though it is God Who has created thee. Then he was asked: "Which sin is next in greatness ?' He replied: Slaying one's child for fear of sharing one's food with him or her.' Then he was asked: 'Which sin is next in greatness?' He replied: "Committing adultery with the wife of one's neighbourer" (*Mishkat,* Babul Kabair)

Lewdness is Hateful to Human Nature and is Disapproved by Society : On account of the monstrosity of lewdness human nature abhors it and human life is never ready to accept it. The Quran syas:

Women impure are for men impure,
And men impure for women impure
And women of purity
Are for men of purity,
And men of purity
Are for women of purity *(XXIV-26)*
Let no man guilty of
adultery or fornication marry
Any but a woman
Similarly guilty, or an Unbeliever:
Nor let any but such a man
Or an unbeliever
Marry such a woman:
To the Believers such a thing
Is forbidden *(XXIV-3)*

It is not the purpose of these Verses to lay down any law; their purpose is to underscore the revulsion of human nature and of society against lewdness. *Roohul Maani* comments by saying that this amounts to the expression of extreme disapproval of the act of lewdness. It goes on to say that the incompatibility of the act has been substituted for the absence of the act.

It is evident that both the male and the female lewd persons are not worthy of marrying a chaste partner because of the stain of corruption they bear. Therefore, marital relation between the chaste and the unchaste is forbidden. In the literature of the Arabs, descriptions like the following are used for indicating the ugliness of some act:

> *A king never tells lies. Which means that a dirty thing like a lie does not become an honourable man like a king.*

Marrying a Lewd Person is Forbidden by Some Jurists : Some scholars of Islamic jurisprudence have argued for the taboo of marriage between the lewd and the chaste. Others have advised separation between the partners after the act of lewdness has been committed inside wedlock. There are some people who do not differentiate between the beginning and the middle of a course. What we imply is that just as it is not lawful for a believer to marry a lewd woman in the same way if the woman commits the act of lewdness after marriage it is not lawful to keep her as a wife. Some scholars have given the verdict of unlawfulness in the case of the beginning or entry into marital career; but if the act is committed in the middle of the marital career they have not given the verdict of unlawfulness or taboo. (Razi, *Tafseer-i-Kabeer; Tafsir-i-Noor)*

This is supported by the following Traditions: The Holy Prophet once said:

> *"The adulterer who has been punished with public flogging should marry a woman like himself." (*Abu Daud, *Kitabul Nikah)*

Murthid b. Abi Murthid Ghanawi once requested the Holy Prophet to get him married to a woman of Mecca (She was Ghasaq, the notorious adulteress). The Holy Prophet kept silent for some time, till the above mentioned Verse (XXIV-3) was revealed, and then he said: "Do not marry her".

The following episode connected with the life of Ali is also enlightening:

> *A man married some woman. The woman committed adultery. She was punished for it. When the matter was brought to the judgement court of Ali, he gave the verdict of separation between them and told the woman to marry somebody like herself. All these punishments do not amount to any prescription of law; the government is authorised to give whatever punishment it likes in accordance with the exigencies of contemporary laws of the Shariah.*

Capital Punishment for Lewdness and the Government Acting as Prosecutor: On account of the monstrosity and seriousness of the offence of lewdness this punishment is capital punishment. The state itself acts as a plaintiff for carrying out the sentence, which means that even if the wronged party Forgoes its claim, the state takes upon itself the duty (the rights of God) to execute the punishment. In Islamic Jurisprudence it is observed:

> *The rulers are justified to punish for this offence even in the absence of having it established by prosecution and even in the absence of any plaintiff. Similarly, it is justified to point witnesses in absence of any plaintiff.*

The standard for the establishment of offences for which the punishment is capital and for which the state itself acts as a plaintiff should be high and invulnerable.

There is wide possibility of escaping the punishment in this case, and the conditions for punishments are very strict and difficult to be fulfilled. In this case, the state is responsible for doing two things: (1) To propose alternative punishments which may be substituted for capital punishment, (2) To establish such courts as would hear to suits cancelled on account of the paucity of firm evidence or the lack of standard witnesses.

For such courts, there are terms like *Waliul Jaraem and Sahibulrad* in the books of jurisprudence. Such courts were supposed to propose alternative punishments in cases where the suits had been rejected because of lack of evidence. These courts adopted an outlook wider than the ordinary courts of justice (which gave the sentence of capital punishment). They adopted this wider outlook in enquiring into the offence and establishing it.

Humility and Honour of the Self

Modesty and self-respect are natural characteristic of human nature which gives rise to many moral virtures and safeguards chastity.

If this virtue is cultivated from childhood it develops and acquires great significance, otherwise it dwindles away. In western civilization, this virtue is not very much valued, nor any arrangement is made for its cultivation. On the other hand, the western way of life tries to eliminate it from the very beginning. But in our scheme of cultural reconstruction it has been commanded to safeguard and cultivate this virtue from the very beginning. For example, the female parts related to sexuality are to be covered; talking of immodest things and looking at them is forbidden; the lowering of glances is commanded; nakedness and nudeness is forbidden, so much that even in bathrooms and bed rooms precautions have to be taken in this regard. All these punishments are there in order to maintain modesty and self-respect.

Modesty and Self-Respect are the Qualities of God and His Prophet: Modesty and Self-respect become God and they are amongst His Attributes:

> *Indeed, Allah would be ashamed to disappoint one who begs Him for some good.*(Baihaqi. *'Kitabul Asma wal Sifet fil Istihya')*

At another place it is said:

> *Nobody is more self-respecting than Allah. This is why He has forbidden lewdness.* (Op. Cit., *'Kitabul Asma Wal Sifat fil, Ghairah')*

Modesty and self-respect were the qualities of Mohammad (peace be upon him).

> *The apostle of God was more modest than a parda-observing virgin.*
>
> (Bukhari, *Kitabul Adab, Babul Haya')*

For the same reason the Quran says that the Holy Prophet was ashamed to dismiss people lingering after dinner:

> *... He is ashamed*
>
> *To dismiss you,* *(XXXIII-53)*

Modesty and self-respect is so much involved with the sense of Prophethood that its violation is not to be tolerated even in the childhood of the Prophet. For example, in his childhood Mohammad (peace be upon him) was engaged in carrying bricks for the reconstruction of the Kaaba. On the advice of his uncle Abbas he loosened his lower garment and put it on his shoulder. But at this incident Mohammad (peace be upon him) fainted out of his sense of modesty.

Modesty and Self-Respect are Constituents of Faith and the Basis of Humanity : In the Traditions, modesty and self-respect have been emphasised in such a way as to indicate that they are the integral constituents of faith and the very basis of humanity. Thus, the Holy Prophet said:

> *Faith branches of have more than seventy dimensions. The highest dimension is the formulation of* La Ilaha Illah *(There is no deity except Allah), and the lowest dimension is marked by acts like removing troublesome things off the way. Modesty is also a dimension of faith. Another Tradition says faith and modesty are mutually involved. If one goes off, the other too does not remain.*

There is a Tradition according to Ibn-i-Abbas which says:

> *"When one of these is lost the other too is lost." Another Tradition says: "Every religion has a specific temperament, and the specific temperament of Islam is modesty." Then there is a Tradition which says: "Modesty leads only to good." Another Tradition declares that "modesty is itself good incarnate." There is still another tradition which defines the psychological quality of immodesty in a manner of premonition: 'If you do not observe modesty, do whatever you like'.*

Honesty and trustworthiness are the very essence of morality and the very basis of humanity. Without them the affairs of life are not set right, nor can mutual trust be established.

This is why the Quran calls the Revelation bearing Angel 'AlAmin' which means one who is 'Faithful to the Trust' or the 'Spirit of Faith and Truth'. For if trust is not reposed in this Angel, the authenticity of the Revelation cannot be ascertained:

> *With it came down*
> *The Spirit of Faith and Truth—* *(XXVI - 193)*
> *With authority there,*
> *(And) faithful to his trust.* *(LXXXI - 21)*

Almost every prophet has manifested to his people his quality of trustworthiness. Thus Shoaib:

> *I am to you an apostle*
> *Worthy of all trust.* *(XXVI -178)*

And the people of Mecca had nicknamed Mohammad (peace be upon him) as 'Amin' or 'The Trustworthy' before he was invested with Prophethood, which indicates the absolute trust they reposed in him.

Honesty and Trustworthiness Hold Good for Every Sphere of Life : In the scheme of cultural reconstruction honesty and trustworthiness are not confined to any one sphere of life; they encompass the economic, the legal, the moral — in fact every sphere of life. For example, the principle of honesty and trustworthiness demands that one must not come slack in fulfilling one's duties (to God's creatures and to God); must return undamaged what has been borrowed; must keep a secret for the sake of the other person's honour; must refrain from being a tell-tale; must give the right advice; must be conscientious; must appoint only the deserving etc. The Quran says:

God doth command you
To render back your Trusts
To those to whom they are due;
And when ye judge
Between man and man
That ye judge with justice *(IV - 58)*

In this Verse, the word 'trusts' encompasses all responsibilities and duties :

Amaanaat (trusts) is the plural of amanat, and so it includes all the duties incumbent on man, the duties to God as well as to fellow-creatures.
(Syed Mahmud Alusi, Ruhul Maani, 'Surah Nisa')

Wider Sense of Honesty and Trustworthiness According to the Quran : The Verses of the Quran testify to the wider sense of honesty and trustworthiness. Thus, the responsibility of vicegerency has been described as a Trust.

We did indeed offer
The trust to the heavens
And the Earth
And Mountains
But they refused
To undertake it,
Being afraid thereof:
But man undertook it;— *(XXXIII - 72)*

Whatever material goods man possesses are as a trust from God. Thus, the Quran:

And spend (in charity)
Out of (substance)
Whereof He has made you
Heirs *(LVII-7)*
Even man's life is a trust from God
God has purchased of the Believers
Their persons and their goods;
For theirs (in return)
Is the Garden (of Paradise): *(IX -111)*

If one lends something to somebody and allows him to keep it, that thing is a trust. It should be returned intact and undamaged:

And if one of you
Deposits a thing
On trust with another,
Let the trustee
(Faithful) discharge
His trust, and let him
Fear his Lord. *(II - 283)*

Duty (in service) is Also a trust. Any slackness in it is the betrayal of trust and dishonesty:

... truly the best
of men for thee to employ is
The (man) who is strong and trusty. *(XXVIII-26)*

Positions and posts are also a trust; to give them to the undeserving is dishonesty and betrayal of trust. Ibn-i-Taimiya while interpreting the Verse: "God doth command you to render back your Trusts..." (IV- 58) includes Government and all the resources of the State in the word "Trusts". Some exegetes have made the following observations while interpreting this Verse: "The fulfilment of the trusts also means that positions should be given only to the deserving". (Mohammad Shafi Deobandi, *Maqala Dastur-i-Qurani*)

Qadi Sanaullah Panipati says:

The fulfilment of the trusts is not confined to giving things that are due because of birth and inheritance; it includes all the duties of man. Whatever is due to somebody should be paid. (Tafsiri Mazhari)

The Wider Sense of Honesty and Trustworthiness according to the Traditions:

The Holy Prophet has included in the term "Trust" many subtleties and particularities of life. For example, he includes advice in this term: 'One who is asked for an advice has been consigned with a trust."

(Bukhari, *Al Adabul Mufrad, Al Mustasharo Motaminun)*

It means that the adviser must give the right advice. Matters related to conferences should be treated as trust: "Conferences are held on trust." It means that the deliberation of one conference should not be reported in another.

From such report are excluded those intrigues that are made for the purpose of torturing or dishonouring anybody. One should convey the reports of such intrigues to the person concerned, otherwise one would incur a sin.

The greatest trust is the secrets between husband and wife, which one does one's duty to hide and honour. The Holy Prophet says:

On Doom's Day, the greatest violation of trust in the eyes of God would be the exposing of secrets about a man's wife before others.

Secret or private affairs are also trust. The Holy Prophet said: "When a man talks to somebody and then turns to the other side this talk is a trust."

All these remarks go to indicate how wide a sense the word "trust" has in Islam.

The Value of the Honesty and Trustworthiness : The value of honesty and trustworthiness and the harm of its violation are brought out by the following saying of the Holy Prophet:

He who is not trustworthy has no faith. He who does not pray has no religion. The religion prayer has the same status as the head has in the body.

(Kanzul, Ummal, *Vol. II, Al Amanat)*

Another Tradition says:

Trustworthiness makes one achieve his sustenance: dishonesty produces poverty. (Ibid)

Still another Hadith says: Trustworthiness is wealth.
(Ibid)

Trustworthiness is not something externally imposed. It is something related to the inner most being of man.

Trustworthiness is related to the very roots of the hearts of the people (it is related to man's inner most nature). People have learnt it from the Quran, and then from the Sunnah. (Mishkat, *Kitabul Fitan, Falt I)*

The loss of trustworthiness is the first thing that happens when *a* community degenerates. Prayer is retained and is the last thing that is lost. A Tradition says:

(By this community) trustworthiness will be lost first; and the thing that is retained in its religion till the very end will be prayer (namaz). But there are many worshippers (namazis) who will have no reward in the eyes of God. (Kanzul 'Ummal, *Vol II)*

Another Tradition says:

The first thing that you will lose in your religion is trustworthiness. (Baihaqi, *Vol. VI)*

Thus in the scheme of cultural reconstruction every duty and every responsibility which has been entrusted is a Trust. Man's status is that of a Trustee, and without fulfilling his Trust he cannot hope to achieve well-being. The other sub-category of Distinctive Attributes, one related to the welfare of human beings, has the following implications:

Impartial Decision

Justice is one of those attributes of God that pervades the whole universe. In fact, the cosmos rests on it. It is the principle of life and the guarantee for its sustenance, progress and survival. Without it develops neither the character of the individual nor of the community. According to etymology of word for justice *'Adl* means dividing something into two equal halves.'

The Quran Uses the Word 'Mizan' (Balance) : In the Quran the reality of justice is brought home to us by the word *Mizan* which means Balance. If one pan of the balance is tilted, disorder results instead of order, and so the Quranic emblem is of tremendous significance :

And the Firmament has He

Raised high, and he has set up

The Balance (of Justice), *(LV - 7)*

We sent aforetime
Our apostles with clear Sings
And sent down with them
The Book and the Balance
(Of Right and Wrong), that men
May stand forth in justice; *(LVII - 25)*

Definition of Justice According to Al Ghazali, Plato and Others : Al Ghazali has defined justice as follows:

> *It controls energy, desire and anger to such an extent that they may function according to Right Reason and the* Sharia. (Ahya, *Vol. III, P. 48)*

> *Shah Waliullah offers the following conception: Justice is, as it were, a Queen, from whom issue forth the actions that make for the smooth management of cities and villages.* (Hujjatullahil Baligha, *p. 58)*

To Plato, the essence of justice is the inner or the spiritual reality, which means that the inner life should be so well-organized that every person does his work in a proper or responsible way, and does not meddle with the work of another. Dewey, James and Rogers see justice as the cream of morality and the crown of essential virtues. If this virtue is lacking all other virtues lose their significance and purpose.

Basis of Justice in Western Culture : In Western culture the basis of justice is nationalism and patriotism, which are adopted on a nation-wide scale for the sake of extolling the nation and its progress.

Basis of Justice in the Scheme of Cultural Reconstruction: In the Islamic scheme of cultural reconstruction, the basis of justice is piety and spiritual purity. It comes into being through the concept of universal welfare and general mercy, as proclaimed by Islam—'All creatures are the children of Allah'— 'All men are brothers'. Owing to such an outlook the standard of justice in our scheme is extremely high, one which would not allow for any discrimination between the close and the distant in relation, the enemy and the friend, the rich and the poor etc. Thus, the Quran says:

O ye who believe!
Stand out firmly
For justice, as witnesses
To God, even as against

Yourselves, or your parents,
Or your kin, and whether
It be (against) rich or poor:
For God can best protect both.
Follow not the lusts
(Of your hearts), lest ye
Swerve... *(IV-135)*
O ye who believe!
Stand out firmly
For God, as witnesses
To fair deasling, and let not
The hatred of others
To you make you swerve
To wrong and depart from
Justice. Be just: that is
Next to Piety: and fear God. *(V-9)*

Once a gentle woman of the clan of Makhzoomia committed a theft. When appeals regarding her reached the Holy Prophets he said:

> *People before you were destroyed (by God) simply for the reason that if a person of high status among them committed a theft he was allowed to go scot free but if a weak person committed a theft he was punished to the utmost limit, By God, if my own daughter Fatima committed a theft her hand would be cut off.*
> (Bukhari, Muslim, Mishkat: *Babul Shafaat fil Hudud)*

Justice is of two kinds: (1) Personal, and (2) Societal.

Chapter 4

Cultural Aspects

The characteristics of culture, as brought out by various scholars and thinkers, can be summed up as follows:

- The habits and manners which produce harmony and beauty in life and constitute the 'good form',
- The things which are products of good taste and good acts,
- The standards by which life is evaluated,
- Principles and laws and social institutions,
- A set of ideals and goals in life,
- A sense of values,
- Arts, sciences, crafts etc.

Cultural Focus

For culture we, in India, use the word *tehzib*. This is originally an Arabic word, and it would be interesting to look into its etymological sense. This is how it has been defined in *Lissanul Arab:*

The root meaning of *tahzib* is the clearing away of the better fruit of *Hanzal of* all its insides and the removing of its bitterness in order to make the seed pleasant to eat.

The seed of *Hanzal* is edible, but all else inside the fruit, which is called *shuhm,* is extremely bitter: The meaning of *tahzib* in *The Tajul Urus* is as follows :

The root meaning of *tahzib* (and *hizb)* was pruning the trees for the sake of beauty and proper growth. Later on the word was used in the sense of cleansing, reforming and purifying a thing of its defects, and this figurative sense became the popular meaning of the word.

Thus, the essential meaning of culture, in the light of the etymology of its Hindustani equivalent *tehzib,* is removing the unpleasant elements of a thing, and shaping or moulding it into some desirable form.

Scope of Culture

The unpleasant elements are found, not in any one department of western culture, but in all its departments. Beginning from the science of psychology we can trace them in every sphere of life—in beliefs, thoughts, feelings, personal life, individual life, family life, social, economic and political life, philosophy, ethics etc. Every sphere of life needs purification, needs culture in this sense. Since all cultural phenomena can be referred back to psychology, we can divide our discussion of culture into two parts: (1) psychological basis of culture and (2) actual construction of culture.

Psychological Aspects

Western Idea of Psychological Constitution : According to the western conception of man his psychological constitution too, like his physical constitution, is a higher form of the animal. In other words, just as Evolution has developed higher forms from lower forms on the physical level, in the same way it has developed higher forms from lower forms on the psychological level. This mechanistic conception of man does not recognize any 'energy' in man except the instincts which are supposed to be common between man and animals. For the specifically human characteristics of man there is no specifically human instinct; no inborn human trait. By nature man has neither self-consciousness, nor is he pervaded by any intelligent spirit. He is nothing but a bundle of instincts and a product of the wonderful combinations of matter and heredity.

According to this conception the 'natural constitution' of man consists of animal instincts (these instincts are supposed to be the source of all human qualities; even will and intellect exist for their appeasement and satisfaction). Hence man's essential nature is supposed to be materialistic and he is supposed to be helpless in the face of the wild forces of matter. So materialism pervades philosophy, history, religion, ethics, in fact every department of culture.

Merely an Explanation

Unfortunately the above interpretation occupies a very important place in modern knowledge but it is only an interpretation and not an established truth. This is what William McDougall himself admits towards the end of his book, *An Outline of Psychology*. He says that his description of psychic structures and processes might have given his readers the impression of cock-sureness. But he believes this is the best possible statement, which he has been able to make after thirty years of study and contemplation. He is aware that his inferences are merely plausible conjectures. It is likely that they are based more on error than on truth. McDougall goes on to say that he would not like to create the impression that the knowledge of psychology has advanced beyond the elementary stage.

Explanation : Same Flans : In the light of experience and observation the above interpretation suffers from the following flaws:

1. Various creative and organizing abilities of man indicate that in his psychological make-up there is some other 'energy', which is inborn and natural and is responsible for the basic distinction between the psychological constitutions of man and the animal from the very beginning.
2. Persistent spiritual phenomena indicates that this 'energy' has some eternal basis, and is not merely a product of evolution.
3. Many times it happens that religious and ethical considerations become so urgently significant for man that in comparison to them he does not give any importance to material or physical considerations. Such phenomena are undeniable facts. But if some 'energy' other than instincts is not posited they cannot be explained.
4. There are moments in life when the guidance of intellect, senses and intuition fails and man stands in dire need of some other guidance. Which points to some hidden and mysterious factors in man's psychological make-up.
5. If all that is there in man is a product of instincts, heredity and tradition, where does the criterion of likes and dislikes come from? We know that man likes some acts and dislikes others, accepts certain traditions and rejects others.

Thus the theory of instincts suffers from many flaws which go to prove that it could not get access to the truth and that there exists some 'energy' other than instincts in the human psyche, by referring to which the above phenomena can be explained. It is by recognising this 'energy' that psychology gets related to ethics, and both get related to spiritualism.

Human Physique : Its Force : The Quran points to the existence of an 'energy' in man's natural constitution. It is called *fitrat* or 'God's pattern' and its essence is numinous:

(Establish) God's handiwork according
To the pattern on which
He has made mankind (XXX-30)

Hence the Holy Prophet says:

> *Every child is born according to God's pattern, then his parents make of him, a Jew, a Christian or a Zoroastrian.*
> (Bukhari; Muslim — *'Mishkat Kitabul Qadr'*)

He goes on to illustrate this pattern by an example:

> *It is like the case of kid which is born whole and normal; it does not have the defect of being 'ear-lopped'.*
> *(Ibid).*

Indeed, man is born immaculate, according to God's pattern or *fitrat.*

The root meaning of *fitrat* is 'kneading flour into a dough and making bread from it before it rises' *(Lughatul Quran).* Hence the following entry in the *Qamus:*

We say *taftaratul ajain* when flour is kneaded into a dough and bread is made from it before it rises.

Later on, by a figurative extension of meaning, the word came to mean 'shaping and moulding of a thing according to a particular pattern *(Majmaul Bihar).*

Thus *fatarallahul Khalq* means:

> *Shaping a thing into such a pattern as to enable it to perform the function for which it is created.*
> *(Imam Raghib,* Mufradatul Quran, *'Fitrat')*

Fatarallah in the above Verse of the Quran should be understood in the light of the following explication:

> *The 'pattern of God' implies the potentiality with which the creature has been endowed for the comprehension of Faith.* *(Ibid)*

This Energy has a Transcendental Source.

The 'energy' we have been talking about is not the product of the combination of instincts and of particles of matter. Its source transcends matter. This is what the Quranic Verse implies:

But He fashioned him (man)
In due proportion, and breathed
Into him something of

His spirit. And He gave
You (the faculties of) hearing
And sight and feeling
(And understanding) *(XXXII-9)*

Indeed, this 'energy' gives to man his specific characteristics and also the ability of bringing the universe under his subjection. Hence God said to the angels:

When I have fashioned him
(In due proportion) and breathed
Into him of My Sprit,
Fall ye down in obeisance
Unto him, *(XV-29)*

A Tradition of the Holy Prophet elucidates further the specific position of man:

The creature whom I made with my own hands and into whom I breathed of my spirit— I am not going to put him on equal terms with creatures which came into being when I said: 'Be'. *(Mishkat)*

Role of Energy : According to our conception of cultural reconstruction, the psychological constitution is God's pattern manifesting itself. Which implies that man's psychological make-up acquires a numinous character, and that life is freed from being a mere product of matter, and its transcendental essence is recognized. This numinous conception of psychological constitution does not deny matter. It simply recognizes the permeation of the spirit in matter, because of which the wild crudity of matter is dispelled and man is enabled to bring it to subjection and maintain his selfhood at the same time. Thus matter itself is transformed into energy and its transcendental reality is established. This provides a firm basis for ethics, and once this basis is established there is no difficulty in relating ethics to psychology.

Nature is a Combination of the Numinous and the Animalistic : When we recognise the factor of the numinous in the natural constitution of man we are led to the recognition of two psychological elements in man: (1) The numinous, and (2) The animalistic. The numinous is the product of God's pattern, and the animalistic emerges from the combinations of matter. The two elements go to make human nature. According to the Western view of man the inborn traits and dispositions are the products of instincts, and it is from instincts that the intellectual faculties emerge. These intellectual faculties are actually the product of the conflict of opposite forces. They emerge from this conflict and become the source of man's thought and intellection, and in this way they sustain his social life.

Disadvantages of Denying the Combination of the Numinous and the Animalistic : If the combination of conflicting forces — the numinous and the animalistic — is not recognised and if man is supposed to have the same instincts as are found in an animal, it becomes difficult to trace the source of the conflicting forces. Which means that the source of the whole dialectic of human nature is obscured. But it is on these conflicting forces and dialectical elements that the superiority of man over other creatures depends.

Of course books of psychology speak of a nature which gradually evolved from the raw material of animal instincts but this nature is not recognised as a spiritual energy and it is not supposed to have anything to do with the constitution of instincts. For this reason this nature has no effective implication for the existence of conflicting qualities in man and for the distinction between man and animal.

Western Concept of Man

The way in which primitive man has been studied in Western thinking confirms the above fallacy. Thus it is said that man is of two type (1) natural man, and (2) civilized man. By natural man is meant the primitive man who has evolved from the animal and reached the status of man but remains still unaffected by the traditions of civilization. The civilized man is one who is a product of industry and traditional knowledge. Beliefs, feelings and thoughts have been accumulated in him.

According to William McDougall, the natural man would be having all the sensible qualities that we have. His faculty of sensing would be quite developed, as it is often the case with savages. He would be having all the instincts that are common to higher mammals, to which category he is supposed to belong. On sensing things and situations he too would be impelled to achieve the natural end of his instincts; experiences the hunger of demands and the motive impulses characteristic of these instincts; and is satisfied or appeased at the success of his impulsive efforts and dissatisfied or unappeased at their failure. All these things he would be having; but for language he would be having nothing but some emotional cries, sounds and signs.

The natural man would not possess the specific civilized characteristics of man. Hence in his kind of life reason, moral principles, conscience, duties — all these things are lacking. In it there is no quest for happiness for the sake of happiness. It does not have a series of unappeased states. It is the life of instinctive impulse and desire. We do not know anything about the habitat and the way of life of the natural man. We cannot say whether he, being what we have conceived of him, lived on trees or on the ground. But his life, thinks McDougall, was the kind of life he has visualized: a life dominated by instinctive impulses, which were similar to the instinctive impulses of other higher mammals. If there was any difference between their mode of living and that of man it was that the latter was marked by foresight and organization.

McDougall goes on to visualize man's gradual evolution. He thinks that in comparison with other animals man should have possessed very superior mental powers. It is because the light of his previous experiences he has greater capacity for foresight and for planning and preparing himself for responding to coming events. In carrying out their plans the human creatures should have co-operated in such effective ways and with such variety of responses as was not possible for any other mammals to do. The superior mental powers of man are also evinced by the fact that he is more self-dependent, can act with greater initiative, and can persist in his efforts for a longer time.

In view of this psychological make up of the primitive man William James observes that man is just an imitating animal and that his ability to learn and make cultural progress proceeds from his imitative character.

Loyd Morgan says that man is a powerfully thinking animal, one who sets goals for his behaviour. But if the operation of the spiritual energy in man is recognised, the picture of the primitive man changes so much as to include civilised human characteristics, self-consciousness and intelligence in his natural constitution.

Culture in the Remaking

According to our conception of the reconstruction of culture, primitive man manifests himself as Adam and his life tells us that all the specific human qualities were present in him from the very beginning.

Thus it is said that when the angels became sceptical about the potentialities of Adam they made the following submission to God:

> Wilt Thou place therein one who will make
> Mischief therein and shed blood? *(II-30)*

At this God said:

I know what ye know not *(II-30)*

But the matter was not left at that. God manifested the truth of His saying by putting man and the angels to a practical test. The angels had to admit:

"Glory to thee: of knowledge
We have none save what thou
Hast taught us: in truth it is Thou
Who is perfect in knowledge and wisdom." *(II-32)*

Man has both Self-consciousness and Intelligence in Him : It is obvious that the earliest life of man was not lost in instinctive experiences and desires. On the other hand Adam had self-consciousness as well as intelligence in him, owing to which he spoke to God, and even his wife did so.

We said:

"O Adam! dwell thou
And thy wife in the Garden *(II-35)*

Both of them had earlier received the following commandment from God:

... but approach not this tree,
Or ye run into harm and transgression *(II - 35)*

In spite of this commandment they approached the tree with the result that their shame became manifest. Their consciousness or sensibility could not bear it and they began to try to cover themselves:

... when they tasted of the tree,
Their shame became manifest
To them, and they began
To sew together the leaves
Of the garden over their bodies. *(VII - 22)*

Their self-consciousness and intelligence was also manifested by the fact that they could not persist in their disobedience for long. On the other hand they bowed themselves in all humility and said:

They said: Our Lord!
We have wronged our souls:
If Thou forgive us not
And bestow not upon us

Thy Mercy, we shall
Certainly be lost. *(VII - 23)*

In Western Thinking Religion is Man's Invention : According to the Western conception of human psychology religion has no place in the natural constitution of man, nor is its invention indebted to any supernatural power. It is, on the other hand, an invention of man and a product of the animal instincts in man. Its genesis is described by McDougall. He says that as consciousness emerged in man he saw amazing and dreadful things around him and, therefore, he was filled with feelings of wonder and fear. He was concerned to protect himself against these things. After a good deal of deliberation he hits upon the idea of placating these things or powers for this purpose. This gave rise to prayer and religious worship and ritual.

As human consciousness and intellect developed, the significance of the objects of nature went on changing till, seeking ways of protection, man reached the present form of religion and came to believe in a God who is the Creator and the Lord of all phenomena. In this picture of the genesis of religion, the question of its relation of God's pattern does not arise. However, the utmost that can be said when it is linked up with instincts is that it is not related to any one instinct but is the most complex and strange result of the interaction of various instincts.

It implies that initially the instincts were not of a religious nature, nor were they specific to man. They were found both in man and in animals. But owing to gradual evolution they began to manifest some sensibility which led to the emergence of religious sentiment and to its inclusion in the instinctive nature of man. The above opinion is expressed by those scholars and thinkers who recognize the operation of metaphysical factors in evolution. The argument is that evolution means progress from the lower to the higher, and that the highest is God. But the reality is that metaphysical factors have no place in the theory of evolution. Hence religion is supposed to be the product of human superstitions and fancies, and God Himself is the invention of an evolved human mind.

In the Islamic Scheme of Cultural Reconstruction, Religion is Related to Natural Constitution : In the Islamic scheme of cultural reconstruction religion is related to the natural constitution of man and is regarded as the voice of God's created nature or *fitrat*. In its manifestation and development there works an Intelligent Power. Thus the instructions that God gave to the First Man are as follows:

1. Man must be beware of the antagonistic forces (instinctive impulses and Satan)—for there is *enmity between yourselves'*. (II-36)
2. Man has to live in this world for a determined *period—'on earth will be your dwelling place'* (II-36)
3. Man must derive benefit from the things of the earth where are 'your means of livelihood—for a *time'* (II-36)

Besides these, some other instructions were also given to the First Man :

Then learnt Adam from his Lord
Words of inspiration, and his Lord
Turned towards him *(II-37)*

It was also pointed out that the work of instruction or Guidance will continue and a system of judgment will be established:

And if, as is sure, there comes to you
Guidance from Me, whosoever
follows My Guidance, on them
Shall be no fear, nor shall they grieve.
But those who reject Faith
And belie Our Signs,
They shall be Companions of the Fire;
They shall abide therein. *(II. - 38-39)*

Recognition of an Intelligent Power Necessary for Understanding the Workings of the Unconscious : In our inner being, there are certain hidden 'chords'; they are directly related to an Intelligent Power, which plays on them, as it were. Unless we recognize this power we cannot understand the notes it sounds. Nor can we have any access to the reality of religion.

Western culture has no idea of this Intelligent Power. This is why the real nature of the unconscious could not be known, and the 'spider's web' that had appeared in the inner being later on was mistaken for the 'chords'. It would be interesting to note what the gnostic saints say about it:

The heart is like a lily. It has two sides, and both the sides are the landing places of the tempting Satan. Spider-like, he has woven a web around the heart and suspended its curtains. He lurks behind these curtains. The heart itself has layers like the petals of the lily. Satan dwells under them.

Freud has divided the human psyche into two parts: the conscious and the unconscious. The conscious is that part of the psyche which is responsible for cognition, thinking, understanding, manipulation etc. The unconscious is the hidden part lying under the conscious, and is the source of all urges and feelings.

The enquiry into the unconscious is based on dreams, falterings, humour, irrationalities and, above all, neurosis. The analysis of these phenomena indicates that the unconscious is constituted of the sex urge. Further enquiry leads to the idea that knowledge, philosophy, ethics etc. are simply ways of the appeasement of the insatiable and suppressed sex urge. In other words, when human nature does not find satisfaction in sex, it seeks satisfaction in knowledge, philosophy, ethics etc.

This enquiry subjects religion to the following explanation:

1. As the child grows up and feels that his parents are unable to look after him, he begins to wish for a heavenly Father. This heavenly Father takes the place of the actual father and issues commandments.
2. Man does not get peace in life unless he sacrifices personal interests for the sake of others. This sacrifice cannot be ensured without some kind of reward. But real reward was not possible in this world, and so a fanciful reward from God was visualized, and the idea of such a reward developed to take the form of religion.

The idea of the unconscious is not a definite and complete discovery. McDougall forcefully denies it. Jung considers it lopsided and attempts to complete it. Adler proposes to replace the sex urge by the urge for superiority. Even Freud had to admit that his theory did not claim to cover the whole life, and that it seeks to explain only that aspect of life which had been ignored by all other theories.

Some Intelligent Power Existing from the Beginning : In our concept of cultural reconstruction there exists some Intelligent Power from the very beginning. Deep down in his inner being, man has an innate desire to worship and obey it. Hence God says:

I have only created
Jinns and men, that
They may serve Me. *(L1 - 56)*

If the unconscious were constituted only of sex desire or desire for superiority, man would have achieved peace from the free satisfaction of either or both the desires. But experience and observation testify that the freedom to satisfy these desires enkindles lustful passions and leads man to greater uneasiness, while prayer and obedience to God leads him to peace. The achievement of peace in this way is so certain that even Freud recognizes the fact of psychic reorganization or re-integration through prayer in the case of the pious and the devoted. He admits that some classes of people can get satisfaction through things other than sex. And this is what the Quran says in this regard:

... for without doubt
In the rememberance of God
Do hearts find satisfaction. (XIII-28)

It is because prayer and remembrance of God and obedience to Him bring the 'chords' of the inner being into relation with the Intelligent Power, and no other mode of satisfaction can do so. For the establishment of this relation the Covenant mentioned in the following Verse is also an operative factor:

When thy Lord drew forth
From the children of Adam—
From their loins—
Their descendants, and made them
Testify concerning themselves, (saying):
'Am I not your Lord
(Who cherishes and sustains you)?'—
They said: 'Yea!...' (VII-172)

The sex desire is related to the animal instincts. But the human psyche reaches a state in which this desire becomes so dominant that doubts arise regarding the essential nature of the psyche itself. This state is pointed out by the Quran:

Then sest thou such
A one as takes
As his god his own
Vain desire? (XLV-23)

This desire invents its own permanent religion:

These are nothing but names
which ye have devised,—

Ye and your fathers,—
for which God has sent
Down no authority (whatever). (LIII-23)

The deeds done in this state seem very pleasing to the doers—

Satan has made their deeds
Seem pleasing in their eyes. (XXVII-24)

But the springs of human life get dried up, and animal life prevails over the being, and manifests itself even in dreams and through the nerves. Regarding this condition the Quran says:

God hath set a seal
On their hearts and on their hearing,
And on their eyes is a veil (II-7)

And at another place it says:

God hath set a seal on their hearts
For their blaspphmy, (IV-155)

Perhaps Freud has been concerned with the study of the same animal state in which a point comes where knowledge, philosophy, ethics etc. become means for the appeasement of sex desire.

Without the Concept of the Spirit Human Psychology Would Remain Incomplete and the Position of Man Undefined.

The West has failed to acquire the knowledge of the real nature not only of the unconscious but also of life and of the spirit. Without such knowledge neither the psychological constitution of man nor his place in the universe can be properly determined.

The enquiry, as we know, began with matter. Now, after about four hundred years, an 'energy' that transcends the world of matter is being conceived. But since no way of going beyond the world of matter is known the conception of this Energy is not clear, and, therefore, many areas of man's psychic life are lying obscure.

The human psyche is like a dark room. Unless it is lit up our sight cannot do much. If research is done without light, certain things will be apprehended, but others will not be apprehended in spite of all attempts. Again, out of the things that are apprehended the real nature of some will be known while the real nature of others will remain unknown—either they will be conceived as things without reality or as things against reality.

Divine Energy as the Source of both the Known and the Unknown.

Our conception of cultural reconstruction recognizes the Energy we have been talking of as living and eternal. It is none other but the Almighty Spirit, who is our Creator and Lord and who does whatever He wills; He is the beginning and the end of all things and He is infinite. The way towards Him is definite. He has himself arranged to light up the dark room of the human psyche. He is the source of all life. He is called Allah. Thus the Quran speaks of Him:

He Who created Death
And Life *(LXVII - 2)*

Again:

Say: He will give them
Life Who created them
For the first time *(XXXVI - 79)*

This Almighty Spirit functions not only as Creator but also as Guide. When Pharoah asked Moses:

...Who, then,
Oh Moses, is the Lord
Of you two. *(XX - 49)*

Moses spoke in reply particularly of two attributes of the Lord:

He said: and our Lord is
He Who gave to each
(Created) thing its form
And nature, and further,
Gave (it) guidance' *(XXII - 50)*

And as for Abraham, he said that it is God

'Who created me, and
It is He Who guides me' *(XXVI - 78)*

At another place the Quran says that it is God:

Who hath created,
And further, given
Order and proportion;
Who hath ordained laws
And granted guidance *(LXXXVII-2-3)*

About the spirit of life the Quran says:

But He fashioned him
In due proportion, and breathed
Into him something of

His spirit. And he gave
You (the faculties of) hearing
and sight and feeling
(and understanding) (XXII - 9)

At another place it is said:

'When I have fashioned him
(in due proportion) and breathed
Into him of My spirit,
Fall ye down, in obeisence
Unto him'. (XV - 29)

God's Pattern is the Manifestation of Divine Energy Who has created Man's Essence as Numinous. After the discovery of the unconscious and the spirit of life' the operation of some Energy in the Psyche becomes an established fact, and it does not remain difficult to determine the real place of man in the universe. God's pattern or *fitrat* is in fact the manifestation of His Energy which has made man numinous in essence and has created his nature basically different from animals. This concept of Divine Energy implies that the means of knowledge do not remain limited to experience and observation but lead us further into another department of knowledge, the knowledge of secret or invisible things. According to gnostics man has access to three kinds of knowledge: (1) Knowledge of sensible realities; (2) Knowledge which proceeds from the known to the unknown; and (3) Knowledge of the secret or invisible things.

God has Appointed Man as the Leader of All Creatures : According to this conception of Divine energy man acquires highest position in creation; no creature is His co-equal. Just as God has no co-equal, in the same way His image, man, has no co-equal. He has been appointed to the position of vicegerency of God and the leadership of all creatures:

I will create
A vicegerent on earth. (II - 30)

The capability required for deserving this status is not found in any other creature. This is why the whole creation except man refused to undertake God's offer Trust:

We did indeed offer
The Trust to the Heavens
and the Earth

And the mountains; but they refused
To undertake it,
Being afraid thereof;
But man undertook it. *(XXXIII - 72)*

According to gnostics 'The right of man for the vicegerency of God is on the basis of his capabilities. He possesses contradictory qualities which he can utilise for the material and spiritual rehabilitation of the world so that they become the manifestation of God's contradictory Names.' *(Akhlaq-i-Jalali)*

In the Mirror of the West the Image of Man is Distorted : After determining the real place of man in the universe man needs a mirror which can show the image not only of material things but also of realities that transcend matter. The West does have a mirror, but it is concerned only with material realities; it does not show the image of transcendental realities. The image of man in this mirror implies that we need not go beyond matter for determining the standard of the capabilities of existence and survival.

Thus according to the theory of the survival of the fittest, only material capabilities are needed for survival. Similarly, for becoming virtuous, moral values are of no significance. On the other hand, the virtuous person is he who is successful and able to survive because of his material capability, no matter if his character is like that of a beast. In the same way, the non-virtuous person is one who has failed in his aims, no matter if his character is angelic.

According to this western conception similarity is shown between man and animal. But it has not been unanimously decided whether man falls down to resemble the animal or the animal rises up to resemble man; in other words, whether the superior includes the inferior or vice-versa. This is rather interesting.

The people who believe that man is like an animal, derive human characteristics and values from the psychological behaviour and organic structure of the animals. This is done to such an extent that even mental capabilities and faculties are also derived from the animals and are supposed to be the result of gradual evolution. Those who suppose that the animal is like man, try to prove that animals have human qualities. They go to the extent of supposing that even religious feelings exist in dogs and monkeys and flies.

Cultural Reconstruction Recognizes Transcendence of Matter : Since in our mirror of cultural reconstruction, transcendental realities are also reflected, it is thought that going beyond matter is a capability which gives us the standard of survival. This transcendental capability has been recognized from the beginning. Hence:

(1) All souls made a Covenant with God in the spiritual world.

(2) In the natural constitution of every man a numinous energy exists, by the help of which he can overcome animal or lustful desires and can transcend matter.

Transcendence has been Underscored in God's Address to Primitive Generations of Man:

(3) In God's address to the primitive human generations transcendence has been particularly emphasised. Thus the Quran says:

Oye children of Adam!
We have bestowed raiment
Upon you to cover
Your shame, as well
To be an adornment to you.
But the raiment of righteousness,—
That is the best. *(VII - 26)*

The particular mention of raiment in the above Verse suggests that the rational and moral consciousness of man had emerged from the very beginning. Here is another Verse pointing to the same truth:

Oye Children of Adam:
Let not Satan seduce you,
In the same manner as
he got your parents out
of the Garden, stripping them
of their raiment, to expose
Their shame: for he
And his tribe watch you
From a position where ye
Cannot see them. *(VII-27)*

Since by transcending material existence, peace is achieved and the right relation with the unconscious established, the earlier address of God to man insisted on removing the obstacles in the way of transcendence and overcoming animal and lustful desires. Also, it was pointed out that special attempts should be made to manipulate and transform the environment into a desirable pattern. This is recorded by the Quran:

Oye Children of Adam!
Whenever there come to you
apostles from amongst you,
Rehearsing My Signs unto you,—
Those who are righteous
And mend (their lives),—
On them shall be no fear
Nor shall they grive. *(VII-35)*

In Western Culture Evolution Stops at the Human Body : In western culture man is supposed to have emerged from the lower forms of life. Previously, he was an ape, and through gradual evolution spanning millions of years he has acquired the present human form. Mental evolution has proceeded on similar lines.

Thus the mind of the man living three thousand years ago was like that of a child: it lacked in the power of intellect. It was through a process of gradual evolution that man became worthy of being called a rational and speech-possessing creature. In this conception of man there is no place for spirituality; nor is there any idea of subsequent evolution in any other dimension. Evolution stops at the human body. Beyond it there is no dimension for evolution to proceed in.

Cultural Reconstruction Begins with the Human Body : Our conception of cultural reconstruction recognizes that man's evolution begins with the body. But it says that a subsequent and never-ending process of spiritual evolution continues. In other words, cultural reconstruction begins where the West ends.

Our conception finds support in various evidences. For example:

1. Man has been gifted with the guidance of Reason and experience and with the knowledge of the nature of things:

   And he taught Adam the names of all things;*(II - 31)*

Exegists have offered various explanations of *al Asma* ('the names of things'). The most plausible one takes the phrase to mean 'the nature of things'. 'Taught' implies man's capability of Knowledge, and, as it should be, this 'Knowledge means intuitive knowledge and not discursive knowledge'.

Owing to Knowledge and the guidance of Reason and experience, all things in the universe have been subjected to man, by Divine Providence.

And he has subjected
To you, as from Him,
All that is in the heavens
And on earth: (XLV-13)

Agency for Senses Not Enough for Apprehending the Supersensible World:

2. Intimations have been given to us of another world, for the apprehension of which the agency of the senses is not enough. This is the supersensible world—

   God is He.....
   Who knows (all things)
   Both secret and open (LIV-22)

The things of the supersensible world are not contradictory to reason; they simply transcend reason. In other words, it is no wonder if reason, which is grounded on knowledge derived from the senses, is unable to apprehend the realities of the supersensible world. Indeed, inability to apprehend something does not go to disprove its existence.

To deny the existence of a thing which cannot be apprehended is a human weakness. But there are many things which are beyond the reach of human reason, and even those things that are within the reach of human reason are not apprehended by a particular person or by the intellectual calibre of a particular age, while some other person of some other age may be able to apprehend them as undeniable truths. If such is the state of affairs, it would be a self-deception to regard the inapprehensibility of a thing as an evidence of its non-existence. The Quran speaks of people who fell into this error:

Nay, they charge with falsehood
That whose knowledge they
Cannot compass, even before
The elucidation thereof
Hath reached them: thus
Did those before them
Make charges of falsehood: (X-39)

Faith in the Supersensible is Necessary : In order to establish relation with the supersensible world it is necessary to have faith in its realities. The most important of these realities is Divine Energy. This Divine Energy partakes of our psychological constitution. Owing to it, infinite possibilities of evolution are opened, and the correspondence between psychological constitution and actual reconstruction of culture is established.

Super Natural Powers

This Divine Energy has always been there and will always be there. It is none other than God whose Knowledge encompasses all things and whose Mercy embraces all creation. His Power is supreme and His Sovereignty is over all the worlds. His Justice is equal for every creature and His Providence works equally in the whole creation:

Praise be to God

The Cherisher and Sustainer of the Worlds;

Most Gracious, Most Merciful;

Master of the Day of Iudgment. *(II - 4)*

All depend on Him, and He depends on none. He is Absolute Act and Absolute Being, and He has no equal or partner:

Say: He is God,

The One and Only;

God, the Eternal, Absolute;

He begetteth not,

Nor is He begotten;

And there is none

Like unto Him. *(CXII 1- 4)*

He is unique in His Essence and Attributes, and there is no one like Him.

.... there is nothing

Whatever like unto Him. *(XLII-11)*

Through Faith in Divine Energy Man Achieves Self-realization : Man achieves self-realization through faith in Divine Energy. He finds his own self which he could not find even after seeking for it for thousands of years. And after he has found his Self, his field of activity does not remain limited to the world of matter but extends beyond it.

He ascends into the transcendental world, in comparison to which this world of matter is inferior and less valuable.

In Western Culture Worldly Life is the Goal of Evolution : In western culture, worldly life is regarded as the last phase or goal of the evolution of life. After it there is death and mere annihilation. The result of such a view is that beliefs, goals, ideals and values are confined to this world of matter. Neither any other world is supposed to exist nor is there any way of ascent into it.

This means that as regards his own self, man is where he was 1400 years ago, and that the light of knowledge has not been able to dispel the darkness of ignorance about himself. The Arabs of the Days of Ignorance also held a similar, materialistic view of life:

And they (sometimes) say:
'There is nothing except
Out life on this earth,
And never shall we be
Raised up again.' (VI - 29)

At another place the Quran speaks of people holding this view:

They say: 'What;
When we are reduced
To bones and dust,
Should we really be raised up
(To be) a new creation?' (XVII - 49)

Life after Death

According to our conception of cultural reconstruction it is believed that beyond death there is another life and another world which is called the Hereafter. To reach this other world one has to pass across a bridge. This bridge is death. In this way life is a continuous process and it does not end in death. On the other hand it goes on from stage to stage.

Man is destined to reach the goal of the Hereafter sooner or later.

How can ye reject
The Faith in God?—
Seeing that ye were without life,
And He gave you life;
And again to Me will ye return. (II-28)

This goal is not a material goal; it is the goal of transcendental and ultimate realities. In the Hereafter the consequences of man's deeds—good or bad—will be manifested in the same way as effects follow causes in this world. There is:

A reward for their deeds *(XXXII-17)*

The good and the bad deeds of man are recorded and their consequences are manifested:

But verily over you

(are appointed angels)

To protect you,— king and honourable,—

Writing down(your deeds):

They know (and understand)

All that ye do. *(LXXXII—10-12)*

The Means of Knowledge of the West are Confined to the Senses : Unfortunately the West does not possess any means of knowing the reality after death. After death nobody comes back to tell of his condition either. The means of knowledge of the West are related only to the senses, but the world of the Hereafter is related to what is beyond the senses. This is why in spite of all the material advancement, the West has ignored the realities of the Hereafter. Man is very fickle-minded. When he does not know anything or is not able to know it, he jumps to the conclusion that it does not exist.

Though the same thing may turn up as an established reality later on. If the judgement of the West regarding transcendental realities were acceptable, the progress of knowledge would have stopped long ago and those hundreds of things which were unbelievable before would not have been discovered as realities now. Just as the impossibilities of yesterday are the possibilities of today, in the same way it would be no wonder if the impossibilities of today become the possibilities (like C.E.M. Joad). These thinkers are seeking the next phase of the evolution of life and they have gone to the extent of saying that the next phase of human life is not material but spiritual.

Knowledge of Transcendental Realities in the Islamic Scheme of Cultural Reconstruction. In the Islamic scheme of cultural reconstruction, there is a means of knowledge which can throw light on the next phase of man's life and which can have access to transcendental realities. This means of knowledge is revelation. It is necessary for us to have faith in it, for its guidance goes beyond the sensible world. The knowledge acquired through revelation is not quantified knowledge. It is intitutive knowledge. Through it the inhabitants of the world get into the secrets of transcendental realities:

> *.....say:*
> *'the Guidance of God, —that*
> *Is the (only) Guidance'.*
> *Wert Thou, to follow their desires*
> *After the knowledge*
> *Which hath reached thee,*
> *Then wouldst thou find*
> *Neither protector nor Helper*
> *Against God.* *(II-120)*

The real subject of Divine revelation is man and its argument is concerned only with human life which continues after death.

Without Transcendental Knowledge the Puzzle of the Universe Remains Unsolved.

If our life is devoid of the guidance of transcendental knowledge, the puzzle of the universe will not be solved, nor will the problems of mankind be resolved. This is why God has given this knowledge to man from the very beginning:

> *And if, as assured, there comes to you*
> *Guidance from Me, whosoever*
> *Follows My Guidance, on them*
> *Shall be no fear, nor shall they grieve.*
> *But those who reject Faith*
> *And belie our Signs,*
> *They shall be companions of the Fire:*
> *They shall abide therein.* *(II— 38-9)*

Through Revelation Man Gets Scientific Knowledge : Through revelation the secrets of life are known and man is led to acquire scientific knowledge. But the materialistic attitude associated with science has created a very unfortunate situation and made life meaningless and futile. The secret of life lies is hidden in the inner being of man. Science has been trying to relate this inner being to some Intelligent Power. To have access to both the inner being and the Intelligent Power is impossible for the man who is merely a creature of reason and selfish desire and who has been further mutilated by industry and the advances of science and technology.

Revelational Knowledge Recognises the Natural Constitution of Man : The culture which has been built up according to revelational knowledge emphasises the shaping of personality according to the natural constitution of man and also the use of the things of the world for human benefit.

Since man is a combination of the material and the transcendental and since in matters related to his own self, his abilities are usually unable to function properly, it is necessary to have such a guidance for the development of personality as may reach beyond reason and sense experience and may encompass both the material and the transcendental. If the guidance of the reason and sense experience is regarded as sufficient only the material part of man's being will be dealt with. The transcendental part will be misunderstood or not understood at all with the result that man will get sick of life, and culture will reach the point of self-destruction. This is being observed in the case of western culture nowadays. But in this case, we may note, even the material part of man's being will not be fully dealt with. The greater part of human life passes in the darkness of passion, and in this state the guidance of reason does not work and sense-experience does not yield any fruit. Moreover, reason and modes of sense-experience, are always subject to change. In such a situation if we rely upon reason and sense experience the state of life and culture will become chaotic. This will be particularly so because there will be no distinction between reason and lustful desire and every human experience will get coloured according to an individual's personal inclination.

The Universe is Easier to Manipulate than Man : In comparison to man the manipulation of the Universe is easier. For man is himself the manipulator and the newer phases of his progress are products of his infinite desires and necessities. As for the manipulation of the Universe, the above-mentioned guidance is not needed. In this case reason and sense-experience can do the job and progress can continue :

Say: and I do admonish you
On one point: that ye
do stand up before God,—
(it may be) in pairs,
Or (it may be) single,—
And reflect (within yourself):
Your Companion is not
Possessed: *(XXXIV - 46)*

The Source of Revelation is Divine Energy : The source of revelation is Divine Energy and for deriving benefit from it the transcendental part of man has to be tuned up. The person to whom the revelation comes is not merely a messenger; he has an insight in the transcendental part of his being, through which he can apprehend super-sensible realities.

Two Kinds of Means of Knowledge : The means of knowledge are of two kinds: (1) Material; (2) Transcendental. The material means are those which are related to the body and the transcendental means are those which are related to what is beyond the body. Pertaining to the first kind of knowledge we have sense perception, axiomatic truths and reason, and to the second kind is revelation and intuition..

The second kind of knowledge begins where the first kind ends and the end of the second kind is the beginning of the Absolute. It means that the end of the first kind is reason, which is related to the physical but is very close to what lies beyond it. The end of the second kind is revelation which is related to the transcendental but is very close to the Absolute.

Revelation is the Highest Form of Non-physical Means of Knowledge : It means that revelation is the highest form of non-physical means of knowledge. It operates on the ultimate frontiers of human consciousness and is a divine gift to man (we shall speak more about it later on):

Such is the Bounty of God,
Which He bestows
On whom He will. *(LXII - 4)*
Again:
God knoweth best where
(And how) to carry out
His mission: *(VI - 124)*

For receiving the divine gift of revelation a particular capability is needed, which is to be trained. Thus the Quran speaks of Moses:

And We tried
The invarious ways.
Then didst thou tarry
A number of years
With the people of Midian.

Then didst thou come hither

As ordained, O Moses!

And I have prepared thee

For Myself (for service) *(XX — 40-41)*

In this verse by *qadar* ('as ordained') is implied the prophetic capability of receiving divine revelation. Exegetes have explained this word as follows:

> *We have determined for the way of knowledge and guidance and also it is proper time. Thou hast come up to our standard.* (Tafsir 'Araisul Bayan')

Another interpretation is as follows:

> *Thou hast reached the highest destiny according to thy capability.* (Tafsir Mohiuddin Ibn-i- Arabi)

For the training of capability, the Prophet passes through circumstances that do not befall ordinary man or are beyond their toleration. The Holy Prophet Muhammad (peace be upon him) was asked: "Who is subject to the greatest test." He replied: 'the Prophet, then he who is close in status to him, and then he who is close in status to the later and so on'. *(Tirmizi; Ibn-i-Majah; Mishkat: Ayadatul Mariz wa Thawabul Maraz).* The ascent of Moses to mount Sinai in the state of fast; the state of Jesus in the wilderness in the state of fast; and the meditation and the prayers of Prophet Muhammad (p.b.u.h.) in the cave of Hira—all these things were meant for the training of their respective capabilities.

Various Forms of Guidance From the Absolute : The Guidance from the Absolute comes according to a particular pattern. For achieving this Guidance, material means do not count. The various forms of Guidance are mentioned in the Quran:

It is not fitting

For a man that God

Should speak to him

Except by inspiration,

Or from behind a veil,

Or by the sending

Of a Message

To reveal, With God's permission,

What God wills: for He

Is Most High, Most Wise. *(XLII - 51)*

It is this Guidance that we spoke about in connection with God's address to the primitive generations of man. Without this Guidance there can be no harmony between man and the Universe, nor can there be a balance between materialism and transcendentalism. The Quran says:

Do they seek
For other than the Religion
Of God?— while all creatures
In the heavens and on earth
Have, willing or unwilling,
Bowed to His will
(Accepted Islam),
And to Him shall they
All be brought back. *(III - 83)*

The process of Guidance has continued in human history and it has been available to every community and every people. Through this Divine Guidance the Right Way has been pointed out and the construction of culture has been taken place —

...and to every people
A Guide. *(XIII - 7)*
At another place it is said:
And there never was
A people, without a warner
Having lived among them
(in the past). *(XXXV - 24)*

There is Continuity and Evolution in the Matter of Guidance : There is continuity and evolution in the matter of Divine Guidance. Thus the Quran says:

Then sent We Our apostle
In succession: *(XXIII - 44)*
Again it is said:
None of Our revelation
Do We ubrogate
Or cause to be forgotten,
But we substitute
Something better or similar: *(II - 106)*

***The Guidance Aims at Perfect Enlightenment of Mankind* :** The continuous process and Guidance was stopped, as it was necessary, after mankind reached perfect enlightenment. Thus a limit was set to the perfection of humanity. The Quran says:

Muhammad is not
The father of any
Of your men, but (he is)
The Apostle of God,
And the seal of the Prophets: *(XXXIII -40)*

The perfection of enlightenment, which is revelation, is achieved in every sense:

The Word of thy Lord
Doth find its fulfilment
In truth and in justice: *(VI - 115)*

There is no question of changing His words:

None can change His word. *(VI - 115)*

In fact the change can be towards the superior or towards the inferior. It cannot be towards the superior because the Words are spoken at the frontiers of human consciousness. It can not be towards the inferior because after this stage of evolution there is no question of retrogression.

***The Perfection of Enlightenment is the Last Phase of Human Consciousness* :** There is no doubt that the Guidance of revelation comes in the last evolutionary phase of human consciousness. The Guidance itself has its stages, the last stage being the perfection of revelation. But every apostle to whom revelation comes is a human being. He is not a partner of the Divine Being, nor is he transformed into a creature other than man:

Their apostles said to them:
And truth, we are human
Like yourself, but God
Doth grant His grace
To such of His servants
As He pleases. *(XIV- 11)*

Prophet Muhammad (p.b.u.h.) is ordained to clarify his position:

Say: 'I am but a man
Like yourself, (but)

The inspiration has come
To me, that your God is
One God.' *(XVIII- 110)*

Again :

Say thou; 'I am
But a man like you:
It is revealed to me
By inspiration, that your God,
Is one God: so stand
True to Him, and ask
For His forgiveness. *(XLI - 6)*

This state of revelation in the history of mankind is as sensitive as it is inevitable. If the apostles were not human beings, they would not be able to guide human beings according to the demands of their nature; and if revelation had not been the last phase of human consciousness, lasting benefits could not be derived from the Guidance. As regards the sensitivity of the state of revelation, it may be noted that in every period of human history various misunderstandings have arisen about it. Sometimes the Prophet is apotheosized into a partner of God or His Manifestation or Autar or even His son. Sometimes the status of apostlehood is so much degraded that every seer has been given the status of the Prophet, no matter if he is not innocent and pure of character.

This is a Very Sensitive and Delicate State : This last phase of the evolution of mankind is so lofty that, let alone mortal beings, even etherial being cannot reach there. A Tradition of the Holy Prophet says: 'I was made to ascend to the Last Lote Tree'. The Lote Tree is the place where any other creature has not reached. Except Muhammad (p.b.u.h.) nobody else reached this place.
(Bukhari, Vol.II, Hadith Isra)

In spite of all this it signifies a state of humanity and creaturehood, one which does not partake of the Divine at all. The Quran speaks about it:

Glory to (God)
Who did take His Servant
For a journey by night
From the Sacred Mosque

To the Farthest Mosque,
Whose precincts We did
Bless,— in order that We
Might show him some
Of Our Signs. *(XVII - 1)*

The following Verse speaks of nearness to the Absolute:

And was at a distance
Of but two bow - lengths
Or (even) nearer;
so did(God) convey
The inspiration to His Servants—
(conveyed) what He (meant)
To Convey. *(LIII — 9-10)*

The laws of the numinous world are different from those of the world of matter. In the case of nearness to the Numinous or Absolute the law of the material world dissolved. So do the categories of space and time. The ultimate reality is revealed, and man becomes a direct recipient of blessings from the Divine Being.

It is obvious that for the apprehension of this state, material means are not enough. If attempt is made to reach there by means of material means, it would result in fallacy in the same way as fallacy results when the intellect of man is approached through the concept of animal psychology. Perhaps it is for this reason that the Quran clinches the argument by saying:

... in order that We
Might show him some
Of Our Signs. *(XVII - 1)*

At another place it is said:

For turly did he see,
All the signs of His Lord,
The Greatest! *(LIII - 18)*

The Need of Guidance has been there in Every Age : After the last phase of the evolution cf human consciousness, the process of revelation came to an end. But its need has always been there and will always be there. Because man is inclined towards his physical nature and is easily entangled in naturalism. Sometimes this entanglement becomes so intense that his intuition and senses are affected and what is sweet and good for him becomes unsavoury. Hence it is very necessary to have some systematic programme of promoting his higher nature and of maintaining a balance between the higher nature and the lower or animal nature. Unless both the higher and the lower chords of his being are struck the desirable music cannot be produced.

In fact, it is for the sake of producing this music that the Guidance of God is needed. It will be needed as long as man exists on this earth. Thus the Quran says:

It is He who has sent
amongst the unlettered
An apostle from among
Themselves, to rehearse
to them His Signs,
to sanctify them, and
To instruct them in Scripture
And Wisdom *(LII-2)*
God did confer
a great favour
On the Believers
When He sent among them
An apostle from among
Themselves, rehearsing
Unto them the Signs
Of God, sanctifying them,
And instructing them
In scripture and Wisdom. *(III - 164)*

At another place God says:

We sent aforetime
Our apostles with Clear Signs
And sent down with them
The Book and the Balance
(Of Right and Wrong), that men
May stand forth in justice; *(LVII - 25)*

Defence of Holy Scriptures

The last Guidance of God is valid for ever and ever, and for this reason God himself has undertaken to protect it. The Quran says:

We have, without doubt,
Sent down the Message:
And We will assuredly
Guard it (from corruption) *(XV - 9)*

Then for translating this Message into a practical form the Holy Prophet's life was presented as a model and God saw to it that it was so:

Ye have indeed
In the Apostle of God
A beautiful pattern (of conduct)
For anyone whose hope is
In God and the Final Day
And who engages much
In the praise of God. *(XXXIII -21)*

Those who assimilated this model or pattern in their own lives were set as models for their successors:

That the Apostle May be
A withness for you,
And ye be witnesses for mankind! *(XXII - 78)*

At another place the Quran says:

These have We made a few
An ummat justly balance
That ye might be witnessed
Over the nations,
and the Apostle a witness
Over yourselves; *(II - 143)*

Even after the Last Phase the Guidance Continues : After the last Message the Guidance still continues. This is why the Quran says:

Ye are the best
Of Peoples, evolved
For mankind
Enjoining what is right,

Forbidding what is wrong,

And believing in God. *(III - 110)*

If man is deprived from Guidance, his life achieves no harmony. Rather it degenerates into self-hatred and self-revulsion. Similarly, if cultural reconstruction is not done, man will not be able to establish relation with the Absolute, nor will it be possible for him to manifest the transcendental dimensions of his life. His culture will be lacking in justice and his civilization will be led to self-destruction.

Man Holds the Most Important Place in the Scheme of in Cultural Reconstruction: According to revelational knowledge, the place of man is of foremost importance in the scheme of the reconstruction of culture. The next importance is given to the understanding of the constitutive principles of culture. After this one can talk about man's individual, social, economic and political life and about philosophy and ethics.

For the understanding of man's place in the universe four things, should be considered:

1. The essence of man;
2. His competence;
3. The nature of his work; and
4. The field of his striving.

The first and the second topics have been discussed under psychological constitution. We shall now discuss the 'nature of man's work' and 'the field of his striving'.

On account of man's competence and essence, the Creator has made him His vicegerent and the leader of the universe. Thus the Quran says:

I will create

A vicegerent on earth *(II - 30)*

At another place it is said:

O David! we did indeed

make thee a vicegerent

On earth: so judge thour

Between men in truth (and justice):

Nor follow thou the lust

(of thy heart), though they will

Mislead thee from the Path

Of God. *(XXXVIII -26)*

The implication is that the nature of man's work is such that through it should be manifested by the nature of the Creator and His Wisdom.

On the one hand man reflects the attributes of God, and on the other he performs creative works and works of subjecting nature to himself, and these works manifest God and His power :

> *His manifestation is thy manifestation, and thy manifestation is His manifestation. Thou shouldst manifest God and God should manifest thee.*
>
> *For man's striving two fields have been set: (1) His self; (2) the universe.*

The Quran speaks of these fields. Thus it is said that there are God's Signs on the earth:

> *As also in your own*
> *Selves: will ye not*
> *Then see?* *(LI-21)*

And again:

> *And He has subjected*
> *To you, as from Me,*
> *All that is in the heavens*
> *And on earth* *(XLV- 13)*

Man and the Cosmos

The relation between the human self and the universe is a mutual relation. It is from both the sides. If anyone side is neglected the result will be destruction. In other words, if an exclusive emphasis is laid on man's exploitation of the universe and higher values are neglected, civilization will be committing suicide. Similarly, if all emphasis is laid on higher values and the scientific and progressive process of comprehending and exploiting nature stops, the survival of man will be in danger. For the sake of maintaining a balance between striving for higher values and exploiting nature, God has sent Guidance through his apostles. With regard to one field of human striving, i.e. the self, detailed instructions were sent down from God.

Regarding the other field, i.e. the universe, only fundamentals were determined.

Man's own self is more complex than the universe. In this matter, human faculties do not work. This is why detailed Guidance was necessary in this regard. But the universe is not so complex. Man is its master and his exploitation of the universe arises from his own desires and necessities. For this reason detailed Guidance in this regard was not necessary, nor would this Guidance keep pace with changes in the universe. It is understandable why God sent down a series of detailed instructions with regard to the human self and pointed out only the fundamentals with regard to man's relation to the universe.

The apostles of God performed their work with regard to both the fields of human striving. With regard to the first field, the human self, they tried to educate man in character building; and with regard to the second field, the universe, they performed some miracles, so as to point to the direction of the exploitation of nature, and left the rest to the Guidance of human reason and experience.

The Teachings of Prophet Muhammad are More Comprehensive : Since Muhammad (peace be upon him) comes at the last phase of the evolution of humanity his teachings are more comprehensive. Thus, on the one hand the Quran gives detailed instructions regarding the education of the human self, and the Traditions provide us with a record of the life of the Holy Prophet, and on the other the Quran mentions the physical realities of life, the beauties of the universe, the objects of nature and man's conception of the universe, and the Holy Prophet's life tells us of certain miracles through which he has pointed to modern discoveries and advances of culture.

Western culture is unfortunate in one respect. It has carried the exploitation of nature to higher and higher stages of advancement but, for certain reason, it has neglected the education and character building (the real psychological constitution of man and the proper development of his personality), with the result that it is cursed with revulsion and hatred of life itself and its civilization is an enemy of civilization itself.

The Gnostics' Way of Knowing the Place of Man : The gnostics have defined the place of man in a different way and have taken a different approach to this subject. Their discussion is brief but very interesting. They say that in the essential being of man there is something which is called *heart*. This is the place where gnosis of God is found like a pearl in an oyster. The relation of the *heart to* the physical heart is like the relation of the content to the vessel or that of the dweller to the house (we are going to discuss this subject later on). The *heart* is the centre of numinous energy in man; it is the dwelling place of love and faith and consciousness. Owing to it man has his distinctive place in creation, and he has become, so to say, the cream of creation and the very purpose of the universe. Again it is owing to the heart that he is worthy of the vicegerency of God. Sheikh Sharfuddin Yahya Muniri observes:

> *There were all kinds of created beings, but with man it was a different matter. When God willed to bring this creature of clay into existence and to exalt him to the place of vicegerency, the angels said: wilt thou bless therein one who will make mischief therein...? The Eternal Love replied: Love does not recognise advice and logic. If we did not accept them what would be the value of all your prayers. And if we are willing to show mercy and forgiveness to manes what harm can his sin do to us? You see that in the affairs of life man has relation with Us, but you do not see that in the matter of love we have relation with him". A Poet has rightly said: 'When the beloved commits some mistake or lapse, her beauty pleads in a thousands ways'.* (Epistle *38)*

In another Epistle Sheikh Sharfuddin Yahya Muniri says : Do not look down on (this creature of) water and clay (man) all the excellencies are there in him and whatever you find in the world has come here along with him. Except him everything else is a shadow on the wall. The gnostics have said that the bird of love took its flight from the nest of Grace. It came near the highest heaven, saw Majesty and passed by. It came near the throne of God, saw infinitude and passed by. It reached heaven, saw loftiness and passed by. Then it reached the dust (man), saw toil and striving and descended there. *(Epistle* 50)

Abu Ali Daqaq says: If the sun of love had not shone on the being and on the *heart of man* his case too would have been like that of other creatures. (Sheikh Muniri, *Epistle 46)*

Man Deserves his Exaltation Because of the Heart : According to the gnostics the exaltation of man is owing to his *heart*. Regarding its value it has been said by Sheikh Muniri:

> *God created the Empyrean and put it under the charge of the highest angels. He created Paradise and put it under the charge of Rizwan. He created Hell and put it under the charge of the Angel of Hell. But when He created the heart of the believer He said: 'The heart, in fact, lies between the two fingers of the Benevolent One.'*
> *(Epistle 43)*

At Another Place the Gnostic Observes : If anything dearer than the heart had been there I (God) would have placed my Gnosis there. *Epistle* 38)

There is a Tradition of the Holy Prophet which is hadith-e-Qudsi: 'I cannot be contained by the heavens, nor by the earth, it is only in the heart of the believer that I can be contained.' Another Tradition says: I can be contained in no other place except in the heart of the believer.

The essence of the Heart cannot be conceived even by Angels:

> *Sheikh Muniri goes on to say that the heart has an essence which is so noble and so much beyond comprehension that, not to speak of material being, even angels can not conceive of it.*

Brother! it is a very big thing that thou hast been made the object of prostration for the angels and of jealousy for the heavens. However, clouded in his physical being man may be, he is so numinous and holy in his essential being that the intelligence of the angels and the speculation of man are unable to comprehend his reality. When his essential being blazes forth, the angels are amazed and the heavens become dizzy. They courtesy to him and are overpowered with awe.

Western culture recognizes its helplessness with regard to the understanding of the essential being of man, in spite of modern psychological researches. It has not been able to explore the *heart* of man. For westerners the *heart* of man is the physical organ, which is merely a pump to supply blood to the various parts of the body. But the above argument brings out that the *heart* is the source of human life and energy and that its influence permeates every department of culture.

The Three Constituent Principles of Western Culture : After understanding the place of man in the universe it is necessary to understand the constituent principles of culture, for without such an understanding the ideals and goals of life cannot be determined, nor can any plan of character building be conceived.

The Constitutive Principles of Western Culture Are:

(1) Freedom of thought and consciousness;

(2) Materialistic tendency;

(3) Test for beauty and the good things of life.

These constitutive principles have been derived from Greeco-Roman culture. They have their potential for good as well as for evil. If they are allowed to operate without any check they can lead to the most appalling manifestations of beastliness and lust; but if certain limits are observed they can be most beneficial for mankind. Unfortunately, in western culture, these constitutive principles have been allowed to operate unchecked. In the beginning the evil consequences were not so prominent because people were more concerned with constructive activity. But later on their power of striving and resistance was weakened and the riot of profligate thought and action broke out to work destruction on humanity. Attempts were made to check it by means of philoscphy. But philosophy was bound to fail where only Faith would have succeeded.

The Three Constitutive Principles of Cultural Reconstruction : The three constitutive principles of cultural reconstruction are: (1) the state of Faith; (2) transcendental concerns; and (3) relation with the Absolute.

These constitutive principles have been derived from the natural constitution of man. If they are allowed to do their proper function in the building up of culture, the spiritual essence of man will be manifested, and the synthesis of reason and the *heart,* of materialism and spiritualism, and of this-worldliness and other-worldliness will be achieved. The achievement of this harmony will help man bring his passions under the control of reason, and enable him to lead his life in a way worthy of his place in creation. On the other hand, if lust for power and sensual enjoyment prevails, mankind will suffer stagnation and degeneration, and will be led to stain with bloodshed and even the Holy places of worship, which has been observed in the case of people in a state of decline. Let us consider each constitutive principle in some detail.

Belief in Islam

The State of Faith is the Result of Synthesis : The state of Faith does not emerge from dead evidence and rigid belief. It is the product of the synthesis of Knowledge and conviction, gnosis and love. After achieving this synthesis man resigns his will to the Will of God. He purifies his *heart* and engages it in devotion to God. The state of Faith is the source of motive power. It is there behind all revolutionary movements. Through it culture is built up and the elements that promote life are activated. For it is directly related to the psychic life of man, where ideas are born and the seeds of revolution are sown.

What has been said about Faith : It has been said that 'owing to Faith the strength of a person is magnified ten times'. The Bible rightly observes that the power of Faith can move mountains. Those who have caused revolutions in history were certain ill-equipped but sincere persons whose Faith was extremely powerful.

That which makes one army victorious over another is not merely physical factors (which also count) but an internal power. Think, it was the power of Faith that made the militarily ill-equipped Arabs, those 'backward inhabitants of the desert', victorious over the immensely large and well-equipped armies of Khosro and Caesar. All the consequences and effects of Faith that the Quran speaks follow from the state mentioned above. For mere dead evidence and rigid belief cannot produce any change in the human psyche or in life.. It would only give some sentimental satisfaction and perpetuate certain empty rituals. This is testified by certain Verses of the Quran which we shall quote.

The Quran says:

But those of Faith are
Over - flowing in their love
For God. *(II-165)*

It means that the heart is purified of the love of everything other than God, the love of idols so to say, and it is engaged fully in the love of God only, valuing no other love before it; neither the love for relations and friends nor the love for power and glory.

In this state of love the Absolute man does not care for any worldly considerations or relations.

Thus the Quran says:

Say: if it be that your fathers,
Your sons, or brothers,
or maids or your kindred.
The commerce in which ye fear
A decline; or the dwellings
In which ye delight—
Are dearer to you then God,
Or His Apostle or the striving
In His cause;— then wait
until God brings about His Decision: *(IX-24)*

If the heart is turned from God's love, the Decision of God is manifested in the form of humiliations for a whole people. It must also be noted that the manifestation of the Decision has various phases corresponding to the degree of the presence or the absence of love for God. The Quran says:

Thou wilt not fing
any people who believe
In God and the Last Day
Loving those who resist
God and His Apostle,
Even though they were
Their fathers or their sons,
Or their brothers, or
Their kindred.
For such,
He has retained Faith
In their hearts, and strengthened
Them with a spirit
From Himself. *(LVIII-22)*

The implication is that the love induced in man as a result of Faith prevails over his will, thought and action and over all his relations with others. In fact this Love can be identified by those of pervading quality.

The Philosophy of Love Resolves the Tangles of Life : The philosophy of love as gnostics have presented it resolves the tangles of life and psychical complexes. Sheikh Yahya Muniri has rightly observed:

> *The monotony and unanimity that you see in the works of angels is there because they are unaware of the lore of love; and the ups and downs that you see in the lives of men are there because they are concerned with love (God loves them and they love God).* (Epistle 46)

At another Place the Sheikh says : "Brother! a broken thing carries no value, but it is a different matter with the heart, the more broken it is the more valuable it becomes. Moses in one of his prayers asked God where he could seek him. God answered:

> *"I am with those whose hearts are broken (because of Me)".* (Epistle *6)*

And this is what Iqbal says : Keep it not secure: let it break. Know that this mirror of thine : The more broken it is the more valuable does it become in its Maker's Eye.

History is Explained through Love of God : The love of God testifies to the realities of the suffering and trails of the prophets.

Their sufferings and trials are meant to show that no other love, even the love of the dearest thing or person is more valuable than the love of God.

Why Setting Partners of God is an Unpardonable Offence: In the light of love it becomes understandable why setting partners of God is such an unpardonable offence:

God forgiveth not
(the sin of) joining other gods
With Him; but He forgiveth
Whom He pleaseth other sins
Than this; one who joins
Other god with God,
Had strayed for, far away
(from the Right). *(IV-116)*

Indeed, it is all because of love. For if the heart which God has made for an exclusive attachment to Himself joins others with God in its love, it is an unforgivable sin.

According to Gnostics Love Encompasses the Whole Universe: The gnostics regard love as all inclusive and eternal. For them it encompasses the whole universe.

Such a conception of love leads to the resolution of all problems. Sheikh Sharfuddin Yahya Muniri observes:

> *The lore of love encompasses every age, the beginning and the end of all time. It is a love that has been and is and will be the same in future. Seekers of Truth have said that this world and the other world both are the worlds of desire. If somebody says that the other world is not the world of desire it is not true. Of course on Doomsday prayer and fasting will not be there and all commandments (of the* Shariah) *shall be obliterated, but two things will always remain: (1) the love of God, (2) the praise of God.* (Epistle *46)*

Faith Demands Sacrifice of Love and Property: It is necessary to present the philosophy of love in modern terms and to consider it as a permanent subject of enquiry. Only after such an attempt its full form will become manifest:

God has purchased of the Believers
Their persons and their goods:

For their's (in return)
Is the garden (of Paradise):
They Fight in His Cause,
And slay and are slain:
A promise binding on Him
In Truth, through the Law,
The Gospel, and the Quran:
and who is more faithful
To his Covenant than God?
Then rejoice in the bargain
Which ye have concluded:
That is the achievement supreme. *(IX-III)*

After achieving Faith in God neither life nor property belongs to the Believer. He resigns them to God, and regards himself only as a trustee of the things that he can dispose only according to the commandment of God.

Self-exile, Holy War and Giving Aid are Obligatory: For this state of Faith self-exile *(hijrat),* Holy war and striving *(jihad)* and giving aid (*nusrat*) to the Believers who have exiled themselves or are righting in the cause of God are obligatory:

Those who believe,
And fight for the Faith,
In the Cause of God,
As well as those
Who give (them) asylum
And aid— these are (all)
In very truth the Believers: *(VIII-74)*

At another place it has been said:

Only those are Believers
Who have believed in God
And His Apostle, and have
Never since doubted, but
Have striven with their
Belongings and their persons
In the Cause of God:
Such are the sincere ones. *(XLIX-15)*

At still another place the Quran proclaims:

Those who believe, and suffer
Exile and strive with might
And main, in God's cause,
With their goods and their persons,
have the highest rank
In the sight of God:
They are the people
Who will achieve (salvation) *(IX-20)*

In these Verses the phrases: 'these are (all) in very truth the Believers', 'such are the sincere ones', and 'they are the people who will achieve (salvation)' testify that without self-exile, striving and fighting in the Cause of God, and giving aid to the Believers who have exiled themselves and are striving and fighting in the Cause of God Quranic Faith cannot be achieved, nor can success in this world and in the next world be achieved by a Muslim.

Holy Injunctions

Self-exile : Self-exile or *Hijrat* is abandoning all things for the sake of Faith — all things that come in the way of Faith and its demands: even if one has to leave his home and family.

Striving or Jihad : It means striving in every way for the cause of Faith—striving in the physical sense, by means of the tongue and the pen, by means of intellectual abilities.

Striving implies all means and modes of human activity; it implies facing every kind of obstacle and not hesitating in making the greatest sacrifice, even the sacrifice of one's own life.

Giving Aid to Believers or Nusrat : It means helping one another and standing by one another in the face of difficulties and hardships. It, therefore, implies mutual cooperation and the spirit of sacrifice. These three factors are the natural modes of progress of all nations. The difference between the Muslims and other nations is that the other nations follow these modes for the sake of power and conquest of lands, but in the cultural reconstruction programme carried out by the Muslims the three modes are followed for the sake of God.

There is no difficulty about understanding the concepts of Hijrat and Nusrat, but the concept of Jihad has been misinterpreted by some bigoted historians as a manifestation of barbarism.

In reply to these historians, it would be enough to refer to the French author Sadeaux. He says that these people have gone deaf to the voice of truth and they are devcid of imaginative insight. It has happened in history that wars among nations have been devoid of moral considerations. As regards western culture, this freedom has taken an extreme form, such as has no precedent in history.

It was the Quran that First Laid Down a Code of War : In the context of cultural reconstruction it can be claimed that the Quran is the first Book that laid down a code of war and brought war under the control of moral principles. It made it clear to the world that the purpose of war should be the removing of corruption and injustice and the propagation of God's message of mercy, and not power or materialistic expansion. Thus the Quran says:

And fight them on
Untill there is no more
Tumult or oppression
And there prevail
Justice and Faith in God *(II - 193)*

The Holy Prophet also said: 'Strive and fight till God prevails'. Since a detailed discussion of the subject is beyond our scope we shall content ourselves with quoting the statement of certain non-Muslims. In the last days of the Caliphate of Omar or the early days of the Caliphate of Osman, a Nestorian Priest recorded his impression as follows:

> *These Tais (Arabs) whom God has made rulers, these Tais have also become our masters. But they are not at all hostile to Christian religion. On the other hand they protect our religion, give regard to our priests and saints and make donations of land and property for our churches.*

Walker in the History of International Law says that it is a common phenomenon in history that barbarous people attack civilized states and conquer them. But in comparison to the Teutonic and Tartarian barbarians, the Bedouins of Arabia who spilled over into other lands cannot be categorised as barbarian conquerors at all.

For these Bedouins, conquerors manifested superior culture and morality than the "civilized people" they conquered." In the history of the law of nations a Roman Catholic priest says that even the Jacobite Christians welcomed the Muslim Arabs as their redeemers. The greatest innovation of these Muslim Arabs was that they regarded the followers of every other religion as an autonomous entity and also appointed the priests of other religions to prestigious posts.

Role of Faith in Integration

It must be noted that it is the Islamic concept of cultural reconstruction that first recognized religious and ethnic minorities as an autonomous entity. According to this concept, the essence of social organization is Faith.

Thus, the Quran says:

But no, by Thy Lord
They can have
No (real) Faith,
Until they make thee judge
In all disputes between them,
And find in their souls
No resistance against
They decision, but accept
Them with fullest conviction. *(IV - 65)*

At another place it is said:

It is not fitting
For a believer,
Man or woman
When a matter has been decided
By God and His Apostle,
To have any option
About their decision: *(XXXIII - 36)*

For the believers the Quran comments:

And hold fast
All together, by the Rope
Which God (stretches out
For you), and be not divided
Among yourselves; *(III - 103)*

Again:

And obey God and His Apostle:
And fall into no disputes,

Lest ye boose heart
And your power depart:
And be patient and persevering:
For God is with those
Who patiently persevere: *(VIII - 46)*

Such Verses indicate that all the three constituents of social organization, allegiance, centrality and unity, emanate from Faith. Psychologists are of the opinion that the following factors are essential for a higher kind of social organization:

1. The members of the community must love one another, and there must be mutual love between them and their leader.
2. They must regard the good of all as the very aim of their life.
3. They must regard consideration for one another as their duty.

The social organization that partakes of these factors will certainly improve moral qualities and prevail over everything else.

Belief and Benefiting

The Quran has repeatedly insisted on the value of good deed alongwith Faith. This combination will certainly result in the vicegerency of man and his mastery in the world. The Quran says:

So lose not heart
Nor fall into despair:
For ye must gain mastery
If ye are true in Faith *(III - 139)*

Again it is said:

God has promised,
To those
Among you who believe
And work righteous deeds,
That He will, of surety grant them
In the land, inherent
(of power), as He granted it
To those before them: that
he will establish in authority
Their religion— one
Which He has chosen for them:

And that He will change
(their state), after the fear
In which they (lived), to one
Of security and peace: *(XXIV - 55)*

These Verses go to prove that without good deeds there can be neither the construction of culture nor the surety of its survival.

Regarding the heading of good deeds we get the following entry in Arabic dictionaries (like *Qamus, Sirah, Lisanul Arab):*

> "Salaah *is the opposite of Fasaad. One who properly carries out ones duties is* Saaleh. *Hence* Salehal kaza *is said when a person has the ability of carrying out some act.* Salahiyat *is the state which produces* Saaleh."

Let us Look at Some Arabic Idioms in this Connection

(1) Such and such a person's condition has become *Saaleh,* which means that the germs of corruption have been eliminated in him.

(2) Such and such a thing is *Saaleh* for thee which means it suits thee.

(3) The thing which was spoiled *(Afsad)* by hail has been restored to good condition by rain (this is said when somebody restores to good conditions what has been spoiled by another person).

(4) The thing which is not right and suitable *(layaslah).* It is better and more proper to abandon it.

(5) Reform *(Aslah)* yourself: People will be in your favour.

(6) He has accomplished sufficient gains *(Saaleh)* out of literature.

(7) A great gift has been obtained *(Saalehata)* from such and such a person.

Except no. 6-7 (where *Saaleh* has been used figuratively) all the above idioms go to prove that in the arabic language *Saaleh* is used in the sense of capability and suitability of accomplishment.

The Quran and the sayings of the Holy Prophet and the interpretations of exegetes also testify to the above mentioned general meaning of the word *Saaleh.* The Quran says:

'If Thou givest us
a goodly child
We vow we shall
(ever) be grateful'
But when He giveth them

A goodly child, they ascribe
To others a share in the gift
They have received: *(VII - 189-90)*

Before a child is born the parents wish that their child may be healthy and comely in every respect. The Quran has used the word *Saaleh* for these qualities, and the exegetes have interpreted accordingly.

At another place the Quran says:

Do not mischief on the earth,
After it hath been
Set in order, *(VII - 56)*

Here for setting in order the word *Islah* has been used, and the setting in order implies setting in order through invitation to the gospel, through which invitation the *hearts* are sown with spiritual capabilities and sensibility and good deeds appear as the fruits of this process. On one occasion the Holy Prophet saw a weary and hungry camel and used the word Saaleh for the animal in a healthy condition.

Thus the Tradition says: Fear God with respect to what you do to these speechless animals. Ride them when they are healthy and strong, and leave riding them in that condition. *(Mishkat)*

It means that you should not leave riding them when they are worn out and not suitable for riding or carrying loads. In another Tradition it is said:

> *In the body of man there is a lump of flesh. When it is healthy and in working order the whole body is healthy and in working order. When it goes out of order the whole body goes out of order. This lump of flesh is the heart of man.* (Bukhari, *Kitabul Iman)*

In this Tradition the health and the right working condition of the heart has been called *Salaah* and the opposite of it is called *Fasaad.* Regarding the word *Saaleh* exegetes have made the following observations:

> *By* Saalehaat *those deeds are implied that are right from the point of view of the Book and the Sunnah.* *(Madarik)*

> *By Saalehaat are implied all those deeds that the Shariah has approved and appreciated.* *(Baizawi)*

> Fasaad *means transgression or the going beyond limits of something, and* Salaah *is its opposit. These (concepts)*

respectively refer to all that is harmful and all that is beneficial. (Baizawi)

Regarding the deeds that are good or Saaleh Sheik. Muhammad Abduhu Misri says:

By them we mean those good deeds which are spelled out in detail in the Quran and are beneficial for oneself, family, community, and for all people in general. (*Tafsir Sura* Wal Asr)

The above explanations indicate that for the manifestation of Faith and the construction of culture, the good deeds that are necessary are not merely rituals, and conventional or outward virtues. Good deeds, in fact, comprehend both the inner and the outward life of man: they comprehend the whole being of man.

But the inner life comes first; for without it a healthy community cannot come into existence, nor can man's use of nature yield any common benefit.

Belief : Consequences

Faith gives rise to a mode of behaviour that combines conviction with good deeds. Through this behaviour man accomplishes what is essential for a progressive society. For one thing this mode of behaviour implies the attitude of right and scrupulous action in every sphere of life. For this attitude the Quran uses the comprehensive term *taqwa* (for which the word 'piety' would be a bad translation).

Taqwa is a pious state, one which is related to the *heart.* It enables a man to distinguish between right and wrong, and to feel pangs of conscience if he goes astray. An episode from Islamic history would bring out the meaning of *taqwa.*

The following dialogue took place between Hadrat Omar and Hadrat Abi bin Kaab:

Omar: *What is* taqwa?

Abi bin Kaab: *Have you ever walked along a thorny way?*

Omar: *I have.*

Abi bin Kaab: *What did you do on that occasion?*

Omar: *I gathered up my garments and tried to save myself from thorns.*

Abi bin Kaab: *Well, this is what is meant by* Taqwa

In other words, taqwa *is saving oneself from dangers of temptation.*

Chapter 5

Islamic Faith and Belief

Fundamentals of Faith

Some people may think that a man becomes a Muslim when he confesses belief in the Oneness of the True God and in Muhammad as His Last Messenger. But this is far from the full meaning of Faith. The full meaning of Faith in Islam is not, by any means, something nominal or a mere formality. Faith in Islam is a state of happiness acquired by virtue of positive action and constructive conceptions as well as dynamic and effective measures.

The Holy Quran and the Traditions of Muhammad define these required measures and establish the standards which build up a meaningful Faith. Thus, the true believers are:

1. Those who believe in God, His angels, His Books as completed by the Quran, His Messengers, with Muhammad being the Last of them all, the Day of Final Judgement.
2. Those who trust God always and enjoy unshakable confidence in Him.
3. Those who spend in the way of God of what He has given them in the form of wealth, life, health, knowledge, experience, and so on.
4. Those who observe their daily prayers regularly as well as the weekly and annual congregations.
5. Those who pay their religious taxes (alms or Zakat) to the rightful beneficiaries (individuals or institutions), the *minimum* of which is two and a half percent of the annual "net" income, or of the total value of stocks if in business—after discounting all expenses and credits.

6. Those who enjoin the right and good, and combat the wrong and evil by all lawful means at their disposal.
7. Those who obey God and His Messenger Muhammad and feel increasing strength of faith when the Quran is recited, and humility of heart when God's name is mentioned.
8. Those who love God and His Messenger most, and love their fellow men sincerely for the sake of God alone.
9. Those who love their near and distant neighbours and show genuine kindness to their guests, especially the strangers.
10. Those who say the truth and engage in good talk or else abstain.

It is clear that the very meaning of Faith makes Islam penetrate deeply and constructively into every aspect of life. According to Islam, true Faith has a decisive effect on the spiritual and material lot of man, and also on his personal and social behaviour as well as his political conduct and financial life. To show how the Quran describes the true believers, here are several of many examples. The Quran contains numerous references like these:

> *They only are the true believers whose hearts feel submissive (and humble) when God is mentioned; and when the revelations of God are recited unto them, they (the revelations) increase and strengthen their Faith; and who trust in their Lord, establish the prayer (as enjoined on them) and spend of what We have bestowed on them (in the cause of God). Those are they who are in truth believers. For them are (high) grades (of honour) with their Lord, and a bountiful provision*
>
> *(Quran 8:2-4).*
>
> *And the believers, men and women, are protecting (and allied) friends of one another; they enjoin the right and forbid the wrong, and they establish worship, and they pay the poor-due, and they obey God and His Messenger. As for these, God will have mercy on them; verily God is Mighty and Wise. God promises the believers, men and women, Gardens under which rivers flow, to dwell therein, and beautiful mansions in Gardens of everlasting bliss. But the greatest bliss is the Good Pleasure of God. That is the supreme felicity*
>
> *(Quran 9:71-72).*
>
> *The true believers are those only who believe in God and His Messenger (Muhammad) and afterward doubt not,*

> *but strive with their wealth and their lives for the cause of God. Such are the sincere* (Quran 49: 15).

Besides these Quranic references, there are many relevant Traditions of Muhammad. For example, he says:

> *None of you can be a true believer unless he loves for his fellow believer what he loves for himself.*

Three qualities are the sign of sound faith, and he who acquires them can really feel the sweet taste of Faith. They are (1) to love God and His Messenger most of all, (2) to love his fellow man for the sake of God alone, and (3) to resent and resist returning to disbelief as much as he does being cast into fire. He who believes in God and the Last Day of Judgement is forbidden to cause any harm to his neighbour, is to be kind to his guests—especially the strangers, and is to say the truth or else abstain. There are many verses and Traditions like the ones cited above. But it should be borne in mind, however, that the given quotations are not and cannot be the exact words of the Quran and Muhammad as they sound in the Arabic Text.

The reason for that is simple. No interpreter, however learned and masterful he may be, can ever convey the spiritual power and charming appeal of the Quran through any language. The Quran is—and so God made it—immitable, and it is beyond human imagination and power to produce anything like it. What is true of the Quran in this respect is also true of the Traditions of Muhammad to a certain extent, because, after the Quran, his words are the most conclusive and eloquent.

Righteousness (Birr)

Islam always warns against superficial concepts and rituals, against lifeless formalities and non-effective beliefs. In one representative verse, God explains the full meaning of righteousness as follows:

> *It is not righteousness that you turn your faces (in prayer) towards East or West; but it is righteousness to believe in God and the Last Day, and the Angels and the Book, and the Messengers; to spend of your wealth—in spite of your love of it—for your kin, for orphans, for the needy, for the wayfarer, for those who ask, and for the ransom of slaves; to be steadfast in prayer and practice regular charity; to fulfil the contracts which you have made; and to be firm and patient, in pain and adversity, and throughout all periods of panic. Such are the people of truth, the God-minded* (Quran 2:177).

In this verse, there is a beautiful and clear description of the righteous man. He should obey all the salutary regulations and should make his sincere motive the love of God and the love of his fellow man for the sake of God. Here we have four elements: (1) our Faith should be true and sincere, (2) we must be prepared to show it in deeds of charity and kindness to our fellow man, (3) we must be good citizens by supporting charitable institutions and social organizations, and (4) we must be steadfast and unshakable in all circumstances.

It is clear, therefore, that righteousness is not merely a matter of void utterances. It must be founded on strong Faith and constant practice. It must cover the person's thinking and action and extend to his inside and outside life, to his individual and common affairs. When the Islamic principle of righteousness is established, it provides the individual with peace in all circumstances, the society with security on all levels, the nation with solidarity, and the international community with hope and harmony. How peaceful and enjoyable life can be when people implement the Islamic Concept of Righteousness! What can be more reassuring than faith in the Beneficent Creator and investing in such good worthy causes? What can be more humane than relieving the deep anxieties of the subjugated, alleviating the sufferings of the exploited, and responding to the needs of the helpless? What is more methodical and honest than the fulfilments of commitments, the preservation of a clear conscience, and the maintenance of integrity? And what is more spiritually joyful than doing all this regularly, as a matter of course, and for the love of God?

Piety (Taqwa)

What has been said about faith and righteousness is generally true of piety. Again, it is not a matter of convenient claims and oral confessions. It is much more serious. As always, the Quran is our best source, and when it speaks of the pious, it describes them as those who believe in the Unseen (which is taught by God), are steadfast in prayer, and spend of what We have provided for them; and who believe in the Revelation sent to you (Muhammad), and sent before your time, and (in their hearts) have the assurance of the Hereafter. They are on true guidance from their Lord, and it is these who will prosper (Quran 2:3-5). The pious are those who spend (freely in the way of God) whether in prosperity or in adversity; who restrain anger and pardon (all men;—for God loves those who do good; and those who—having done something to be ashamed of, or wronged their own souls—earnestly bring God into mind, and ask for forgiveness for their sins,— and who can forgive sins except God?—and are never obstinate in persisting knowingly in (the wrong) they have done. For such the reward is forgiveness from their Lord, and Gardens with rivers flowing underneath,—an eternal dwelling. How excellent a recompense for those who work (and strive) (Quran 3:134-136).

In these verses, we find that piety requires a proper use of the mind by grasping the truth of God and life, a proper use of wealth by spending in the way of God under all circumstances and a proper use of the spiritual as well as the physical abilities of man by observing the prayer. It also demands a high degree of self-control over one's anger and emotions, a moral capacity for forgiveness and patience, and a conscious urge to make the sinner return to God in regret and repentance. To be pious is to be a man of true and fine convictions, of determination and character, of will and courage and, above all, to be a man of God. Piety, righteousness and meaningful Faith are interrelated and all pour into one channel. They lead to Islam and build up the true Muslim.

Prophethood (Risalat)

The Merciful and Loving God has sent many Prophets at different times of history. Every known nation has had one or more Prophets. All of the Prophets of God were men of good character and high honour. They were prepared and chosen by God to deliver His Message to mankind. Their honesty and truthfulness, as well as their intelligence and integrity, are beyond doubt. They were infallible in that they did not commit sins or violate the Law of God. But as mortals, they might have made unintentional mistakes in some human affairs and decisions. Their private judgments were not necessarily always right.

The sending of these Prophets from God is a clear manifestation of a strong link between Heaven and Earth, between God and man. It means that man is reformable and that there is much good in him. The purpose of Prophethood is to confirm what man already knows or can know, and to teach him what he does not or cannot know by his own means. It is also to help man to find the Straight Path of God, and to do the right and shun the wrong. Prophethood is an eloquent expression of God's love for His creations and His will to guide them to the right way of belief and behaviour. It is an emphasis of His justice to man, because He shows him true guidance first and then holds him responsible for his deeds. He gives warnings through His Prophets, and if man fails to see the dangers of his wrong deeds, his behaviour becomes punishable. This is in complete accord with God's love and justice, and the worth and capability of man of being responsible to his Lord.

The Source of Prophethood and the Sponsor of all the Prophets are One and the Same: God. Their aim is to serve God, to acquaint man with God and His Divine teachings, to establish truth and goodness, to help man to realize the true purpose of his existence and help him to conduct his life in a purposeful way. It is on this basis that the Muslims make no discrimination among the Prophets and accept their teachings as consistent and complementary. And this is the reason why the Muslims believe in all the Divine Books and accept all the Prophets of God as already mentioned.

Life (Hayat)

Life is a brilliant demonstration of God's wisdom and knowledge, a vivid reflection of His art and power. He is the Giver and Creator of life. Nothing comes into existence by chance, and nobody creates himself or anybody else. Life is a dear and cherishable asset, and no sensible or normal person would like to lose it by choice. Even those who feel so desperate that they take their lives by committing slow suicide try, at the last minute, to regain their existence and wish to capture a second chance to live. Life is given to man by God, and He is the only Rightful One to take it back; no one else has the right to destroy a life. This is why Islam forbids all kinds of suicide and self-destruction, and recommends patience and good Faith when a dear soul passes away. When a murderer is executed in punishment, his life is taken away by the right of God and in accordance with His Law.

When God gives life to man, it is not in vain that He endows him with unique qualities and great abilities. Nor is it in vain that He charges him with certain obligations. God means to help man to fulfil the purpose of life and realize the goal of existence. He means to help him to learn the creative art of living and to enjoy the good taste of life according to the Divine guidance. Life is a trust from God, and man is a trustee who should handle his trust with honesty and skill, with mindfulness of God and with consciousness of responsibility to Him.

Life may be likened to a journey that starts from a certain point and ends at a certain destination. It is a transitory stage, an introduction to the Eternal Life in the Hereafter. In this journey, man is a traveller and should be concerned only with what is of use to him in the Future Life. In other words, he should do all the good he can and make himself fully prepared to move any minute to Eternity. He should consider his life on this earth as a chance provided for him to make the best of it while he can, because when his time to leave comes he can not delay it even for one second. If his term expires, it will be too late to do anything about it or to extend it. The best use of life, therefore, is to live it according to the teachings of God and to make it a safe passage to the Future Life of Eternity. Because life is so important as a means to an ultimate end, Islam has laid down a complete system of regulations and principles to show man how to live it, what to take and what to leave, what to do and what to shun, and so on. All men come from God, and there is no doubt that they shall return to Him. In one of His comprehensive statements. Prophet Muhammad wisely advised man to consider himself a stranger in this life or a traveller passing through the world.

Religion (Deen)

Throughout history religion has been abused and misunderstood. Some people use it as a means of exploitation and suppression, as a pretext for prejudice and persecution. Some other people use it as a source of power and domination over the elite and the masses alike. In the name of religion unjustifiable wars have been launched, freedom of thought and conscience has been oppressed, science has been persecuted, the right of the individual to maturity has been denied, and man's dignity and honour have been flagrantly debased. And in the name of religion injustice has been inflicted upon humanity, with the result that religion itself has suffered many losses.

These are historical facts which no one can deny. But is this the proper function of religion or the right approach to religion? Could this be the purpose of religion? The indisputable answer is an emphatic no. There are many religions in the world, and each one claims to be the one and only true religion. Each religion is supposed to have come from God for the right guidance of man. But these claims contradict each other and have caused dissensions among people and vehement reactions to religion, instead of welding mankind into one universal brotherhood under the One Universal Benevolent God. This situation makes any neutral observer confused and perhaps averse to all kinds of religion. The Islamic concept of religion is unique in the broadest sense of the word. It is true that genuine religion must come from God for the right guidance of man. And it is equally true that human nature and major human needs are basically the same at all times. This conception leads to one conclusion, and that is: There is only one true religion coming from the One and the Same God, to deal with the outstanding human problems of all times. This religion is ISLAM. But it should be borne in mind that Islam was not taught by Prophet Muhammad alone. On the contrary, Islam had been taught by all the Prophets before Muhammad, and the true followers of Abraham and Moses as well as those of Jesus and the rest were all called MUSLIMS.

So Islam has been, and will continue to be, the true universal religion of God, because God is One and Changeless, and because human nature and major human needs are fundamentally the same, irrespective of time and place, of race and age, and of any other considerations.

Bearing this in mind, the Islamic concept maintains that religion is not only a spiritual and intellectual necessity but also a social and universal need. It is not to bewilder man but to guide him. It is not to debase him but to elevate his moral nature. It is not to deprive him of anything useful, or to burden him, or to oppress his qualities but to open for him inexhaustible treasures of sound thinking and right action. It is not to confine him to narrow limits but to launch him into wide horizons of truth and goodness. In short, true religion is to acquaint man with God as well as with himself and the rest of the universe. This is by no means an over-simplification of the function of religion. Here is what it means. When the purpose of true religion is carefully examined, it will be found that religion satisfies the spiritual and moderate material needs of man. It unties his psychological knots and complexes, sublimates his instincts and aspirations, and disciplines his desires and the whole course of life. It improves his knowledge of God—the Highest Truth in the universe—and of his own self. It teaches him about the secrets of life and the nature of man and how to treat them, about good and evil, about right and wrong. It purifies the soul from evil, clears the mind of doubt, strengthens the character and corrects the thinking and convictions of man. All this can be achieved only when man faithfully observes the spiritual duties and physical regulations introduced by religion.

On the other hand, true religion educates man and trains him in hope and patience, in truthfulness and honesty, in love for the right and good, in courage and endurance, all of which are required for the mastery of the great art of living. Moreover, true religion insures man against fear and spiritual loss and assures him of God's aid and unbreakable alliance. It provides man with peace and security and makes his life meaningful:

> *That is what true religion can do for humanity, and that is the concept of religion in Islam. Any religion which fails to bear these fruits is not Islam or, rather, is not religion at all, and any man who fails to draw these benefits from religion is not religious or God-minded. God is absolutely truthful when He says in the Holy Quran: "Verily the religion with God is Islam. Nor did the People of the Book dissent therefrom except through*

> *envy of each other, after knowledge had come to them. But if any deny the Signs of God, God is swift in calling to account" (Quran 3:19) and "If anyone desires a religion other than Islam, never will it be accepted of him; and in the Hereafter he will be in the ranks of those who have lost (all spiritual good)" (Quran 3:85).*

Sin (Gunah)

One of the major troublesome areas of human existence is the problem of sin or evil in the world. It is commonly believed that sin started with Adam and Eve during their life in the Garden of Eden. That event led to the Fall and has ever since branded the human race with guilt, stigma, and bewilderment.

Islam has taken a unique position oft the whole issue, a position which is not shared by any other religion we know. The Quran states that Adam and Eve were directed by God to reside in the Garden of Eden and to enjoy its produce as they pleased, assured of bountiful supplies and comfort. But they were warned not to approach a particular tree so that they would not run [into harm and injustice. Then Satan tricked them into temptation and caused them to lose their joyful state. They were expelled from the Garden and brought down to earth to live, die, and be taken out again at last for the Final Judgement. Having realized what they had done, they felt shame, guilt, and remorse. They prayed for God's mercy and were forgiven (Quran 2:35-38; 7:19-25; 20:117-123).

This symbolic event is significantly revealing. It tells us that the human being is imperfect and ever-wanting, even if he were to live in paradise. But committing a sin or making a mistake, as Adam and Eve did, does not necessarily deaden the human heart, prevent spiritual reform or stop moral growth. On the contrary, the human being has enough sensibility to recognize his sins and shortcomings. More importantly, he is capable of knowing where to turn and to whom he should turn for guidance. Much more important is the fact that God is ever-prepared to respond to the sincere calls of those who seek His aid. He is so Gracious and Compassionate that His Forgiveness is Encompassing and His Mercy all-Inclusive (Quran 7:156). One last revealing reading of the event is that discrimination on the basis of sex and hereditary guilt or sin are alien to the spirit of Islam.

The idea of Original Sin or hereditary criminality has no room in the teachings of Islam. Man, according to the Quran (30:30) and to the Prophet, is born in a natural state of purity or *fitrah,* that is, Islam or submission to the will and law of God. Whatever becomes of man after birth is the result of external influence and intruding factors. To put the matter in terms of modern thought, human nature is malleable; it is the socialization process, particularly the home environment, that is crucial. This process plays a decisive role in the formation of the human personality and the development of moral character. This does not deny to the individual the freedom of choice or exempt him from responsibility. Rather, it is a relief from that heavy burden of hereditary criminality or instinctual sin.

God, by definition, is Just, Wise, Merciful, Compassionate, and Perfect. He has created man by breathing into him of His own Spirit (Quran 15:29; 32:9; 66:12). Since God is the absolute infinite good and His Spirit the absolute perfect one, and since man, through creation, received of the Spirit of God, then man was bound to retain at least some portion of this good Spirit of the Creator. This may account for the good dispositions of man and his spiritual longings. But, on the other hand, God created man to worship Him, not to be His equal or rival, or the perfect incarnation or absolute embodiment of His goodness. This means that no matter how good and perfect man may be, by the grace of creation, he is still far short of the goodness and perfection of the Creator. Man is not without such qualities, to be sure. But they are limited and proportionate to man's finite nature, capacity, and responsibility. This may explain the imperfection and fallibility of man.

However, imperfection and fallibility are not the equivalent of sin or synonymous with criminality—at least not in Islam. If man is imperfect, he is not left helpless or deserted by God to fall victim to his shortcomings. He is empowered by revelation, supported by reason, fortified by the freedom of choice, and guided by various social and psychological dispositions to seek and achieve relative perfection. The constant gravitation between the forces of good and evil is the struggle of life. It gives man something to look forward to, ideals to seek, work to do, and roles to play. It makes his life interesting and meaningful, not monotonous and stagnant. On the other hand, it pleases God to see His servants in a state of spiritual and moral victory.

According to the moral scale of Islam, it is not a sin that man is imperfect or fallible. This is part of his nature as a finite limited creature. But it is a sin if he has the ways and means of relative perfection and chooses not to seek it. A sin is any act, thought, or will that (1) is deliberate, (2) defies the unequivocal law of God, (3) violates the right of God or the right of man, (4) is harmful to the soul or body, (5) is committed repeatedly, and (6) is normally avoidable.

These are the components of sin, which is not innate or hereditary. It is true, however, that man has the potential capacity of sin latent in him; but this is not greater than his capacity of piety and goodness. If he *chooses* to actualize the potential of sin instead of the potential of goodness, he will be adding a new external element to his pure nature. For this added external element, man alone is responsible.

In Islam, there are major and minor sins as there are sins against God and sins against both God and man. All sins against God, except one, are forgivable if the sinner sincerely seeks forgiveness. The Quran has stated that truly God does not forgive the sin of *shirk* (polytheism, pantheism, the Trinity, and other similar doctrines). But He forgives sins other than this and pardons whom He wills. Yet if the polytheist or atheist comes back to God, his sin will be forgiven. Sins against men are forgivable only if the offended pardons the offender or if the proper compensations and/or punishments are applied. In conclusion, sin is acquired and not inborn, emergent and not built-in, avoidable and not inevitable. It is a deliberate conscious violation of the unequivocal law of God. If man does something that is truly caused by natural instinct or absolutely irresistible drives and uncontrollable urges, then such an act is not a sin in Islam. Otherwise, God's purpose would be pointless and man's responsibility would be in vain. God demands of man what lies within the human possibility and reach.

Freedom (Azadi)

Freedom, both as a concept and as a value, has been denied many individuals, groups, and nations. It has been often misunderstood and abused. The fact is that in no human society can man be free in the absolute sense of the word. There must be some limitations of one sort or another if the society is to function at all.

Apart from this general idea, Islam teaches freedom, cherishes it, and guarantees it for the Muslims as well as for the non-Muslims. The Islamic concept of freedom applies to all voluntary activities of man in all walks of life. As already stated, every man is born free as regards his *fitrah* or in a pure state of nature. This means that man is born free from subjugation, sin, inherited inferiority, and ancestral hindrance. His right of freedom is sacred as long as he does not deliberately violate the Law of God or desecrate the rights of others.

One of the main objectives of Islam is to emancipate the mind from superstitions and uncertainties, the soul from sin and corruption, the conscience from oppression and fear, and even the body from disorder and degeneration.

The course which Islam has enjoined on man to realize this goal includes profound intellectual endeavour, constant spiritual observance, binding moral principles, and even dietary regulations. When man follows this course religiously, he cannot fail to reach his ultimate goal of freedom and emancipation.

> *The question of freedom with regard to belief, worship, and conscience is also of paramount importance in Islam. Every man is entitled to exercise his freedom of belief, conscience, and worship. In the words of the Quran, God says: "Let there be no compulsion in religion. Truth stands out clear from Error. Whoever rejects Evil and believes in God has grasped the strongest bond that never breaks; And God knows and hears all things" (Quran 2:256).*
>
> *Islam takes this attitude because religion depends upon faith, will, and commitment. These would be meaningless if induced by force. Furthermore, Islam presents the Truth of God in the form of an opportunity and leaves the choice for man to decide his own course. The Quran says: "The Truth is from your Lord. Let him who will, believe, and let him who will, disbelieve" (Quran 18:29).*

The Islamic concept of freedom is an article of faith, a solemn command from the Supreme Creator. It is built on the following fundamental principles. First, man's conscience is subject only to God, to Whom every man is directly responsible. Second, every human being is personally responsible for his deeds and he alone is entitled to reap the fruits of his work. Third, God has delegated to man the responsibility to decide for himself. Fourth, man is sufficiently provided with spiritual guidance and endowed with rational qualities that enable him to make responsible, sound choices. Such is the foundation of the Islamic concept of freedom and such is the value of freedom in Islam. It is a natural right of man, a spiritual privilege, a moral prerogative, and, above all, a religious duty. Within the framework of this Islamic concept of freedom, there is no room for religious persecution, class conflict, or racial prejudice. The individual's right of freedom is as sacred as his right of Life; freedom is the equivalent of Life itself.

Equality (Masawat)

One basic element in the value system of Islam is the principle of equality or, better yet, equity. This value of equality is not to be mistaken for or confused with identicalness or stereotype. Islam teaches that, in the sight of God, all men are equal, but they are not necessarily identical. There are differences with regard to ability, potential, ambition, wealth, and so on. Yet none of these differences can by itself establish a status of the superiority of one man or race to another. The stock of man, the colour of his skin, the amount of wealth he has, and the degree of prestige he enjoys have no bearing on the character and personality of the individual as far as God is concerned. The only distinction which God recognizes is that of piety, and the only criterion which God applies is that of goodness and spiritual excellence. In the Quran, God says:

> *O mankind, verily We have created you from a single (pair) of a male and a female, and have made you into nations and tribes, that you may know each other. Verily the most honoured of you in the sight of God is the most righteous* *(49:13).*

The differences of race, colour, or social status are only accidental. They do not affect the true stature of man in the sight of God. Again, the value of equality is not simply a matter of constitutional rights or a gentleman's agreement or condescending charity. It is an article of faith which the Muslim takes seriously and to which he must adhere sincerely. The foundations of this Islamic value of equality are deeply rooted in the structure of Islam. It stems from such basic principles as: (1) All men are created by One and the Same Eternal God, the Supreme Lord of all; (2) All mankind belongs to the human race and shares equally in the common parentage of Adam and Eve; (3) God is just and kind to all his creatures. He is not partial to any race, age, or religion. The whole universe is His dominion and all people are His creatures; (4) All people are born equal in the sense that none brings any possession with him, and they die equal in the sense that they take back nothing of their worldly belongings; (5) God judges every person on the basis of his own merits and according to his own deeds; and (6) God has conferred on man, man as such, a title of honour and dignity.

Such are some of the principles behind the value of equality in Islam. When this concept is fully utilized, it will leave no place for prejudice or persecution. And when this Divine ordinance is fully implemented, there will be no room for oppression or suppression. Concepts of chosen and gentile peoples, words such as privileged and condemned races, expressions such as social castes and second-class citizens will all become meaningless and obsolete.

Brotherhood (Ukhuwwat)

Another fundamental element in the value system of Islam is the value of human brotherhood. This value is founded on the same principles which have been discussed in connection with freedom and equality. In addition to those foregoing principles, human brotherhood in Islam is based on an unshakable belief in the Oneness and Universality of God (the worshipped), the unity of mankind (the worshippers), and the unity of religion (the medium of worship). For the Muslim, God is One, Eternal and Universal. He is the Creator of all men, the Provider for all men, the Judge of all men, and the Lord over all men. To Him, social status, national supermanship and racial origin are insignificant. Before Him, all men are equal and are brothers of one another.

The Muslim believes in the unity of mankind with regard to source of creation, original parentage, and final destiny. The source of creation is God Himself. The original common parents were Adam and Eve. To this first parentage, every human being belongs and of it he partakes. As for the final destiny, there is no doubt in the Muslim's mind that it will be to God, the Creator, to Whom all men shall return. The Muslim believes in the unity of God's religion. This means that God does not confine His religion or favours to any particular nation, race, or age and that there can be no contradiction or fundamental differences in the Religion of God. When this is interpreted properly, it leaves no ground for pretended supremacy or presumptuous exclusivity. When it is imparted to the human mind, it provides man with a clear concept and a solid basis of human brotherhood. Because the Muslim believes in the Oneness of God, the unity of mankind, and the unity of religion, he believes in all the Messengers and Revelations of God without discrimination.

Peace (Amn)

To appreciate how Islam approaches the question of peace, one has only to consider a few basic facts about Islam. Peace and Islam are derived from the same root and may be considered synonymous. One of God's names is Peace. The concluding words of the daily prayers of every Muslim are words of peace. The greeting of the Muslims when they return to God is peace. The daily salutations among the Muslims are expressions of peace. The adjective "Muslim" means, in a sense, peaceful. In Islam, Heaven is the abode of peace.

This is how fundamental and dominant the theme of peace is in Islam. The individual who approaches God through Islam cannot fail to be at peace with God, with himself, and with his fellow men. Taking all of these values together, putting man in his proper place in the cosmos, and viewing life in the Islamic perspective, men of good faith and principles cannot fail to make our world a better place, to regain human dignity, to achieve equality, to enjoy universal brotherhood, and to build a lasting peace.

Community (Millat)

The word "community" has acquired certain connotations, some of which are romantic and nostalgic, some derogatory and reactionist. But since we intend to deal with the basics, we shall confine our discussion to the most fundamental meanings of this word.

In one basic sense, it means "all forms of relationship that are characterized by a high degree of personal intimacy, emotional depth, moral commitment, social cohesion, and continuity in time ... It may be found in ... locality, religion, nation, race, occupation, or (common cause). Its archetype ... is the family."

In another basic sense, a community is a comprehensive group with two chief characteristics: (1) it is a group within which the individual can have most of the activities and experiences that are important to him and (2) The group is bound together by a shared sense of belonging and a feeling of identity. The historical master trend has been a movement from the community's intimate, deep, moral relationships to mass society's impersonal, formal, utilitarian relationships. The movement has been designated by different phases and marked by far-reaching consequences. From this historical trend, one can infer certain conclusions. First, this historical evolution has not been totally negative or completely positive and constructive. Both negative and positive consequences have affected different people in different degrees. Secondly, modern society is far from perfect, and there is a great task yet to be performed. Thirdly, the human condition is not a lost cause or a hopeless case. True, there are crises and travail, but the situation is not entirely out of control. Finally, mankind has grown more interdependent and human societies more intertwined. Whatever happens in one segment of society is bound to affect the rest. We should keep this in mind when we discuss the Islamic concept of community.

It is generally correct to state that the Islamic concept of community has certain unique characteristics that relate to the foundation or basis of the community, its historic mission and purpose, its status among other communities, its identity, and its continuity.

The community in Islam is not founded on race, nationality, locality, occupation, kinship, or special interests. It does not take its name after the name of a leader or a founder or an event. It transcends national borders and political boundaries. The foundation of the community in Islam is the principle which designates submission to the will of Allah, obedience to His law and commitment to His cause. In short, an Islamic community is present only when it is nourished and fostered by Islam.

The Islamic community has a historic mission far beyond mere survival, sheer power, breeding, or physiological continuity. Such a mission is described in the Holy Quran as follows:

> *Let there be a community (of ummah) among you, advocating what is good, demanding what is right, and eradicating what is wrong. These are indeed the successful* *(3:104)*

and:

> *You are the best community brought forth for mankind; you enjoin what is right, forbid what is wrong, and believe in Allah* *(3:110).*

The historic role of the Islamic Community is to be the true embodiment of all that is virtuous, wholesome, and noble. A truly Islamic community is the alert guardian of virtue and the bitter enemy of vice. What is required of the community at large is likewise required of every individual member. This is because the whole community is an organic entity and every individual is accountable to Allah. The role of the individual Muslim is best described by the statement of the Prophet:

> *Whoever of you sees something wrong must seek to rectify it by action or deed; if he cannot, let him try to change it by word; if he cannot, let his feelings of disapproval and condemnation intensify and this is the minimal degree of faith.*

As we can see, this description is very significant and comprehensive. In this age of revolutionary media, no one in his right mind can underestimate the power of concerted action, communicable words, or of feelings. The historic role of the Islamic community is further restated in Quran 2:143:

> *We have made you a middle nation, [a well-integrated community,] a balanced* ummah, so *that you may be witnesses over other people and the Messenger a witness over you.*

Such a role of witnessing is both highly significant and extremely demanding. It means that the community of Islam must be exemplary. It must set the highest standards of performance and be the reference point for others. It must avoid excesses and extravagances, static rigidity and instant evaporation. To strike a middle course of action, to be steadfast and consistent, to know what to accept and what to reject, to have principles and at the same time to remain adaptable is probably the hardest test of the human character and social viability. But this is the role of the Islamic community and the historic mission of the Muslims. And it is this very criterion that qualifies the Muslims as the best human community ever to evolve. The identity of the Islamic community centers upon the principles of consistent balance, exemplary conduct, unity of purpose, reciprocity of feelings, solidarity, and equity. There are many statements in the Quran and Sunnah to this effect (see, for example, 4:135, 21:92, 23:52).

With regard to the continuity of the Islamic community, certain points are noteworthy. It is the duty of Muslims to do everything within their means to insure that continuity. The rules of marriage and inheritance, the duties of *Zakat* and *Hajj,* the mutual rights and obligations of kin, the individual conscientiousness and social belonging —all of these are oriented to the healthy continuity of the community of Islam:

> *On the other hand, Allah has pledged to protect this continuity in several ways. First, He has pledged to preserve the Quran and protect its purity (15 :9). This means that there shall always be a community to follow the Quran —the Quran shall not be without followers even though there may be followers of other books. Second, Islam itself is a continuity. Whenever a nation deviated from the path of Allah, He restated His word, reaffirmed His truth, and commissioned new Prophets or reformers to continue. Third, Allah has issued a strong warning to the effect that if Muslims turned away from the right path, they would be the losers and that He would replace them by other people*
>
> *(Quran 47:38).*
>
> *Again, the believers are warned that if any of them turns back from their Faith, soon will God produce people whom He will love and they will love Him,—humble toward the believers and mighty against the disbelievers, fighting in the way of God and never afraid of reproaches*
>
> *(Quran 5:57).*

Morality (Khulq)

The concept of morality in Islam centers around certain basic beliefs and principles. Among these are the following: (1) God is the Creator and Source of all goodness, truth, and beauty; (2) Man is a responsible, dignified, and honourable agent of his Creator; (3) God has put everything in the heavens and the earth at the service of mankind; (4) Because of His Mercy and Wisdom, God does not expect the impossible from man or hold him accountable for anything beyond his power. Nor does God forbid man to enjoy the good things of life; (5) Moderation, practicality, and balance are the guarantees of high integrity and sound morality; (6) All things are permissible, in principle, except what is singled out as obligatory (which must be observed) and what is singled out as forbidden (which must be avoided); and (7) Man's ultimate responsibility is to God and his highest goal is the pleasure of his Creator.

The dimensions of morality in Islam are numerous, far-reaching, and comprehensive. Islamic morals deal with the relationship between man and God, man and his fellow men, man and the other elements and creatures of the universe, as well as with man and his innermost self. The Muslim has to guard his external behaviour and his manifest deeds, his words and his thoughts, his feelings and intentions. In a general sense, his role is to champion what is right and fight what is wrong, seek what is true and abandon what is false, cherish what is beautiful and wholesome and avoid what is indecent. Truth and virtue are his goal. Humbleness and simplicity, courtesy and compassion, are his second nature. To him, arrogance and vanity, harshness and indifference, are distasteful, offensive, and displeasing to God.

More specifically, the Muslim's relationship with God is one of love and obedience, complete trust and thoughtfulness, peace and appreciation, steadfastness and active service. This high-level morality will, undoubtedly, nourish and reinforce morality at the human level. In his relationship with his fellow men, the Muslim must show kindness to his kin and concern for his neighbour, respect for the elderly and compassion for the young, care for the sick and support for the needy, sympathy for the grieved and cheer for the depressed, joy with the blessed and patience with the misguided, tolerance toward the ignorant and forgiveness of the helpless, disapproval of the wrong and the ability to rise above the trivial. Moreover, he must respect the legitimate rights of others as much as he does his own. His mind must be occupied with constructive ideas and serious pursuits, his heart must beat with compassionate feelings and good will, his soul must radiate with peace and serenity, and his counsel must be sincere and courteous.

The Muslim's moral obligation is to be a vivid example of honesty and perfection, to fulfil his commitments and perform his tasks well, to seek knowledge and virtue by all possible means, to correct his mistakes and repent his sins, to develop a good sense of social consciousness and nourish a feeling of human response, to provide for his dependents generously without extravagance and to meet their legitimate needs. Nature and the world are the fields of exploration and the objects of enjoyment for the Muslim. He must utilize their elements and ponder their marvels, read them as signs of God's greatness and preserve their beauty, explore their wonders and discover their secrets. But whether he uses them for utility or for sheer enjoyment, he must avoid waste and excess. As a responsible agent of God and a conscientious trustee, he must always be mindful of others who share the world with him and who will succeed him in the future.

The moral principles of Islam are sometimes stated as positive commitments which must be fulfilled and sometimes as negative prescriptions which must be avoided. Whether they are stated positively or negatively, they are designed to build in the human being a sound mind, a peaceful soul, a strong personality, and a healthy body. There is no doubt that these are necessary requirements of the general welfare and prosperity of mankind. And to help man satisfy these requirements, Islam has, among other things, laid down the following regulations:

1. To bear witness to the Oneness of God and the Messengership of Muhammad in a meaningful committal way;
2. To observe the daily prayers regularly;
3. To pay the religious tax, known as alms or the poor-due (zakat);
4. To keep the fast of the Holy Month of Ramadan;
5. To make a pilgrimage to the Holy City of Mecca at least once.

In addition to these positive measures, there are others which may be characterized as preventive and precautionary ones. To protect man from insanity and degeneration, from weakness and indulgence, from indecency and temptation, Islam has prohibited certain things pertaining to food, drinking, recreation, and sex. Among these are the following:

1. All kinds of intoxicating wines, liquors, and spirits *(Quran 2:219: 4:43; 5:93-94);*
2. The meat and products of swine (pork, bacon, ham, lard), of wild animals that use claws or teeth to kill their victims (tigers, wolves, leopards, etc.), of all birds of prey (hawks, vultures, crows, etc.), of ro dents, reptiles, worms and the like, of dead animals and birds that have not been slaughtered properly *(Quran 2:172-173; 5:4-6);*
3. All forms of gambling and vain sports *(Quran 2:219; 5:93-94);*
4. All sexual relations out of wedlock and all manners of talking, walking, looking and dressing in public that may instigate

temptation, arouse desire, stir suspicion, or indicate immodesty and indecency . *(Quran 23:5-7; 24:30-33; 70:29-31).*

This Act of Prohibition is introduced by God for the spiritual and mental well-being of man as well as for the moral and material benefit of humanity. It is not an arbitrary action or a self-imposed intrusion from God. On the contrary, it is a sign of God's interest in the welfare of humanity and an indication of His good care of man. When God prohibits certain things, it is not because He wants to deprive man of anything good or useful, but because He means to protect man and allow him to develop a good sense of discrimination, a refined taste for the better things in life, and a continued interest in higher moral values.

To achieve this, good care must be taken of man's spirit and mind, soul and body, conscience and sentiments, health and wealth, physique and morale. Prohibition, therefore, is not deprivation but enrichment, not suppression but discipline, not limitation but expansion.

> *To show that all prohibitions are acts of mercy and wisdom, two Islamic principles are worth mentioning in this connection. First extraordinary circumstances, emergencies, necessities and exigencies allow the Muslim to do what is normally forbidden. As long as these circumstances exist and to the extent that he cannot help the situation, he is not to blame if he fails to observe the moral rules of God (see Quran, 2:173; 5:4). Second, God has inscribed for Himself the rule of mercy: "Any who do evil out of ignorance, but thereafter repent and amend their conduct, will be forgiven; surely, God is Merciful and Oft-forgiving" (Quran 6:54).*

In a remarkable and typical passage, the Quran has laid down the grounds and philosophy of sound moral conduct. The passage may be rendered as follows:

> *O Children of Adam! Wear your beautiful apparel at every time and place of prayer; eat and drink, but waste not by excess, for God loves not the wasters. Say: "Who has forbidden the beautiful gifts of God, which He has produced for His servants, and the things, clean and pure, (which He has provided) for sustenance?" Say: "They are, in the life of this world, for those who believe, (and) purely for them on the Day of Judgement." Thus do We explain the Signs in detail for those who understand. Say: "The things that my Lord has indeed forbidden are: shameful deeds, whether open or secret,*

> *sins and trespasses against truth or reason; assigning of partners to God—and saying things about God of which you have no knowledge"* *(Quran 7:31-33).*

The range of morality in Islam is so inclusive and integrative that it combines at once faith in God, religious rites, spiritual observances, social conduct, decision making, intellectual pursuits, habits of consumption, manners of speech, and all other aspects of human life. Because morality is such an integral part of Islam, the moral tone underlies all Quranic passages and the moral teachings are repeatedly stressed in various contexts throughout the Holy Book.

This makes it hard to devise any reasonably brief classification of these moral teachings according to their citations in the Quran. Every principle is mentioned many times and in various contexts. It appears either as a single significant principle or as an element of a total system of morality, which itself is an element of a complete religious super-system.

In view of this, the following passages must be taken only as representative selections from the Quran, rendered and interpreted by human endeavour which, inevitably, fall short of the perfection of the original and complete version of the Book:

> *Serve God, and join not any partners with Him; and do good; —to parents, kinsfolk, orphans, the needy ones, neighbours who are near, neighbours who are strangers, the companion by your side, the wayfarer (you meet), and what your right hands possess (captives, slaves, animals, birds, etc.): For God loves not the arrogant, the vainglorious;— (Nor) those who are niggardly or enjoin niggardliness on others, or hide the bounties which God has bestowed on them; for We have prepared for those who resist Faith a punishment that steeps them in contempt; (Nor) those who spend of their substance (out of hypocrisy) just to be seen of men, but have no faith in God and the Last Day. If any take the Evil One for their intimate, what a dreadful intimate he is!*
>
> *(4:36-38).*

Say (O Muhammad): "Come, I will rehearse what God has (really) prohibited you from": join not anything as equal with Him; be good to your parents; kill not your children on a plea of want;—for We provide sustenance for you and for them;— come not nigh to the orphan's property, except to improve it, until he attains the age of full strength; give measure and weight with full justice;—no burden do We place on any soul, but that which it can bear; and whenever you speak, speak justly, even if a near relative is concerned; and fulfil the Covenant of God. Thus does He Command you, that you may remember. Verily, this is My Way, leading straight; follow it; follow not (other) paths: They will scatter you about from His Right Path. Thus does He command you, that you may be righteous" (6:151-153). God commands justice, the doing of good, and kindness to kith and kin; and He forbids all shameful deeds, and injustice and rebellion: He instructs you, that you may receive admonition. Fulfil the Covenant of God when you have entered into it, and break not your oaths after you have confirmed them; indeed you have made God your surety; for God knows all that you do—whoever works righteousness, man or woman, and has Faith, verily, to him will We give a new Life, a life that is good and pure, and We will bestow on such (workers) their reward according to the best of their actions (16:90-91, 97).

Invite (all) to the Way of your Lord with wisdom and beautiful preaching; and argue with them in ways that are best and most gracious; for your Lord knows best, who have strayed from His Path, and who are truly guided (16:125).

Who is better in speech than one who calls (others) to God, works righteousness, and says: "I am one of those who bow in Islam." Nor can Goodness and Evil be equal. Repel (Evil) with what is best. Then the one between whom and you there was hatred will become, as it were, your friend and intimate! (41:33-34).

Whatever is given to you (here) is (only) a convenience of this Life. But that which is with God is better and more lasting. (It is.) For those who believe and put their trust in their Lord; those who avoid the greater crimes and shameful deeds, and, when they are angry even then forgive; those who hearten to their Lord, and establish regular prayer; who (conduct) their affairs by mutual consultation; who spend out of what We bestow on them for sustenance; and those who, when an oppressive wrong is inflicted on them, (are not cowed but) help and defend themselves. The recompense for an injury is an injury equal to it (in degree), but if a person forgives and makes reconciliation, his reward is due from God, for God loves not those who do wrong. But indeed if any do help and defend themselves after a wrong (done) to them, against such (persons) there is no cause of blame. The blame is only against those who oppress men with wrong doing and insolently transgress beyond bounds through the land, defying right and justice. For such (oppressors and transgressors) there will be a penalty grievous. But indeed if any show patience and forgive, that would truly be an exercise of courageous will and resolution in the conduct of affairs (42:36-43). If any do wish for the transitory things (of this Life), We readily grant them such things as We will, to such persons as We will, but in the end have We provided Hell for them where they will burn, disgraced and rejected. And those who do wish for the (things of) the Hereafter, and strive therefore with all due striving, and have Faith,—they are the ones whose striving is appreciable (by God). Of the bounties of your Lord We bestow freely on all these as well as those: the bounties of your Lord are not closed (to anyone) .... Take not with God another object of worship: or you (man!) will sit in disgrace and destitution. Your Lord has decreed that you worship none but Him, and that you be kind to parents. Whether one or both of them attain old age in your life, say not to them a word of contempt, nor repel them, but address them in terms of honour. And out of kindness, lower to them the wing of humility, and say: "My Lord! Bestow on them Your mercy even as they cherished me in childhood." Your Lord knows best what is in your hearts.

If you do deeds of righteousness, verily He is Most Forgiving to those who turn to Him again and again (in true penitence). And render to the kindred their due rights, as (also) to those in want, and to the wayfarer. But squander not (your wealth) in the manner of a spendthrift. Verily spendthrifts are brothers of the Evil Ones; and the Evil One is to his Lord ungrateful. And even if you have to turn away from them (the said people), in pursuit of the Mercy from your Lord which you do expect, yet speak to them words of easy kindness. Make not your hand tied (like a niggard's) to your neck, nor stretch it forth to its utmost reach (like an irresponsible squanderer, if you choose either way), you will become blameworthy and destitute (respectively). Verily your Lord does provide sustenance in abundance for whom He pleases, and He provides in a just measure; for He does know and regard all His servants. Kill not your children for fear of want.

We shall provide sustenance for them as well as for you. Verily the killing of them is a great sin. Nor come nigh to adultery; for it is a shameful deed and an evil, opening the road (to other evils). Nor take life—which God has made sacred—except for just cause. And if anyone is slain wrongfully, We have given his heir authority (to demand equal punishment or to forgive). But let him not exceed bounds in the matter of taking life; for he is helped (by the Law). Come not nigh to the orphan's property except to improve it, until he attains the age of full strength; and fulfil (every) engagement: for (every) engagement will be enquired into (on the Day of Reckoning). Give full measure when you measure, and weigh with a balance that is straight. That is the most fitting and the most advantageous in the final determination. And pursue not that of which you have no knowledge (idle and useless curiosity); for every act of hearing, or of seeing or of (feeling in) the heart will be enquired into (on the Day of Reckoning. Nor walk on the earth with arrogance; for you cannot rend the earth asunder, nor reach the mountains in height. Of all such things the evil is hateful in the sight of your Lord. These are among the (precepts of) wisdom, which your Lord has revealed to you. Take not, with God, another object of worship, lest you should be thrown into Hell, blameworthy and rejected (17:1839).

We bestowed wisdom on Luqman: "Show your gratitude to God." Any who is grateful does so to the profit of his own soul. But if any are ungrateful, verily God is free of all needs, worthy of all praise .... And We have enjoined on man (to be good) to his parents. In travail upon travail did his mother bear him, and in two years was his weaning. (Hear the command), show gratitude to Me and to your parents. To Me is your final Goal. But if they strive to make you join in worship with Me things of which you have no knowledge (or do any wrong), obey them not; yet bear them company in this life with justice (and consideration), and follow the way of those who turn to Me (in love). In the end the return of you all is to Me, and I will tell you the truth (and meaning) of all that you did .... "O my Son!" (said Luqman): "Establish regular prayer, enjoin what is just (and right) and forbid what is wrong; and bear with patient constancy whatever be falls you; for this is firmness (of purpose) in (the conduct of) affairs. And swell not your cheek (for pride) at men, nor walk in insolence through the earth; for God loves not any arrogant boaster. And be moderate in your pace, and lower your voice; for the harshest of sounds without doubt is the braying of the ass" (31:12-19). O you who believe ! Intoxicants and gambling ... are an abomination, of Satan's handiwork. Avoid such (abomination), so that you may prosper. Satan's plan is only to excite enmity and hatred between you, with intoxicants and gambling, and hinder you from the remembrance of God and from prayer. Will you not then abstain? (5:93-94).

But seek, with that which God has bestowed on you, the Home of the Hereafter. Nor forget your portion in this world. But do you good, as God has been good to you, and seek not mischief in the land; for God loves not the mischief makers (28:77).

These selections can be supported by many others from the Quran and the Traditions of Muhammad. In themselves they are sufficient to portray the fundamental morals of Islam, which are unique in their nature under all circumstances. They are introduced by God not simply to be admired occasionally, but to be enforced and effective. They are meant to help the individual to develop his personality and cultivate his character in the most wholesome manner, to strengthen his bonds and consolidate his association with God, the Source of all Goodness. Never were the Islamic morals designed to intimidate the individual and make him passive or indifferent.

One example will illustrate the point. If a Muslim is wronged or oppressed, he has the free choice either to resist and retaliate in an equal measure or to forgive and entrust God with the results of his deed. He knows that he is authorized to take either action, and he equally knows that it is better for him to forgive. So when he forgives, he does so of his own free choice out of his love for God. Similarly, when he retaliates he is not violating the Law or acting unjustly; he is defending his rights, an attitude which is a sacred duty in itself, and is helping the rightful authorities to establish order and justice. If Islam were to demand absolute forgiveness, as some other creeds do in theory, many undisciplined people would be tempted to do wrong and exceed all limits. Likewise, if Islam were to demand only retaliation, as some other creeds ruthlessly teach, there would be no room for either mercy and patience or for spiritual reform and moral maturity, in which case many fine qualities of man would subside and many moral potentials may never be actualized.

It is common knowledge that those people who are taught to forgive under all circumstances do not, and probably cannot, practice their teachings, because it is not in the interest of humanity in the long run, nor is it in the interest of morality itself. Likewise, the people who are taught to practice stern retaliation have little or no respect for human virtues and careless for moral values as universal rules. But Islam, the Divine fosterer of human nature, has given the right answers to human problems. To those wrong doers who are looking for a second chance, who may improve or benefit by granting them pardon, forgiveness is recommended and preferable. But against those who might misunderstand the motives of forgiveness or be tempted to pursue the wrong course, equal retaliation is authorized. Thus, the attitude of the Muslim in either case is sound and beneficial. When he forgives, he pleases God, retains the upper hand and contributes to the reformation of the delinquent. And when he retaliates, he defends the right, establishes order and justice, and helps to arrest evil. Now, which one reflects sound morality? The attitude of one who is a ruthless avenger indiscriminately or the attitude of a Muslim who makes room for mercy and forgiveness, and who allows for extraordinary circumstances? And who is morally sound? One who forgives because he knows that he is not allowed to retaliate or a Muslim who forgives while he is fully aware that he can lawfully retaliate? Which one reflects real forgiveness? The one resulting from external compulsion and prohibition not to act otherwise or the one resulting from freedom of choice and freedom of action? It is no wonder that the moral principles of Islam are sound, unique, and adaptive. They are the instructions of God, the Source of all goodness and morality.

Perception of Universe

In the foreword, we briefly discussed the position of the Muslims and the future of Islam in the Western hemisphere. In this part, we shall discuss the position of man in the contemporary world, the general human situation, and the Islamic concept of the universe or world view. This will reaffirm the concepts that have already been discussed, add some new ideas, and tie together the various dimensions of the subject in a summary recapitulatory fashion.

The present human situation is alarming, to say the least. It demands concern and active response on the part of all people of good will and God-mindedness. But this does not, and should not, lead to despair or resignation. The spirit of hope is, and has always been, an integral part of Islam (see, for example, Quran 12:87; 65:3). The problems and crises of modern times are not entirely unique or peculiar. It is true that they are difficult, complex, and agonizing. Perhaps this is even more so now than ever before. But the difference, however, between this age and those of previous centuries is basically a difference of degree rather than of kind. The ever-increasing complexity of our contemporary predicaments may be largely due to a similar, proportionate rise in our expectations and capacities.

For many centuries and in numerous regions of the globe, the chief source of the most difficult crises has essentially been a kind of inflexible, exclusive, and intolerant attitude toward the unfamiliar, the different, and the foreign. This orientation fostered racism, elitism, bigotry, prejudice, and a whole host of other equally distasteful attitudes. Few people can really deny that humanity is facing an unusual crisis. This present human crisis seems to emanate from a serious imbalance between our external, outward, material explorations and our internal, inward, moral gropings. Nothing is simpler than calling for the maintenance of an equilibrium, advocating a "middle range," or crusading for the "golden means." Yet nothing has been harder to attain. In the past, utterances such as "man cannot live by bread alone" were sometimes so distorted as to connote disregard for man's material welfare. Similarly, trust in God has been misunderstood, for it has often taken to mean helpless fatalism or categorical denial of human free will and self-realization. An overemphasis on spirituality and resignation is bound to give rise to a counter emphasis on materialism, rationalism, "free will," and so on. Stressed beyond certain limits, spirituality may become superstition and confusion. Likewise, a counter stress may turn materialism into laxity, free will into libertinism, and rationalism into sheer vanity. The intellectual history of the last few centuries demonstrates these tendencies only too well.

Over the span of recent decades, the spiritual scale tipped up and down. In the sixties, and now in the seventies, the news-making events are those of the unsurpassed, unprecedented, outer space explorations. Equally sensational are the unprecedented explorations in the inward, internal realms of being, however faddish, cultic, or neurotic they may seem to be.

The rise of these two unprecedented and unbalanced types of exploration is exceptionally alarming. The reason probably lies in the fact that they do not seem to relate to each other, let alone converge. There is no apparent reciprocity, mutual reinforcement, or cross-fertilization. Besides, their precarious, unbalanced existence is a constant threat to the majority of people. It may very well drive them into ambivalence and confusion which may, in turn, intensify the problems of society and harden the lot of modern man. But such a precarious course can be changed if the outward scientific explorations and the inward moral gropings are somehow reconciled. Man does not live by bread alone. That is true enough. But neither does he live by prayers only. He is both a political or materialistic animal and a religious explorer of the holy.

As already mentioned, the contemporary world is clearly baffled by numerous problems. But it is equally baffled by the conflicting diagnoses and prescriptions to cope with these problems. Some people sing along with the popular lyric, "What the world needs now is love ... etc." Some call for a human rebirth. Others turn to Marxism, Humanism, Satanism, or Scientism as the ultimate solution. Still more are awaiting the arrival of some future Savior. Yet this long list does not even include the indifferent, the hopeless, and the apathetic who may in fact outnumber the optimist clubs combined. But it seems that the greatest need today is the pressing need for "understanding." What man needs most of all is to understand himself and his nature, his potentials and limitations, his place in the universe and his relationships with its elements.

The question now is how can Islam help man to understand himself, unclog his mind, and clear his blurred vision? In our attempt to answer this question, it will be necessary to keep in mind the basic concepts of Islam which have been discussed and to elaborate further upon some elements of its value system. This analysis will hopefully show how they may relate to modern man in his contemporary predicament and how they may help him to find his way through.

The principle of "moderation" is most characteristic of Islam. It is probably best expressed in the way Islam views human nature, the meaning of life, and the idea of God. Islam does not subscribe to the one-sided "humanistic" philosophy, which almost deifies man and recognizes nothing beyond. Neither does Islam endorse the equally one-sided verdict that human nature is inherently vicious, wicked, or sinful. Islam rejects the idea that life is nasty, brutal, short, and miserable. It also rejects the idea that life is an end in itself, pleasurable, and carefree. Islam does give life a positive meaning, a purpose. It would devalue life on earth *only* relative to the Hereafter. It is not concerned exclusively with the here and now, instant hedonism, and immediate pleasures. Nor does it completely bypass the here and now in pursuit of a future paradise in a hereafter. It addresses itself to both the human condition here on earth and the human destiny in the Hereafter. Such concern is, of course, proportionate; it values each phase of existence according to its relative effect on the general well-being of man (Quran 7:33; 17:18-21; 28:77; 57:20-21). In the Quran, there is a passage (2:27-39) which is typical of so many others. This passage contains some of the fundamental principles of Islam, and represents the foundations of the world view of Islam. Outstanding among these principles are the following:

1. The world is a becoming entity, created by the will of a Designer and sustained by Him for meaningful purposes. Historical currents take place in accordance with His will and follow established laws. They are not directed by blind chance, nor are they random and disorderly incidents.
2. Man also is created by God and is commissioned to be God's viceroy on earth. He is so chosen to cultivate the land and enrich life with knowledge, virtue, purpose, and meaning. And to achieve this goal, everything in the earth and the heavens is created *for* him and is made subservient to him. Life on this

planet is not a prison for man; his coming into the world was not an arbitrary punishment for previously committed sins. Nor was he expelled from another world and cast into this one. His existence was no mere chance or undesigned occurrence.

3. Knowledge is the unique faculty of man and is an integral part of his personality and his being. It is knowledge that qualifies man to be the viceroy of his Creator and entitles him to command the respect and allegiance even of the angels of God.
4. The first phase of life on earth began not in sin or rebellion against the Creator. The "Fall" from the Garden of Eden and what followed thereafter—the remorse of Adam and Eve, their repentance, God's forgiveness of and compassion for them, the enmity between man and Satan—all of this was no surprise to the Creator. Nor was it an accident. It was too meaningful to be accidental. Rather, it seems to have been designed to discipline the first man, to give him actual experience of falling and rising, moral defeat and triumph, straying from and reconciliation with the Creator. In this way, man would become better prepared for life and more enlightened to face its uncertainties and trying moments.
5. Eve was not the weaker party of the first human couple. She neither tempted Adam to eat of the forbidden tree nor was she alone responsible for the expulsion from the Garden of Eden. Both Adam and Eve were equally tempted and equally responsible; both were remorseful, repented, and were blessed with the forgiveness and compassion of God. This is significant, as it liberates Eve from the curse that has followed her and her sex throughout the ages, and acquits her of the charge that she alone bears all or most of the responsibility for the Fall. Furthermore, it declares in no uncertain terms that the belief in the moral inferiority of women is unfounded and that the resulting double standard is totally unjustifiable. Here, as elsewhere, the Quran makes it very clear that both man and woman are equally capable of virtue and weakness, equally sensitive, and equally meritorious.
6. Man is a free agent endowed with a free will. This is the essence of his humanity and the basis of his responsibility to his Creator. Without man's relative free will, life would be meaningless and God's covenant with man would be in vain. Without human free will, God would be defeating His own purpose and man would be completely in capable of bearing any responsibility. This, of course, is unthinkable.

7. Life emanates from God. It is neither eternal nor an end in itself, but a transitional phase, after which all shall return to the Creator.
8. Man is a responsible agent. But responsibility for sin is borne by the actual offender alone. Sin is not hereditary, transferable, or communal in nature. Every individual is responsible for his own deeds. And while man is susceptible to corruption, he is also capable of redemption and reform. This does not mean that Islam prefers the individual to the group. Individualism means little or nothing when severed from social context. What it means is that the individual has different sets of roles to play. He must play them in such a way as to guard his moral integrity, preserve his identity, observe the rights of God, and fulfil his social obligations.
9. Man is a dignified and honourable being. His dignity derives from the fact that he is infused with the spirit of his Creator. What is more important is that such dignity is not confined to any special race, colour, or class of people. It is the natural right of man, every man, the most honourable being on earth.
10. The passage, finally, points to the deep seated roots of the Oneness of God and the unity of mankind. It shows, further, that man's highest virtues are piety and knowledge and that when such knowledge is acquired and invested according to the divine guidance, man's blissful destiny will be assured and his life will be serene.

Chapter 6

Social Behaviour in Islam

Almighty and His Messengers

Meaning and Importance : The basis of the Islamic teaching and way of life are various obligatory acts of worship, Ibadat which are often referred to as the Five Pillars of Islam. These consist of:

a. Declaration that there is no god but Allah.

b. The prescribed prayers, five times a day.

c. Fasting, once a year in the month of Ramadan.

d. Zakat, helping the needy by giving alms.

e. Hajj, pilgrimage to Mecca, if and when circumstances permit.

Just as the pillars bear the burden of a building, these principles, according to the teachings of the Prophet (PBUH) are the basis of piety and of a virtuous worldly life; as the Prophet (PBUH) has taught that the only difference between individuals is the extent of their piety and not their colour or the social status that they enjoy in this world.

The purpose of the Islamic worship is to strengthen the Muslim faith and sense of submission to Allah, to discipline a Muslim for his role as Allah's faithful servant and vicegerent on earth, and to reinforce the ties of brotherhood and affection among Muslims. These acts of worship require the participation of all aspects of man's nature — his soul, his mind, his feelings, his body, his time, his energy and his possessions. Thus, they demand the worship of Allah with all the faculties of an individual. For example, the declaration of faith is to be always present in the mind and heart of the Muslim and is to be uttered again and again with the tongue during his daily prayers. Prayers are to be performed five times daily, everyday of a man's life.

Fasting is for a full month every year, while Zakat or "poor-due" is to be paid once yearly; and the pilgrimage is to be performed once in a lifetime, if possible. These aspects of Islamic worship and the total involvement of human beings make them extremely unique. They are a complete expression of man's dependence and submission to His will, his humility before His Creator and his desire to serve and obey Him alone.

In these religious institutions, there is punctuality, regularity, orderliness, uniformity and an exhibition of complete equality.

Tauhid-Unity of Allah

The first part of the declaration that there is no god but Allah attests not only to the Oneness and Uniqueness of Allah, but it also signifies the Oneness of Lordship, the Sovereignty and the Authority in the universe and in this world. As there is no other Creator and Sustainer of the universe, there can likewise be no other Ruler, Law-giver and Supreme Authority for mankind.

Allah is the Lord of all creation; He creates what He pleases, giving each of His creatures the nature, role and function which He desires for it; in this He is accountable to no one and all things are under His absolute control.

The primary emphasis of the Quran is upon the doctrine of Tauhid. There are numerous verses in the Quran which highlight the concept of *Tauhid* which is the cardinal principle of Islam. In the very opening chapter of the Holy Quran, Surah Fatiha, it is said:

> *"Thee do we worship and thine aid we seek." (1:5)*

Similarly, verse 36, it is said:

> *"Serve Allah, and join not any partners with Him." (4:36)*

The most concise expression of this principle is to be found in Surah Ikhlas. This Quranic Surah as translated by Abdullah Yusuf Ali says:

> *"Say: He is Allah,*
> *The One and Only;*
> *Allah the Eternal, Absolute,*
> *He Begetteth not,*
> *Nor is He begotten;*
> *And there is none*
> *Like unto Him. (112:1-4)*

True unity of Allah means that Allah is:

(a) *Unique in Person:* This signifies that Allah is only One and there is no plurality of gods. The Quran says:

Allan has said:

"Take not (for worship) two gods: for He is just one God."
(16:51)

(b) *Unique in Attributes:* This signifies that no other being can be equal to Allahin attributes. For example, man may attain a degree of perfection in the attribute of kindness, but only Allah possesses the perfection of the attribute of kindness.

(c) *Unique in Action:* No one can do the works which Allah has done or may do. All the messengers of Allah have conveyed the message of His unity:

"O my people, " said they, "Worship Allah. You have no other god but Him." *(7: 59, 73, 85)*

The role of the Prophet of Islam was to bring about the acceptance of this principle of religion by entire mankind. The Quran says:

"Not a messenger did We send before thee without this inspiration sent by US to him: that there is no god but I; therefore, worship and serve Me." *(21: 25)*

The doctrine of *Tauhid* confers dignity on man who is otherwise a slave to every manifestation of power. Only Allah becomes his refuge, security and stability. Associating partners with Allah is called Shirk. *Shirk* is not only the worship of idols, but also offering prayers and supplications to anyone, dead or living, believing that they hold the same attributes in a lesser degree than Him.

Thus, the belief that Allah is not Sovereign or Independent and Sole Dispenser of affairs of the world and that other deities can intercede with Him and that any attempt to implore any other being besides Allah for the grant of any wishes of the believer or to answer his prayers is *Shirk*. The Quran considers *Shirk* to be an unpardonable sin. It says:

"Allah forgives not that partners should be set up with Him; but He forgives anything else to whom He pleases; to set up partners with Allah is to devise a sin most heinous indeed. " *(4: 48)*

Man has been created as lord of creation and everything in nature has been placed under his control. By worshipping other beings besides Allah man debases himself, the Quran says:

"Shall I seek for you a god other than the (true) God, when it is Allah Who hath endowed you with gifts above the nations." *(7:140)*

In Surah Luqman, ascribing partners to Allah is regarded as a tremendous wrong.

The Holy Prophet (PBUH) is reported to have said:

"Shirk is the greatest of all sins".

Meaning and Importance of Prophethood

The next basic requirement of Islam is belief and faith in all the prophets of Allah. This means that a Muslim believes that the prophets are devoted servants of Allah, selected and appointed by Him, to convey His Commands to mankind without any addition or deduction. Prophethood is a gift of Allah and only He can bestow this gift on whom He wishes.

Allah deputed prophets in different periods of time to communicate His guidance to human beings. They were raised from the nations to whom they were sent as messengers. They preached in the language of their nations, the Quran says:

"We sent not a messenger except (to teach) in the language of his (own) people, in order to make (things) clear to them." *(14:4)*

And again:

"And there never was a people without a warner having lived among them (in the past)." *(35:24)*

According to the Quran, all prophets sent by Allah were men, had human bodies and were mortal. At the same time, the Quran tells us that the prophets were Allah's chosen and selected. Allah chose them and guided them and gave them the Book and the prophethood. They all received revelation from Allah and were sent for the guidance of their people.

They all did good deeds and were truthful. The Holy Quran insists that the prophets were raised to be obeyed and followed. They called their followers to profess and follow the Divine code of rules to regulate their life. There are numerous verses in the Quran in which emphasis is laid on obedience to the prophets and following their example.

It says:

"We sent not a messenger, but to be obeyed, in accordance with the will of Allah." *(4:64)*

"He who obeys the messenger obeys Allah. " *(4:80)*

"Say, (O Muhammad!), if you do love Allah, follow me; Allah will love you and forgive you your sins. " (3:31)

Many prophets came to this world. The last in the line of prophets is the Holy Prophet Muhammad (PBUH) who is termed as "the seal of the prophets."

The Quran says that the appearance of the Holy Prophet (PBUH) was foretold by previous prophets.

His distinguishing feature was that he confirmed the truth of all the prophets that preceded him. He not only conveyed the message revealed to him, but also explained and acted upon it himself and after demonstration, urged the people to follow it for their own benefit.

The Prophethood of Hadrat Muhammad (PBUH) is distinguished in many ways:

1. It is universal which means that the Holy Prophet (PBUH) was not sent for any particular country or community but for the whole world and the entire mankind. Allah says in the Holy Quran:

   " We have not sent thee but as a universal (Messenger) to men, giving them glad tidings and warning them (against sin)." (34:28)

And the Holy Prophet (PBUH) also confirmed this:

"Every prophet who preceded me was sent especially to his own people but I have been sent as a Prophet for all mankind. "

2. The Prophethood of the Holy Prophet (PBUH) is eternal. With him, the chain of revelation and Prophethood has come to an end. There will not be any other prophets.

   "But he is the messenger of Allah and the Seal of the Prophets. " (33:40)

The Holy Prophet (PBUH) said:

"With me the edifice of prophethood has been completed and with me the chain of prophethood has come to an end. "

"No doubt, no prophet will come after me. "

At another place, he said:

" When a prophet died, another prophet took his place; but there will be no prophet after me."

3. The religion and the Divine law which the Holy Prophet (PBUH) brought is perfect in all respects. This distinction was not enjoyed by any other religion. The Quran says:

   "This day have I perfected your religion for you, completed my favour upon you, and have chosen for you Islam as your religion. " *(5:3)*

Through the Holy Prophet (PBUH) a perfect law was given to suit the requirements of all ages and for all countries and this law that is, the Holy Quran was guarded against all corruptions. The life of the Holy Prophet (PBUH) is an explanation of the Holy Quran as confirmed by his wife Hadrat Aishah:

"His morals are the Quran. "

It means that while the Holy Quran was the command, the Prophet's (PBUH) life was an example of the teachings of the Quran.

The Quran compares his personality to the sun, while the previous prophets were like lamps. Just as the light of the sun cannot be substituted by any other light and is universal, similarly, after the advent of the Holy Prophet (PBUH), no necessity is felt of any other prophet to follow him.

Five Time Worshipping

Meaning and Importance : The importance of prayer in Islam is great as it is the foremost duty of the Muslims and the chief of the pillars on which the structure of Islam stands. It is the distinguishing feature between a Muslim and a non-Muslim. The Holy Prophet (PBUH) said:

"What stands between a man and disbelief is the abandonment of salat. "

And again:

"Know that among your duties, prayer is the best. "

A unique service that the Prophet (PBUH) rendered to humanity was that he made prayer to Allah not only the foundation stone of the individual development of a man but also the basis of a vast brotherhood of humanity.

The first revelations were in the following order:

To read and write; to warn the people and declare the Greatness of Allah; and to pray to Allah not only during the daytime but also during night.

The Quran says:

> *"Establish regular prayers - at the Sun's decline till the darkness of the night —And pray in the small watches of the morning —"* *(17: 78-79)*

The object of prayer is to remember Allah. It is, therefore, the chief reason why prayer was dearest to the Prophet (PBUH), he said:

> *"Prayer has been made a coolness for my eyes."*

He declared prayers to be the pillar of Islam and said:

> *"He who gives up prayer has indeed disbelieved."*

The Quran mentions prayer many times and has laid the greatest emphasis on it; therefore, the sin of giving up prayer is great as also praying carelessly or with an absent mind.

> *"So woe to the worshippers who are neglectful of their prayers. "* *(107: 4-5)*

Observance of prayer five times a day is compulsory. Basically, it consists of recitations from the Holy Quran and glorification of Allah accompanied by various bodily postures, such as standing, bowing, prostrating and sitting. Through these postures, Muslims express submission, adoration and humility to Allah.

The self-discipline which is needed to perform salat regularly and at proper times, to perform the ablution which precedes prayer and to carry on these prayers in the early morning when sleep is so attractive, during the busy daylight hours when one is preoccupied with work and other activities, and at night when one is tired and wants to sleep reaffirms the human being's total dependence on his Creator and his position as His slave.

The Holy Prophet (PBUH) exhorted his followers to offer their prayers as if they were standing in front of Allah, looking at Him. In prayer, the Divine presence is to be felt as a reality:

> *"You should worship Allah, as if you see Him; if you do not see Him, He surely sees you."*

Prayer is further meant to seek help as well as guidance from Allah. This seeking of help and guidance is linked up in the daily prayer of the Muslims:

> *"Thee do we worship and thine aid we seek. Show us the straight way."* *(1: 5-6)*

In the Holy Quran, prayer is referred to as a sustenance for the human soul so that the man who does not pray to Allah must be regarded as spiritually dead.

Prayer protects one from sins and shameful deeds. Prayer purifies him and brings him closer to Allah. The Quran says:

> *"Establish prayer, for prayer restrains from shameful and unjust deeds. "*

This continuous reminder keeps the conscience alive, functioning in a proper manner. Without the regular performance of prayer, it is likely to become inactive and easily corrupted. It will be obvious that prayer once a week or even once or twice a day, does not fulfil this purpose and is only a partial and insufficient expression of the human being's relationship with his Sustainer, who in the words of the Quran is *"nearer to him than his jugular vein."*

The three conditions of the believers as given in the Holy Book are:

> *"Those who believe in the unseen, are steadfast in prayer and spend out of what we have provided for them."*
> *(2:3)*

It will be seen that belief in Allah, the Great Unseen, is immediately followed by the keeping up of prayer, thus showing that by means of prayer, belief is turned into a certainty of the Divine existence. This is again followed by spending out of what Allah has given to man, for the benefit of others, in charity. Thus, faith in Allah is translated into practice by prayer, which in turn, leads to the service of humanity. According to the Holy Prophet (PBUH), self development of a man depends upon prayer:

> *"The believers must (eventually) win through— those who humble themselves in their prayers." (23: 1-2)*

The Holy Prophet (PBUH) further explained what the Holy Quran taught. On one occasion, he thus addressed his companions:

> *"Tell me, if there is a stream at the door of one of you in which he washes himself five times a day, what do you say, will it leave any dirt on him?"*

And on receiving the reply that it would not, he added,

> *"This is the likeness of the five prayers with which Allah washes away all faults. "*
>
> *" When one of you ", said the Prophet (PBUH), "says his prayers, he holds confidential intercourse with his Lord."*

A Muslim is required to pray at the prescribed times wherever he may be. But it is preferable and meritorious to pray in congregation with his fellow Muslims if possible. This gathering of all Muslims living in the same locality five times daily, is a step towards the establishment of healthy social relations.

In the daily service, these relations are limited to a narrow circle i.e., to members of the same neighbourhood. The circle becomes wider in the weekly Friday service which gathers together all Muslim members of a particular locality, and still more extensive in the two annual gatherings of Muslim festivals of Eid-ul-Fitr. Thus, prayer promotes social relations between different sections of the Muslim community.

Salat is the central point of the life of a Muslim, without which he would not be able to maintain a strong and vital link with his Lord or continue his inner struggle against wrong doing or temptation. Because of all these aspects, Salat is the principal means whereby the Muslim keeps in mind the limited and temporary nature of this world's life and the certainty of death and life to come. Thus, he is able to maintain a sense of balance and proportion between the needs and claims of this world and the Hereafter.

Cleanliness : A true Muslim must be pure and clean in mind, body and heart. Islam enjoins strict cleanliness and purity on its followers. We are told in the Quran:

> *"He loves those who keep themselves pure and clean." (2:222)*

And again:

> *"Allah loveth those who make themselves pure."*
>
> *(9:108)*

The Holy Prophet (PBUH) is reported to have said:

> *"Purification is the key to prayer," and also, 'Religion is built on cleanliness', and again, "Purification is one half of faith. "*

In the light of the Quranic verses and traditions, it becomes clear that a person should be clean inwardly as well as outwardly at all times, especially at the time of saying prayers. Inward purification is to rid the mind of all corrupt ideas and evil thoughts. Outward purification is attained by taking a bath or performing ablution. If a man cleans himself five times a day, he would undoubtedly be in a constant state of physical purity.

There are certain conditions regarding cleanliness of body, clothes, place of worship, etc. that have to be fulfilled before a person can say his prayers. The Holy Prophet (PBUH) said:

> *"Surely Allah does not accept prayers without purification."*

Filth : Apart from waste products discharged from the body which are regarded as filth, other impurities recognized by Islam are semen, flowing blood, pus, swine and everything associated with it and wine. All these are included in the definition of Najasat Ghaleezah. If even the smallest quantity of Najasat Ghaleezah falls in any article of food or drink, the whole of it is polluted and becomes unclean and unfit for use by a Muslim. If some Najasat Ghaleezah falls on the clothes, they must be removed and washed thrice, squeezing the cloth each time.

Wudu or Ablution : Ablution or Wudu in the prescribed manner is necessary for a person who intends to say his prayers as the Quran says:

> *"O you who believe! When you prepare for prayer, wash your faces and your hands to the elbows, rub your heads (with water) and (wash) your feet to the ankles." (5:6)*

Ablution consists of some practices that are obligatory or Farz i.e., those specifically mentioned in the Quranic verses; others that are traditional i.e., the Holy Prophet's (PBUH) practice or sunnat, and others that are termed desirable or mustahab entitling a person to spiritual recompense or Sawab. The approved method of performing Wudu is as under:

> *Making the intention or Niyyat, of Wudu, i.e. to say: 'I intend to perform the Wudu for securing Allah's good pleasure and in compliance with His command.' Then recite the following:*
>
> *In the name of Allah, the Beneficent, the Merciful.*
>
> *Allah! Forgive my sins."*

If possible, one should sit facing the Qibla. The water to be used for Wudu should be absolutely clean.

First the right and then the left hand should be washed upto the wrists thrice. The wet fingers should be passed in between each other. If there are any bangles on the wrists or rings on the fingers, as in the case of females, they should be moved around so that the skin under them does not remain dry.

After this rinse the mouth thrice. Next, some water should be taken in the right hand and sniffed into the nostrils thrice and then blown out. The left hand should be used for cleaning the nose. Then the whole face should be washed with both hands, thrice from the forehead down to the lower portion of the chin and from the lobe of one ear to that of the other.

No portion of the face should remain dry. For males, the wet fingers of the right hand should be passed through the hair of the beard. Thereafter, first the right arm and then the left arm upto the elbows should be washed thrice. After washing the arms wipe the head with wet hands from front to back, and pass the back of wet hands over the nape of the neck. Clear the inner side of ears with forefingers and outer with thumbs. Finally wash the feet, right and then left upto the ankles.

The Wudu should be a continuous process, each part being washed and cleaned in the prescribed order, without any break or interval. No part should be allowed to dry up before the other is washed. After the Wudu, the Kalima-e-Shahadat should be recited:

> *"I bear witness that there is no god except Allah, who is One, Who has no partners, and I bear witness that there is no god except Allah, who is One, Who has no partners, and I bear witness that Muhammad is His servant and apostle.*

And then the following prayer may be recited:

> *"O Allah! Make me one of those who repent for their sins; and make me one of those who keep themselves pure; and make me one of Your righteous servants."*

Wudu may be performed before every prayer. But the necessity for it arises only when a person has passed urine, stool or wind or if he has been fast asleep.

The items that are specifically mentioned in the Holy Quran i.e., Faraiz-e-Wudu are four in number. These are:

1. To wash the face from the top of the forehead to the chin and as far as each ear.
2. To wash the hands and the arms upto the elbow.
3. To wipe the head with wet hands.
4. To wash the feet upto the ankles.

The items established on the example of the Holy Prophet (PBUH) i.e., Sunan-e-Wudu are fourteen in number. They are:

1. To make the intention of Wudu.
2. To wash the hands upto the wrist.
3. To say one of the names of God at the commencement of the Wudu.

4. To brush the teeth.
5. To rinse the mouth three times.
6. To put water into the nostrils thrice.
7. To do all the above items in proper order.
8. To do all the above items without any delay between the various acts.
9. Each part is to be washed thrice.
10. The space between the fingers of one hand must be rubbed with the wet finger of the other.
11. The beard must be combed with the fingers.
12. The head must be wiped once.
13. The ears must be washed with the water remaining on the fingers after wiping the head.
14. To rub between the toes with the little finger of the left hand starting from the little toe of the right foot.

There are five Mustahab or desirable acts in Wudu. They are:

1. To begin from the right to the left.
2. To rub the neck.
3. To perform Wudu without the help of another person.
4. To face the Qiblah while performing Wudu.
5. To sit on a high and clean place while performing Wudu.

There are four Makruhat or undesirable acts in Wudu. They are:

1. To perform Wudu in an impure place.
2. To clean the nose with the right hand.
3. To talk about worldly affairs, while performing Wudu.
4. To perform against the rules and regulations laid down by the Holy Prophet (PBUH). A person's Wudu becomes ineffectual on becoming subject to the state of Hads-e-Asghar i.e., the state of impurity or uncleanliness which is brought about by answering the call of nature, by passing wind or by vomiting or Hads-e-Akbar i.e., the state of impurity or uncleanliness which is caused by sexual intercourse, menstruation or the period of childbirth. In addition to these, the following acts and circumstances also render the Wudu void:

1. Discharge of intestinal worms or stone.
2. Flowing of any impurity from any part of the body.

3. Taking a nap, or going to sleep by resting the body against any object.
4. Laughing loudly during prayers.
5. Losing consciousness or fainting due to some illness.
6. Becoming insane or mad.

Dry Ablution

Regarding Tayammum (Dry Ablution) the Holy Quran says:

> *"If ye are ill or on a journey And ye find no water, then take for your selves clean sand or earth and rub therewith your faces and hands. Allah doth not wish to place you in a difficulty, but to make you clean...."* *(5: 6)*

It will be seen from the above mentioned verse of the Holy Quran that permission for resorting to Tayammum is granted on the grounds of illness, travelling and the non-availability of water. It can be performed instead of Wudu or Ghusl (bath). If one is suffering from a disease in which the use of water would be injurious and there are chances that the use of water would aggravate the illness; or if one cannot find water for *Wudu* or *Ghusl;* or if one is travelling in a place where there is no one to indicate where water could be found; or if there is a danger that the enemy might attack while one is performing ablution or taking a bath, then one can perform *Tayammum* instead of *Wudu* or *Ghusl.*

The approved, traditional method of Tayammum is as under: First to recite and then to make the following Niyyat: "I intend to make tayammum with the object of removing impurity and acquiring purity."

After this, both hands should be struck on some clean and pure earth or sand, the excessive dust blown off and both the hands rubbed on the face is such a way that no part of the face which has to be washed with water in *Wudu* is left out.

In the case of males, it is desirable to pass the fingers through the beard. Again, both hands should be struck on the clean earth or sand, the excess dust blown off and first the right arm and then the left arm be rubbed upto the elbows. This completes the *Tayammum. A* dry stone free of dust, brick or an earthen pot may also be used for the purpose.

As in the case of *Wudu,* several prayers can be said with one *Tayammum.* The acts and circumstances which nullify *Wudu* also nullify *Tayammum.* If *Tayammum* is done because of the non-availability of water, then it would become ineffectual as soon as water is available. Similarly, if *Tayammum* was done on account of illness, then as soon as the disability to use water ceases, *Tayammum* will become void.

The Bath : The Holy Quran says:

> *"O you who believe! Do not approach prayers in a state of ceremonial impurity (except when travelling on the road) until after washing your whole body. "* *(4: 43)*

The Arabic word for bath is *Ghusl* derived from *Ghasl* which means to wash. In religious terminology, it is the act of washing the whole body after Hads-e-Akbar or greater impurity which is caused by sexual intercourse, menstruation or the period of childbirth. Other occasions of taking a bath founded on the practice of the Holy Prophet (PBUH) are upon the admission of a convert to Islam; before Friday prayers and on festivals and after washing the dead.

The approved, traditional method of *Ghusl* is as follows:

1. Make the Niyyat i.e., to say: "I intend to take a bath for seeking purification;"
2. Both hands including the wrists should be washed;
3. Any impurity that there may be on any part of the body should be removed.
4. *Wudu* should be performed in the prescribed manner taking special care about gargling and ensuring that water reaches the throat; but if one is fasting, care must be taken to see that water does not enter the throat while cleaning the nose.
5. Water should be poured thrice on the entire body from the head to the feet, first on the right-hand side and then on the left, taking care to rub the body well.

No portion of the body should remain dry and water should reach even the roots of the hair. In case of females, care should be taken about bangles and rings. There are three faraiz in a bath. They are:

1. Gargling.
2. Putting the water into the nostrils.
3. Pouring of water over the entire body, at last once in such a way that not even a hair's breadth of the body remains dry.

The acts in a bath established on the example of the Holy Prophet (PBUH) are:

1. To wash both hands upto the wrists.
2. To wash those parts of the body where impurity is found.

3. To make the intention of removing the impurity.
4. To perform *Wudu*.
5. To wash the whole body thrice with water.

The *Wudu* performed while taking a bath is sufficient for saying prayers.

Call to Prayers : Every prayer with the exception of the two Eid prayers and funeral prayers is preceded by a call or Adaan. When it is time for a particular prayer, the *Adaan* is called out. *The Muazzin* i.e., the person who calls out *the Adaan* should be a Muslim, male, adult. It is preferred that he should perform the *Wudu* before calling the *Adaan* and stand on a raised platform with his face towards the Qibla. Inserting the tips of his forefingers in his ears, he should give the *Adaan* in a loud and clear voice pronouncing the words correctly and distinctly. The words of the *Adaan* are as under:

1. "Allah is Great." (4 times)
2. "I do bear witness that there is no god except Allah." (Twice)
3. "I do bear witness that Muhammad is the Apostle of Allah" (Twice)
4. "Come to prayer." (Twice; turning the face to the right)
5. "Come to success. " (Twice; turning face to the left)
6. "Allah is Great." (Twice)
7. "There is no god except Allah." (Once)

In the Adaan for the Fajr prayers, after saying item no 5, the following words are included:

8. "Prayer is better than sleep." (Twice)

Except when : A person is saying his prayers; The Imam is delivering the Khutba; A person is answering the call of nature; it is compulsory on all those who hear the *Adaan,* to repeat in a low voice, the words of the *Muazzin.* When he hears and the listener should say:

> *"The strength to shun evil and to do good deeds is only from Allah." When he hears he should say:*
>
> *"You have spoken the truth and said a good thing. "*

When the Adaan is over, the listener should pray in the following words:-

> *"O Allah! Lord of this perfect call and the prayer to be offered presently, grant Muhammad the way of approach unto Thee and also eminence and raise him unto the glorious station Thou hast promised him and bestow his*

intercession on us on the Day of Judgement. Verily Thou never go back on Thy word."

The words of the *Adaan* in the order in which they are pronounced have come down to us unchanged from A.H. I., when the *Adaan* was said for the first time in the presence of the Holy Prophet (PBUH).

Iqamat - Announcement for Congregational Service

When the congregational prayers are about to start, people stand up and form rows and the Muazzin recites the *Iqamat*. The words of the *Iqamat* are the same as those *of Adaan,* but the person reciting the *Iqamat* does not insert the tips of his fingers in his ears nor does he turn his face to the right or the left while reciting:

After which he says:

"Prayer has indeed begun." (Twice) after which the people present in the mosque say:

"May Allah make the prayer well-established and permanent."

Names and Times of Prayers

The names of the five obligatory prayers are:

1. *Fajr:* This is an early morning prayer.

   The time of this prayer commences after the break of dawn and ends just before sunrise. It is makruh or undesirable to say prayers when the sun is rising. No nafil prayer is to be said till the sun has risen well.

2. *Zuhr:* (Early afternoon)

   The time of this prayer commences when the sun begins to decline and the shadows of things cease to decrease. It ends when the shadow of everything becomes equal to twice the shadow of a thing at noon or mid-day.

   No prayer is to be said or the Quran recited at the time of the decline of the sun.

3. *Asr:* (Late afternoon)

   The time of this prayer commences after the end of the time for Zuhr prayers and ends before sunset.

4. *Maghrib:* (Evening)

   The time of this prayer commences immediately after sunset and ends on the fading of twilight.

   No prayer is to be said or the Quran recited at the time of the setting of the sun.

5. *Isha:* (Early night)

The time of this prayer commences after the fading of twilight and ends before dawn but it is desirable to say this prayer before midnight. Number of Rakat in the Five Daily Prayers The five daily prayers consist of:

(a) Farz or obligatory

(b) Sunnat (traditional) i.e., the Holy Prophet's (PBUH) practice.

(c) Wajib

(d) Nafal

The Sunnat is again divided into Sunnat Muakkadah and Sunnat Ghair Muakkadah.

By Sunnat Muakkadah is meant an act which the Holy Prophet (PBUH) always did except for some valid reason.

The *Rakat* which are *Sunnat Muakkadah* must be offered.

By Sunnat Ghair Muakkadah is meant an act which the Holy Prophet (PBUH) did but which he sometimes did not do without any valid reason.

The offering of *Rakat* which are *Sunnat Ghair Muakkadah* entitles a person to spiritual reward.

1.	*Fajr:*	2	Pre-Farz Sunnat (Muakkadah)
		2	Farz
	Total =	4	Rakat
2.	*Zuhr:*	4	Pre-Farz Sunnat (Muakkadah)
		4	Farz
		2	Post-Farz Sunnat (Muakkadah)
		2	Nafil
	Total =	12	Rakat
3.	*Asr:*	4	Pre-Farz Sunnat (Ghair Muakkadah)
		4	Farz
	Total=	8	Rakat

4. *Maghrib:*	3	Farz
	2	Post-Farz Sunnat (Muakkadah)
	2	Nafil
Total =	7	Rakat
5. *Isha:*	4	Pre-Farz Sunnat (Ghair Muakkadah)
	4	Farz
	2	Post-Farz Sunnat (Muakkadah)
	2	Nafil
	3	Witr-Wajib
	2	Nafil
Total =	17	Rakat

Components of Salat (Arkan) : Each Rakat consists of:

a. Six items which are Farz:

(1) Takbir Tahrima, (2) Qiyam, (3) Qirat, (4) Ruku, (5) Sajda, (6) Qaada Akhira.

If any item (Ruku) is left out, the Salat shall have to be repeated.

b. Thirteen items which are Wajib.

If any item is left out then Sajda Sahw (Prostration due to forgetfulness) becomes necessary and this shall remove the defect.

c. Twenty items which are *Sunnat.*

If any item classified as *Sunnat* is left out due to mistake, no *Sajda Sahw* is necessary and the *Salat* does not become void.

d. *Mustahab.*

Conditions of Salat : Before a person can say his regular prayers, the following conditions must be fulfilled; otherwise the prayers would be void:

a. The body of the person must be clean.

b. The clothes worn must be clean and free from all impurities.

c. The place where the prayers are to be said must be clean and free from all impurities.

d. The 'Satar' (those parts of the body which should be kept covered) must be properly covered. For a male, the *Satar* consists of the portion of the body from the navel to the knees. For a female, her entire body with the exception of her face, hands and feet is *Satar*.

e. It must be the time for the particular prayer to be offered.

f. The *Qiblah* must be faced while saying the prayers.

g. Intention or *Niyyat* must be declared for saying the kind of prayer i.e., *Farz, Sunnat* etc., of the particular prayer time i.e., Fajr, Zuhr etc. that one is offering.

Method of Salat

The approved traditional method of *Salat* is as follows:-

1. Standing erect with the face towards the *Qibla* i.e., the Kaaba in Mecca, with both hands hanging down the sides of the body and with feet nearly four inches apart. The Niyyat should be made in the following words:

   "I intend to offer two/three/four Rakat of prayer Farz/ Sunnat/Nafal of Fajr/ Maghrib/Isha (as the case may be) for Allah the Most High and I am facing the Holy Kaaba."

2. Eyes should be kept at the spot where the forehead will touch the ground while doing the *Sajda*. This is a *Mustahab*.

3. Raising both hands, with the palms and the fingers open and facing the *Qibla,* as far as the ears in such a way that the thumbs of both hands are in line with the lobes of the ears. Females may raise their hands upto the shoulders, but the hands

4. With hands still raised, *Takbir Tahrima* i.e." God *is Great"* is to be said once. If a person is Munfarid, i.e., praying alone, the Takbir may be said in a fairly loud voice; but if he is a Muqtadi, i.e. saying the farz prayer in congregation under the leadership of an Imam, who shall say all the Takbirs in a loud voice, the *Takbir Tahrima* should be said in a low voice inaudible to the other members of the congregation.

5. While saying the *Takbir Tahrima,* both hands should be brought down and folded on the navel in such a way that the palm of the right hand sets on the back of the palm of the left hand with the thumb and the little finger of the right hand making a circle and holding the wrist of the left hand, and the remaining three fingers of the right hand resting on the left forearm.

Females are to fold their hands on their breasts. This is called Qiyam. The eyes should be kept at the spot where the forehead will touch the ground while doing the *Sajda,*

6. While standing in the position of *Qiyam* the *Sana* is to be recited which is as follows:-

   "Glory to Thee O Allah; and Thine is the Praise and Blessed is Thy name and Exalted is Thy Majesty; and there is no one worthy of worship except (Thee)."

7. Then the Tawwuz i.e..

   "I betake myself to Allah for refuge from the accursed Shaitan, is to be recited.

8. After the Tawwuz, the Tasmiyah i.e.,

   "In the name of Allah, the Beneficent, the Merciful" is to be recited.

   Serial Numbers: 6, 7 and 8 are Sunnat.

   If a person is Munfarid all three-Sana, Tawwuz and Tasmiyah are to be recited; but if he is a Muqtadi, only Sana should be recited. The Imam shall recite all the three in a low voice, not audible to the congregation.

9. After the Tasmiyah, Surah Fatiha is to be recited:-

   "Praise be to Allah, the Cherisher and Sustainer of the worlds. Most Gracious, Most Merciful. Master of the Day of Judgement. Thee do we worship and Thine aid we seek. Show us the straight way. The way of those on whom Thou hast bestowed Thy Grace, those whose (portion) is not wrath, and who go not astray."

   After the last word of Surah Fatiha, (amen) is to be said in a low voice. This is *Sunnat.*

   If a person is *Muqtadi,* he is not to recite *Surah Fatiha.* The Imam shall recite it in a loud voice and the congregation should hear the recitation of the Imam with attention and shall only say at the end.

10. Immediately after the *Surah Fatiha,* some other *Surah* is recited. The voice should neither be too loud nor too low. If a person is *Muqtadi,* he is not to recite any Surah but should hear the Imam's recitation. This is called Qirat.

11. After the *Qirat* is over, *"God is Great"* is said. While doing so, hands are unfolded and the Ruku performed. *Ruku* is to bow down, hold the knees with the open fingers of the two hands, keeping the back straight and in line with the head. The arms

should be kept away from the ribs and the legs should be kept straight. In this position, the Tasbih Ruku, viz.

"Glory to my Lord, the Great " is said three times. This is Sunnat. The Imam, Muqtadi and Munfarid shall all say the Tasbih Ruku in a low voice.

12. After saying the *Tasbih Ruku,* and standing erect, the *Tasmiyah* is recited viz:

    "Allah listens to him who gives praise." This is Sunnat.

13. After the Tasmiyah, the Tahmid viz:

    "O our Lord! All praise is due to Thee alone" is recited.

This is *Sunnat.*

If it is a congregational prayer, the Imam shall say the *Tasmiyah* in a loud voice and the members of the congregation - the *Muqtadis* shall say the *Tahmid,* in a low voice.

But if a person is *Munfarid,* he should say both the *Tasmiyah* and the *Tahmid* while rising from the Ruku and standing straight. This is *Sunnat.* Standing straight for a short while after Ruku is called Qaumah.

This is *Wajib.*

14. After the *Tahmid,* the Takbir i.e., *"God is Great "* is said once. The Imam shall say the *Takbir* in a loud voice, and the *Muqtadis* in a low voice.

15. While saying the *Takbir,* the prostration or *Sajda* is performed. For this, both knees, then both hands, then the nose and lastly the forehead are placed on the ground. The face should be between both palms and the two thumbs should be in line with the two ears.

    The fingers of the hands should be kept close to one another, but not closed; the finger tips should face the *Qibla.*

    The elbows should be kept away from the ribs and the stomach away from the legs. The elbows should not be put on the ground. Females are to perform the *Sajda* in such a way that they do not raise the rear portion of their body, but rest it on their calves. They are allowed to put their elbows on the ground.

16. While doing the *Sajda,* the Tasbih Sajda i.e., *"Glory to my Lord, the Most High"* is to be recited thrice, in a low voice. This is *Sunnat.*

17. After the *Tasbih Sajda,* first the forehead, then the nose and finally the hands are to be raised and the *Takbir viz: "God is Great "* is to be recited once.

This is *Sunnat.*

Next is to sit straight by folding the left foot and sitting on it and keeping the right foot erect, with the toes of the right foot facing the *Qibla.* The hands should be kept on the thighs close to the knees. Females should keep both feet on the right side and sit on their buttocks. This short sitting between two Sajdas is called Jalsa.

This is *Wajib,*

The eyes should be kept on the back of the hands. This is mustahab.

18. Then the *Takbir "God is Great"* is to be said once and the second *Sajda* performed in the same manner as the first *Sajda* reciting the Tasbih Sajda again at least thrice.
19. The *Takbir* is to be recited while rising from the second *Sajda.*
20. Next is to stand straight and repeat the whole procedure from S. No 5 till S. No. 19.
21. Then the next position is to sit erect as explained in S. No 17. If *the Niyyat was* for two *Rakat,* this will be called Qaada Akhira which is Farz, but if the *Niyyat* was for three or four *Rakat,* this sitting will be called Qaada Ula.

This is *Wajib.*

22. In the Qaada Ula, first the Tahiyya

    "All prayers and worship rendered through words, actions and wealth are due to Allah alone. Peace be on you, O Prophet, and the mercy of Allah and His blessings. Peace be on us and the righteous servants of Allah." And then the Tashhaud viz:

    "I bear witness that none deserves to be worshipped except Allah; and I bear witness that Muhammad is His servant and apostle."—are to be recited.

Both these items are *Wajib.*

While reciting the *Tashhaud, a circle* with the thumb and the middle finger of the right hand should be made and the third and the little finger of the same hand should be closed. While uttering the words, the forefinger of the right hand should be raised and while saying, it should be lowered. The position of the circle should be retained till the end of the Qaada Ula or Qaada Akhira, as the case may be. The tips of the fingers of both hands should face the *Qibla.*

23. If the *Niyyat* was for three or four *Rakat,* after reciting the *Tashhaud, Takbir* viz *"God is Great"* is to be said once and the person is to rise from the Qaada Ula for the Qiyam of the third *Rakat.*

The third and fourth *Rakat* are to be completed in the same manner as the second *Rakat*.

After the second *Sajda* of the fourth *Rakat*, is the *Qaada Akhira*, in which first the *Tahiyya*, then *Tashhaud* and finally the Darood viz:-

> *"O Allah! Exalt Muhammad and the true followers of Muhammad as Thou exalted Ibrahim and the true followers of Ibrahim, for surely Thou art praised and magnified. O Allah! Bless Muhammad and the true followers of Muhammad as Thou blessed Ibrahim and the true followers of Ibrahim, for surely Thou art praised and magnified "is to be recited. This is Sunnat.*

24. After the *Darood*, the following prayer is to be recited:-

    "O my Lord! Make me one who establishes regular prayers and also among my progeny. O Our Lord! Accept my prayer. O One Lord! Cover (me) with your forgiveness - me, my parents and believers on the Day of Judgement."

25. After this prayer, the *Salat* is to be ended with *Salam*. For this the face is first turned to the right. Looking over the right shoulder

    "Peace be upon you and the mercy of Allah "- is to be said. Then turning the face to the left and looking over the left shoulder, the same words are to be repeated.

Chapter 7

Social Obligations in Islam

Offer devotions to Allah

Appoint no one His Partner

Be Good to :

- Your Mother and Father,
- Your Kith and Kin,
- The Orphans,
- The Needy,
- The Neighbour — who is a relative, and
- The Neighbour — who is not a relative,
- The Companion — in whose fellowship you spend some time, however brief it may be, and
- Be kind to the traveller,
- The captives (slaves) who are under your charge. (4:36)

Regards for Parents

1. Behave well towards your father and mother and consider this good conduct as a propitious act which will earn Allah's grace in this world as well as in the next. Next to Allah, man owes the greatest obligation to his parents. The greatness and value of this obligation towards one's parents may be realised from the fact that the Holy Quran at several points mentions the rights of parents and the rights of Allah simultaneously at one place. Furthermore, the Holy Quran has ordained the duty of offering thanks to the parents along with thanksgiving to Allah.

"Thy Lord hath decreed that ye worship none save Him and (that ye show) kindness to parents." *(17: 23)*

Hadrat 'Abdullah ibn Masud [R.A.A.] relates: "I submitted to the Holy Prophet [S.A.W.] which deed will win the highest favour of Allah?" The Holy Prophet [S.A.W.] answered: "The prayer which is offered at the appointed hour." I submitted again: "Next to this which other deed will win the greatest favour of Allah?" The Holy Prophet [S.A.W.] affirmed: "Good conduct towards father and mother." I again submitted: "And next to this?" The Prophet of Allah [S.A.W.] observed: "Jihad (Fighting) in the way of Allah." *(Bukhari, Muslim)*

Hadrat 'Abdullah [R.A.A.] reports: "One day a person went to the Holy Prophet [S.A.W.] and submitted: "I give my hand into your hand and swear allegiance for performing Hijrat and Jihad and I beseech a reward from Allah in return for this." The Holy Prophet [S.A.W.] enquired: "Is one of your parents alive?" He submitted: "Yes, praise be to Allah, both my father and mother are alive." Thereupon the Prophet of Allah [S.A.W.] observed: "Well then do you really want to receive a reward from Allah for performing Hijrat and Jihad'?" The man replied: "Yes, indeed, I beseech reward from Allah in return for these acts." The Holy Prophet [S.A.W.] observed: "Go then. Attend to your parents and serve them well." *(Muslim)*

Hadrat Abu Umama [R.A.A.] relates: "A man enquired from the Holy Prophet [S.A.W.]: "O Prophet of Allah [S.A.W.]! What are the rights of parents over their offspring?" The Holy Prophet [S.A.W.] affirmed: "Your entry into Paradise or Hell depends on your good or bad conduct towards your parents. " *(Ibn Majah)*

In other words, if you treat them well, you will be sent to Paradise and if you violate the rights that your parents have over you, you will be consigned to serve as fuel for Hell-Fire.

2. Be grateful to your parents. Thanksgiving and an acknowledgement of debt and gratitude are the first duties which a beneficiary owes to the Benefactor. It is a fact that the parents are the palpable cause for our existence. Again, it is under their protection and upbringing that we grow up to an age of maturity. The extraordinary self-sacrifice, unparalleled devotion and deep

affection with which they patronise us demand that our hearts should be filled with sentiments of reverence, indebtedness, love and an acknowledgement of their magnanimity and every fibre of our heart should pulsate with feelings of gratitude to them. It is for this reason that Allah has ordained offering of gratitude to parents along with thanksgiving to Him.

"(We willed) that you should offer thanks to Me and remain grateful to your father and mother."

3. Always try to make your parents happy. Do not say anything in opposition to their will or temperament which may displease them, especially when they are advanced in age they acquire a peevish and irritable temperament. In old age the parents start making unexpected demands and begin proffering impossible claims. In this case also tolerate their behaviour in good cheer and do not say anything in anger in response to their demands which may cause them pain and may injure their feelings.

"If one or both of thy parents reach an advanced age with thee, say not 'fie' unto them nor repulse them."

As a matter of fact, the strength to tolerate unpleasant things is sapped during old age and weakness increases the sense of self-importance in old people. Hence they react sensitively to even the minor offensive matters. Keeping in view their delicate and sensitive nature, do not let your parents feel angry by any of your words or deeds.

> *Hadrat 'Abdullah b. Amr [R.A.A.] relates that the Holy Prophet [S.A.W.] affirmed: "The pleasure of Allah is contained in the pleasure of the father even as His displeasure is contained in the displeasure of the father."*
> *(Tirmidhi, Ibn Habban, Hakim)*

In other words, any one who wants to please Allah should seek the pleasure of his father, for if the father is angry, the favour of Allah cannot be earned. The one who makes his father angry provokes the wrath of Allah."

> *Another statement of Hadrat 'Abdullah [R.A.A.] runs as follows: "A man left his parents weeping and came to the presence of the Holy Prophet [S.A.W.] for the purpose of offering allegiance to the Prophet [S.A.W.] for Hijrah. The Holy Prophet [S.A.W.] observed to him: "Go back to your parents and return after making them happy as you came after leaving them crying." (Abu Daud)*

4. Do service to your parents with heart and soul. If Allah has afforded you the opportunity to serve your parents, it is in fact a favourable opportunity for you to earn entitlement to Paradise and to win the Pleasure of Allah. Good service to parents secures blessings and grace in both worlds and man obtains salvation from the calamities of this world and the next. Hadrat Anas [R.A.A.] relates:

   "Any man who desires that his life should be prolonged and his subsistence may be increased ought to do good service to his parents and show kindness to them."
   (Al-Targhib-wat-Tarhib)

The Holy Prophet [S.A.W.] has observed:

"Let that man be disgraced, and disgraced again and let him be disgraced even more." The people enquired: "O Prophet of Allah [S.A.W.]! who is that man?" The Prophet of Allah [S.A.W.] affirmed: "I refer to the man who finds his parents old in age both of them or one of them - and yet did not earn entitlement to Paradise by rendering good service to them." *(Muslim)*

On one occasion, the Holy Prophet [S.A.W.] gave precedence to the obligation of looking after one's parents over one of the supreme forms of worship like Jihad. The Holy Prophet [S.A.W.] forbade a companion [R.A.A.] to proceed on Jihad and urged him to look after his parents.

Hadrat 'Abdullah ibn 'Amr [R.A.A.] relates that a person came to the presence of the Holy Prophet [S.A.W.] with the intention of participating in the Jihad. The Holy Prophet [S.A.W.] enquired from him: "Are your father and mother alive?" He submitted: "Yes, they are alive." The Holy Prophet [S.A.W.] thereupon observed: "Go and render good service to them. This is the Jihad."
(Bukhari, Muslim)

5. Respect and adore your parents and do not show disrespect to them by a single word or action. The Holy Quran affirms:

   "But speak to them a gracious word." *(17: 23)*

   On one occasion Hadrat 'Abdullah b. 'Umar [R.A.A.] enquired from Hadrat Ibn 'Abbas [R.A.A.]: "Do you wish to ward off Hell and gain entry into Paradise?" Ibn 'Abbas [R.A.A.] answered: "Yes, why not, I swear in the name of Allah I cherish this desire." Hadrat Ibn 'Umar then asked: "Are your parents alive?" Ibn 'Abbas [R.A.A.] replied: "Yes, my mother is alive." Ibn 'Umar [R.A.A.] remarked: "If you talk to them in a polite manner and look after their needs and feed them well, you will certainly be admitted to Paradise provided you abstain from capital evils." (Al-Adab-ul Mufrad)

Hadrat Abu Hurrayrah [R.A.A.] once saw two men. He asked one of them: "What is your relationship with the other man?" The person replied: "He is my father." Hadrat Abu Hurrayrah [R.A.A.] thereupon advised him, "Look, never call him by his proper name, walk ahead of him nor sit before he takes his seat."
(Al-Adab-ul Mufrad)

6. Be faithful and humble towards your parents.

   "And lower unto them the wing of submission through mercy." (17: 23)

To offer humble obedience to parents implies to pay constant regard to their dignity. Do not assume a haughty attitude towards them, nor treat them with insolence.

7. Love your parents and consider this act as a privilege and a source of reward in the eternal world. Hadrat Ibn 'Abbas [R.A.A.] relates that the Holy Prophet [S.A.W.] observed:

   "The pious offspring who casts a single look of affection at his parents receives a reward from Allah equal to the reward of an accepted Hajj." The people submitted: "O Prophet of Allah [S.A.W.]: If someone casts a hundred such glances of love and affection at his parents, what then?" The Holy Prophet [S.A.W.] observed: "Yes, indeed, even if one does so a hundred time a day, he will get a hundredfold reward. Allah is far greater than you imagine and is completely free from petty narrowmindedness. (Muslim)

8. Obey your parents with full devotion. Even if they show some intransigence, obey their will cheerfully. Keeping in view the great favours which they have done to you, try to fulfil all their demands willingly which may be offensive to your own taste or temperament, provided, of course, they are not derogatory to the tenets of religion.

   Hadrat Abu Said Khudri [R.A.A.] narrates that a person came to the presence of the Holy Prophet [S.A.W.] from

Yemen. The Prophet of Allah [S.A.W.] enquired from him: "Do you have any relations in Yemen?" He submitted: "Yes, my father and mother are there." The Holy Prophet [S.A.W.] then asked: "Did they give you permission to leave?" He submitted: "No, I did not take their permission." The Prophet of Allah [S.A.W.] thereupon observed: "Go back then and ask the permission of your father and mother. If they agree, come back and join the Jihad, otherwise, attend on them and render good service to them." *(Abu Daud)*

Realise the value of rendering obedience to parents from the facts that a man came from miles intending to join the Holy Prophet [S.A.W.] in Holy war for the glory of religion, yet the Holy Prophet [S.A.W.] turned him back saying: "You can join the Holy War only if both your father and mother allow you to do so."

Hadrat Ibn 'Abbas [R.A.A.] reports that the Holy Prophet [S.A.W.] observed: "The man who wakes up in the morning having previously discharged all the duties and obligations laid upon him by Allah concerning his parents, he will find the two gates of Paradise open for him on waking up in the morning; and in case there is only one parent, the person will find one door of Paradise open for him. And in contrast if a man wakes up in the morning having previously disregarded any obligations or duties laid upon him by Allah concerning his parents, then he will find two gates of Hell open for him on waking up in the morning; and in case one of the parents is alive, then the man will find one gate of Hell open for him." The man submitted: "O Prophet of Allah [S.A.W.], if the parents are treating him wrongly, what then?" The Holy Prophet [S.A.W.] affirmed: "Yes, even if they are treating him wrongly; yes, indeed even if they are treating him wrongly." *(Mishkat)*

Consider your own goods as the property of your parents and spend your capital on them with an open hand. The Holy Quran affirms:

"They ask thee, what they shall spend. Say what ye spend for good must go to parents."

On one occasion a man came to the presence of the Holy Prophet [S.A.W.] and complained that his father took whatever goods he wanted from him. The Holy Prophet [S.A.W.] sent for that man's father. An old, infirm man came walking with the help of a stick. When the Holy Prophet [S.A.W.] interrogated him on the point, the old man submitted: "O Prophet of Allah [S.A.W.]! There was a time when I was strong and he was weak and helpless. I had money and he was empty-handed. I never forbade him then to lay his hands on anything that I possessed. Today, he is strong and healthy and I am old and infirm. He has money and I am empty-handed. He now denies me access to his goods." Upon hearing this tale of the old man, the Benefactor of the humanity [S.A.W.] burst into tears and addressing the son of the old man observed: "You and your goods are the property of your father."

10. Even if your father and mother are non-Muslims, treat them well. Continue to pay them respect and devotion and serve them faithfully. However, in case they command you to become a polytheist or indulge in a sinful act, refuse to obey them and sternly repulse their demand.

"And if your (parents) pressurise you to associate some one with Me of which you have no knowledge, obey them not, yet continue to treat them well in the world."

Hadrat Asma' [R.A.A.] states: "In the sacred lifetime of the Holy Prophet [S.A.W.], my mother visited me on one occasion. She was a polytheist at that time. I submitted to the Holy Prophet [S.A.W.]: "My mother has come to pay me a visit and she is an unbeliever in Islam. How should I treat her?" The Holy Prophet [S.A.W.] observed: "Yes, you should continue to show kindness to your mother." (Bukhari)

11. Offer prayers begging grace for your parents. Bring to mind their fervent appeals to the Allah and beg His mercy for them with a zealous and sincere heart. Allah ordains:

"And say: My Allah! Have mercy on them both as they did care for me when I was little." In other words, say: "O Creator, with mercy, devotion, affection and love my Allah they reared me in childhood and sacrificed their own pleasure and ease for my sake but, they, in their infirmity and helplessness of old age, are more deserving of kindness and love than I ever was. Allah! I can pay them no recompense. Do patronise them and show them mercy in their miserable state."

12. Observe special care in looking after your mother. By nature, the mother is weak and more sensitive and needs your better

treatment and devotion. Moreover, her favours and sacrifices are comparatively far greater than the father. Hence religion has conceded preferential rights to the mother and has enjoined upon the believers to treat their mothers with special consideration. The Holy Quran affirms:

"And We have commanded unto man kindness towards parents. His mother beareth him with suffering, bringeth him forth with suffering, bearing of him and weaning of him is thirty months." *(46: 15)*

While enjoining upon the believers to show good behaviour towards both father and mother, the Holy Quran has drawn a poignant picture of constant suffering of pain and hardships by the mother and has excellently pointed out in a psychological manner the fact that the devoted mother deserves comparatively more of your service and kind behaviour than your father. The same fact has been elucidated in greater detail by the Prophet of Allah [S.A.W.].

Hadrat Abu Hurrayrah [R.A.A.] reports: "A man came to the presence of the Holy Prophet [S.A.W.] and submitted: "O Prophet of Allah [S.A.W.]! Who deserves the noblest treatment from me?" The Holy Prophet [S.A.W.] observed: "Your mother." He again submitted: "And next?" The Holy Prophet [S.A.W.] observed: "Your mother." When the man submitted for the fourth time: "And who next?" The Holy Prophet [S.A.W.] observed: "Your father." *(Al-Adabul Mufrad)*

Hadrat Jahma [R.A.A.] paid a call on the Holy Prophet [S.A.W.] and submitted: "O Prophet of Allah [S.A.W.]! I wish to join you in the Jihad and have come to solicit your guidance in this matter. I seek your command." The Holy Prophet [S.A.W.] enquired from him: "Is your mother alive?" Jahma [R.A.A.] submitted: "Yes, she is alive." Thereupon the Holy Prophet [S.A.W.], said "Return to her then and devote yourself to her service, for Paradise lies under her feet." *(Ibn Majah, Nasai)*

Hadrat Awais [R.T.A.] was a contemporary of the Holy Prophet [S.A.W.], but he could never attain the privilege of calling on the Holy Prophet [S.A.W.]. He had an old mother to whose service he devoted himself day and night. He cherished a great desire to see the Holy Prophet [S.A.W.] and it was but natural for every Muslim to have a burning desire to catch a glimpse of the Prophet of Allah [S.A.W.]. Hadrat Awais [R.T.A.] indeed wanted to pay a call, yet the Holy Prophet [S.A.W.] forbade him to come. Similarly, Hadrat Awais [R.T.A.] cherished an ambition to discharge the obligation of Hajj, yet as long as his mother remained alive, Hadrat Awais [R.T.A.] never set out for the Hajj alone. He fulfilled the desire to perform Hajj after his mother's demise.

13. Treat your foster mother well. Do service to her and show her respect and adoration. Hadrat Abu Tufail [R.A.A.] states: "I once witnessed the Holy Prophet [S.A.W.] distributing meat at a place called 'Jarana'. Presently, a lady arrived and approached near the Holy Prophet [S.A.W.]. The Holy Prophet of Allah [S.A.W.] spread out his sheet for her and the lady sat on it. I enquired from the people, "Who is this lady?" The people told me: "This lady is the foster mother of the Holy Prophet [S.A.W.]. (Abu Daud)

14. Remember your parents after they have passed away. Observe the following etiquettes to render good service to your deceased parents:

(i) Offer prayers continuously invoking mercy of Allah upon your dead father and mother.

The Holy Quran enjoins upon the pious to say this prayer:

"O our Allah! Grant forgiveness to me and my parents and pardon all the faithful on the day of Reckoning."

Hadrat Abu Hurrayrah [R.A.A.] states: "When the deceased is elevated to high degrees of favour, he enquires in astonishment: "How so?" He is informed by Allah, "Your offsprings have been offering prayers, begging mercy for you (and Allah has accepted those petitions of mercy)."

Hadrat Abu Hurrayrah [R.A.A.] also states:

"The Holy Prophet [S.A.W.] observed: The opportunity to do something ends with one's death yet there are three things which continue to afford benefit to him after death- a recurring charitable act; knowledge which he has imparted to others from which people derive benefit and thirdly, pious offsprings who continue to offer prayers invoking mercy of Allah upon him."

(ii) Fulfil all the contracts and promises made by your parents and carry out their will. Your parents must have made many agreements with some people, they might have made a covenant with Allah; they might have taken a vow; they might have promised to deliver goods to someone; they might have owed a debt to somebody but were unable to discharge it before death overtook them; they might have made a will at the time of their death. Fulfil all these obligations to the extent of your means.

Hadrat 'Abdullah b. 'Abbas [R.A.A.] narrates: "Hadrat Sad b. Ubaba [R.A.A.] submitted to the Holy Prophet [S.A.W.], "O Prophet of Allah [S.A.W.]! My mother had taken a vow, but she expired before discharging it. Can I carry out the vow on her behalf?" The Holy Prophet [S.A.W.] affirmed: "Why not! You must carry out the vow taken by her."

(iii) Show good conduct to the friends of your father and the female companions of your mother. Treat them with respect. Seek their advice just as you seek the advice of your elders and pay due regard to their opinions and advice. On one occasion, the Holy Prophet [S.A.W.] observed: There is no superior deed of piety than that man should do good service to the companions and friends of his father."

Once Hadrat Abu Darda [R.A.A.] fell ill and his condition continued to aggravate till they lost all hopes of his life. Hadrat Yusuf b. 'Abdullah [R.A.A.] made a long journey and came to enquire after his health. On seeing him, Hadrat Abu Darda asked in astonishment: "How are you here?" Yusuf b. 'Abdullah [R.A.A.] replied: "I have come here only to enquire after your health, for you were on terms of deep friendship with my late father."

Hadrat Abu Darda [R.A.A.] relates: "When I arrived in Medina, 'Abdullah b. 'Umar [R.A.A.] paid me a visit and said: "Abu Darda, do you know why I have come to see you?" I replied: "No. I have no idea why you have come here." Thereupon Hadrat 'Abdullah b. 'Umar [R.A.A.] said: "I have heard the Prophet of Allah [S.A.W.] as affirming: "The man who wishes to render good service to his father, who is in the grave, ought to show good treatment to his father's companions and friends." Having related this saying of the Holy Prophet [S.A.W.] 'Abdullah b. Umar [R.A.A.] remarked: "Brother, my father 'Umar and your father [R.A.A.] were on terms of deep friendship. I wish to commemorate this friendship and fulfil its duties." *(Ibn Habban)*

(iv) Show constant good treatment to the relations of your parents and entertain full respect and pay due regard to the sanctity of these connections. An indifferent and irresponsible conduct towards these relations is tantamount to treating your own parents with indifference and negligence. The Holy Prophet [S.A.W.] observed: "Do not observe indifference towards your forefathers. To show carelessness in your conduct towards your parents is to display ingratitude to Allah."

15. If, Allah forbid, you have been guilty of negligence in treating your parents well or discharging your full obligations towards them during their lifetime, do not despair of Allah's mercy. Offer prayers constantly invoking blessings of Allah upon your deceased parents. It is possible Allah may forgive your sin of negligence and admit you among the ranks of the pious people. Hadrat Anas [R.A.A.] relates: The Holy Prophet [S.A.W.] affirmed:

    "If a person does not observe filial devotion to his parents during their lifetime, and both parents or one of them passes away, the person ought to offer prayers for his deceased parents and beg His Mercy and beseech Him to grant salvation to them till Allah in His Mercy ordains their admission to the rolls of the pious people."

Familial Matters

The sublime culture and civilisation which Islam envisages can only come into existence when we succeed in building up the structure of a righteous society. And a stable and well-organised family system is a prerequisite for the birth of a righteous society. Family life begins with the sacred matrimonial connection between husband and wife and the development of this connection into a permanently happy and pleasant matrimonial life chiefly depends on the full awareness of the etiquettes and duties of marital life in both husband and wife and their zeal, sincerity and devotion to observe those etiquettes and discharge obligations of married life. Let us in the first place deal with those etiquettes and obligations which concern the husband and then we shall proceed to discuss the etiquettes and duties to be observed by the wife.

1. Treat your wife well in life. Discharge your obligations towards her with a liberal heart and adopt a favourable and self-sacrificing attitude in every matter concerning your wife. Allah ordains:

"And live with them in a good manner."

In a sermon to a mammoth congregation on the eve of Hajjatul-Widah (Last Hajj) of the Prophet [S.A.W.], the Holy Prophet [S.A.W.] enjoined upon the Muslims:

"O people! Listen! Behave well towards women, for they are like captives with you. You have no right to give them harsh treatment save in the case when they show open disobedience. If they are guilty of disobedience, keep away from them in the bed room. In case you punish them, take care not to cause them severe injury. When they come round and obey your will, do not find pretexts to harass them. Listen carefully! you have some rights over your wives and your wives have some rights over you. They owe an obligation to you not to let your beds be trampled by anyone whom you dislike and not let anyone trespass into your house whose visit you do not like. And listen, you owe a duty to them to feed them well and provide good clothing to them." *(Riyad-us-Salihin)*

In other words, make such provisions for their feeding and clothing as are befitting to a marital relationship of unique intimacy, union of hearts and a spirit of companionship.

2. Entertain a good opinion about your wife as far as possible and adopt an attitude of politeness, toleration and magnanimity for the sake of amicable living with her. If she lacks beauty of face or person or is deficient in good manners, morality, good sense or skill in household affairs, bear these faults with patience. Look to her virtues and maintain a harmonious relationship by means of generosity, liberality of mind and self-sacrifice. Allah ordains:

   "And amity contains goodness."

   And the believers are enjoined upon as follows:

   "For if ye hate them it may happen that ye hate a thing wherein Allah hath placed much good." *(4: 19)*

   The same subject has been elucidated by the Holy Prophet [S.A.W.] in the following Tradition:

   "No believer should hate his pious wife. If he dislikes one habit of his wife, it is possible he may like her for some other aspects of her character."

As a matter of fact, each woman has some weakness of one sort or another and if the husband turns against her on account of her bearing a certain deficiency and conceives a hatred for her, a pleasant home life becomes impossible for the couple. Common-sense dictates that man should adopt a liberal attitude and reposing his trust in Allah should endeavour to live amicably with his wife. It is possible that Allah may vouchsafe to that man merely for the sake of this woman, such bounties which his limited mind cannot comprehend.

For instance, this woman may possess excellent virtues of religion, faith, character and morality in reward for which Allah may shower blessings upon her own family or may be a pious soul is born of this woman who may prove beneficial for the whole mankind and may serve as a Sadaqa-e-Jariah (Continuing Charity) in favour of the father till the end of his life, or perhaps the woman may serve as a means of reforming the character of her man and thus may help him to gain proximity to Paradise or it may be that Allah may bless this man with large subsistence and prosperity because such a blessing of prosperity was destined for his wife. At any rate, do not ruin your married life impetuously on the grounds of an apparent defect in the woman. On the other hand, be wise and try to promote gradually an atmosphere of happiness and concord in the home.

3. Adopt an attitude of forgiveness and kindness. Forget all the faults of omission, stupid actions and disobedient attitude of your wife. The woman is deficient and weak in wisdom and Common-sense and bears an extremely passionate temperament. Hence try to bring her round with patience, calmness, kindness, affection and devotion. Try to get along with her with patience and restraint. Allah ordains:

   "O ye who believe! verily, among your wives and your children, there are enemies for you, therefore beware of them. And if ye efface and overlook and forgive, then Allah is Forgiving, Merciful." (Attaghabun: 14)

   The Holy Prophet [S.A.W.] affirmed:

   "Be good to women. The woman has been created out of the rib and the uppermost part of the rib ends in a curve; so if you try to straighten out the curve, it will break, yet if you leave it alone, the curve will remain. Hence, be good to women." (Bukhari, Muslim)

4. Treat your wife politely and show love and affection to her. The Holy Prophet [S.A.W.] has affirmed:

"The believers who possess perfect faith are those who display the best manners, and the best among you are those who treat their wives in the best possible manner."
(Tirmidhi)

Politeness and tenderness of behaviour can best be judged in the home. People are constantly living amidst their family members and the real temper and moral conduct of man is completely revealed in the free and uninhibited atmosphere of the home.

It is a fact that only such believers possess perfect faith who display civility, kindness, and affectionate behaviour towards their family members and who support, sympathises, love and adore inmates of their household.

Hadrat 'Aishah [R.A.A.] reports: "I used to play with dolls along with my playmates in the house of the Holy Prophet [S.A.W.]. On the arrival of the Holy Prophet [S.A.W.] all of them used to hide themselves in the nooks and corners of the house. The Prophet [S.A.W.] used to search out each one of them and send them to join me in the play." (Bukhari, Muslim)

Once on the occasion of Hajj, the camel of Hadrat Safiyah [R.A.A.] sat down on the ground and she was therefore left behind while the entire caravan passed on. The Holy Prophet [S.A.W.] came to her and found her weeping without restraint. The Holy Prophet [S.A.W.] stood there wiping off her tears with the edge of a sheet with his own holy hands. While the Prophet of Allah [S.A.W.] wiped off tears from her eyes, she [R.A.A.] continued to weep unrestrainedly for a long time."

5. Make liberal provisions for all the needs of your wife and do not stint in expenses. Feel a sense of pleasure and comfort in spending your lawful earnings on members of your family. You owe an obligation to your wife to provide her with food and clothing and to struggle energetically, in order to earn enough money to discharge this obligation, is the most pleasant duty of a husband. The performance of this duty with an open and cheerful heart earns for the believer the reward of a happy marital life in this world and a favourable recompense and bounty in the world to come. The Holy Prophet [S.A.W.] has affirmed:

   "You spend a dinar in the way of Allah; you spend another dinar to ransom a slave; you give away one dinar as alms to a beggar; and there is one dinar which you spend

on your family. Among all these, the dinar that will earn the best reward and blessings of Allah is the one which you have spent on your family."

(Muslim)

6. Teach your wife the rules and manners enjoined by religion. Let her observe Islamic morality and make her life graceful. Make every possible effort to train and mould her according to the Islamic pattern of life so that she may prove to be a good wife, good mother and a pious devotee of Allah and may discharge her duties as a wife efficiently and faithfully. Allah affirms:

   "O ye who believe! Save yourselves and your family from the Fire of Hell."

   As the Holy Prophet [S.A.W.] devoted himself to preaching and teaching the laws of religion outside the home, likewise he continued to perform the same function inside his home. Making an illusion to this fact, the Holy Quran addresses the wives of the Holy Prophet [S.A.W.] in these words:

   "And remember the verses of Allah and the matters of wisdom that are conveyed to you in your house." The Quran has advised the believers through the ministry of the Holy Prophet [S.A.W.]:

   "And urge upon the inmates of your house to observe prayers and fully abide by this obligation yourself too."

   The Prophet of Allah [S.A.W.] affirms:

   "When a man wakes up his wife during the night and they offer two Rakats of Prayers together, Allah ordains that the man's name should be included in the rolls of the male remembers of Allah and the woman's name in the register of those females who offer praises to Allah and remember Him." *(Abu Daud)*

The second Caliph Hadrat 'Umar [R.A.A.] used to stand all night offering devotions to Allah. Near the hour of dawn he used to wake his wife saying: "Rise, get up and say prayers," and later he [R.A.A.] used to recite this verse also:

"And urge upon the inmates of your house to observe prayers and fully abide by this obligation yourself."

7. If you possess several wives; show equal treatment to all of them. The Holy Prophet [S.A.W.] used to observe great care in

dispensing equal treatment to his wives. On the eve of setting out for a journey the Prophet of Allah [S.A.W.] used to draw lots and took with him the wife whose name was decided by the toss. Hadrat Abu Hurrayrah [R.A.A.] states that the Holy Prophet [S.A.W.] observed:

"If a man has two wives, but does not treat them with equality and even-handed justice, he shall be resurrected on the Day of Judgement in such a condition that half of his body is paralysed." *(Tirmidhi)*

'Justice' and 'equality' imply to treat them equally in all matters and show the same kind of behaviour to each wife. As regards the fact that a man may be specially attracted towards one wife or may be drawn to her or cherish deeper feelings of love for her, Allah will award no punishment to the man for it.

8. Obey your husband with a willing heart and feel pleasure and satisfaction in being faithful to him. This is what Allah commands a wife to do and the believing woman. Who acts according to the will of Allah wins His Favour. The Holy Quran affirms:

   "The pious wives are those who show obedience to their husbands."

   The Holy Prophet [S.A.W.] observed:

   "No woman should keep fast without the permission of her husband." *(Abu Daud)*

   Stressing the importance of rendering obedience and devotion to her husband, the Holy Prophet [S.A.W.] has warned the woman:

   "There are two types of persons whose prayers do not rise above their heads-the prayer of a slave who deserts his master until he returns to his service and the prayer of a woman who shows disobedience to her husband until she recants from this behaviour."
   (Al-Targhib-o-Al-Tarhib)

9. Protect your honour and chastity. Keep away from all matters of activities which contain a possible threat to violate your honour or chastity. This is what Allah commands and it is also an essential prerequisite for making your marital life happy and pleasant. No amount of devotion and obedience of the wife can win the heart of her husband if the seeds of suspicion about her infidelity are once sown in his mind. Even an ordinary act

of carelessness on the wife's part may prompt the devil to fill the heart of her husband with indelible doubts and suspicions. Hence keeping in view this human weakness, exercise utmost vigilance in such matters.

The Prophet of Allah has affirmed:

"If the woman offers prayers five times a day, protects her honour and chastity, remains faithful to her husband, she may enter Paradise by whichever gate she likes." (Al-Targhib-o-Al-Tarhib)

10. Do not go out of the house without leave or permission of your husband. Do not call at homes of which your husband disapproves, nor admit anyone into your house whom your husband dislikes.

Hadrat Muadh ibn Jabal [R.A.A.] narrates that the Prophet of Allah [S.A.W.] observed:

"It is not lawful for a woman who believes in Allah to admit a man into her house whose visit is disapproved of by her husband or that she should go out of the house against her husband's will or she should obey the will of someone else in opposition to her husband's wishes." (Al-Targhib-o-Al-Tarhib)

In other words, obey the wishes of your husband, even watch and be mindful of the slightest indications of his approval or disapproval. Do not follow the counsels of others which are in opposition to the will of your husband.

11. It should be your permanent concern to make your husband happy by your words, actions, behaviour and manners. This is not only the real secret of a successful marriage, but a means to win the favour of Allah and admittance into Paradise. The Holy Prophet [S.A.W.] has affirmed:

"The woman who dies in such a state that her husband was entirely satisfied and in concord with her, will certainly enter Paradise." (Tirmidhi)

Furthermore, the Holy Prophet [S.A.W.] observed:

"When a man calls his wife to fulfil the sexual urge and she declines and for this reason the husband remains angry with her all night, the angels send curses upon such a wife till dawn." (Bukhari, Muslim)

12. Love your husband and value his companionship. He is the adornment of your life, your life's support and a great companion

and helper in the course of your life. Give thanks to Allah for this great Bounty and value this Bounty too with all your heart and soul. The Holy Prophet [S.A.W.] observed on one occasion:

"For the two who love one another there is no better thing than the 'Nikah' (matrimonial tie)."

Hadrat Safiyah [R.A.A.] cherished deep love for the Holy Prophet [S.A.W.]. When illness overcame the Holy Prophet of Allah [S.A.W.], Hadrat Safiyah [R.A.A.] spoke with genuine concern: "Would Allah that I had fallen ill instead of you, O Holy Prophet of Allah [S.A.W.]!" At this expression of deep love by Hadrat Safiyah [R.A.A.], the other wives of the Holy Prophet [S.A.W.] looked towards her in astonishment. Thereupon the Holy Prophet [S.A.W.] observed:

"She is not merely making show of her affection; she is expressing her genuine love."

13. Acknowledge the debt of gratitude you owe to your husband and remain grateful to him. Your greatest benefactor is your husband who is always concerned with making you happy, providing for your needs and feels satisfied when he has made all provisions for your comfort.

    Hadrat Asma [R.A.A.] narrates the Tradition: I was once with my neighbour friend when the Holy Prophet [S.A.W.] passed near me. He [S.A.W.] said 'Salam' [peace be on you] to us and observed: "Avoid being ungrateful to those whom you owe a debt of gratitude. One of you, for instance, lives with her parents in an unmarried state for a long period. Then Allah confers upon her a husband. Subsequently, Allah grants her offspring. Yet in spite of all these favours when she feels enraged with her husband on some matter, she utters, 'Never have I received anything good from you." (Al-Adabul Mufrad)

    The Holy Prophet [S.A.W.] in a warning statement to an ungrateful and unthinking wife observed:

    "On the Day of Judgement, Allah will not even look at a woman who is ungrateful to her husband, despite the fact that a wife can never get along without her husband." (Nasai)

14. Feel happy in doing service to your husband and afford maximum comfort to him at the expense of your own inconvenience. Devote yourself to his welfare in all matters and

by means of this sincere service capture the deep affections of his heart. Hadrat 'Aishah [R.A.A.] used to wash the clothes of the Holy Prophet [S.A.W.] with her own hands, anointed his sacred head with oil, combed his hair, and rubbed perfume on his holy person. The other contemporary pious ladies [R.A.A.] served their husbands in the same manner.

On one occasion, the Holy Prophet [S.A.W.] observed:

> *"It is unlawful for a human being to prostrate before another human. If it had been permissible, the wife would have been ordained by Allah to offer prostration to her husband. The husband has the supreme right over his wife, and such is the optimum degree of this right that in case a husband's whole body is covered with wounds and the wife licks them all with her tongue, the obligation she owes to her husband is even then not discharged in full measure."* *(Musnad Ahmad)*

15. Safeguard the home, property and goods of your husband. After marriage consider the husband's home as your own and spend the wealth of your husband wisely and economically on the adornment of your home, on the enhancement of the prestige of your husband and on securing a better future for your children.

Consider the advancement and prosperity of your husband as your own personal achievements. Praising the virtues of the women of the tribe of Quraish, the Holy Prophet [S.A.W.] observed:

> *"How excellent are the women of the tribe of Quraish! They are most affectionate towards children and most efficient guardians of their husband's homes."*
> *(Bukhari)*

Describing the virtues of a pious wife, the Holy Prophet [S.A.W.] observed:

> *"Next to the fear of Allah the most useful and the bountiful reward for a believer is a pious wife. When he asks her to do something, she does it cheerfully. When he looks at her, she pleases him to the core of his heart. When he swears upon her trust, she fulfils his oath. When he goes away, she protects her honour and chastity in his absence and finally in superintendence of her husband's goods and property she remains truly faithful and devoted to his interest."* *(Ibn Majah)*

16. Observe cleanliness, manage you household affairs wisely and look after the decoration and furnishing of your homes. Keep your house clean. Arrange everything tidily and use things with proper care and skill. A clean and tidy home, neatly furnished rooms, good management of household affairs and home economy and a beautifully dressed and adorned wife wearing a pleasant smile on her lips ....:all this charges the home atmosphere with currents of deep love and affection and the marital life is enriched with happiness and blessings. This is the only way for a wife to gain her personal salvation and to win the favour of Allah.

On one occasion during a meeting Hadrat 'Aishah [R.A.A.] saw that the wife of Uthman b. 'Mazun [R.A.A.] was dressed in plain clothes and wore no adornments. Hadrat 'Aishah [R.A.A.] was taken aback and enquired:

"My good lady! Has your husband 'Uthman gone out on a journey?"

You can judge from the exclamation of Hadrat 'Aishah [R.A.A.] what a propitious act it is for a married woman to adorn and beautify herself for her husband.

Once a Muslim lady of Medina [R.A.A.] presented herself before the Holy Prophet [S.A.W.]. She was at that time wearing gold bangles. The Holy Prophet [S.A.W.] expressed his disapproval of her wearing the gold bangles. The lady submitted:

> *"O Prophet of Allah [S.A.W.]! If a woman does not adorn herself and make her person attractive for her husband, she would soon lose her value for him."*
>
> *(Nasai)*

Children under Care

1. Consider your children as a bounty of Allah. Celebrate the birth of a child with joy and exchange messages of congratulation on such occasion. Welcome the birth of children with prayers for grace and blessings of Allah. Offer thanks to Allah that He has conferred upon you the favour of rearing one of His creatures and that He has afforded you the opportunity of leaving behind an heir to represent you in spiritual as well as mundane life.
2. If you are childless, pray to Allah for favour of granting you pious offspring in the same manner as the venerable Prophet of Allah Hadrat Zakriya [A.S.] had prayed to Allah for the grant of pious offspring.

"Allah! Bestow upon me by Thy bounty goodly offspring. Lo! Thou art the Hearer of prayer." *(3: 38)*

3. Do not feel downcast on the birth of a child. Strictly guard against feeling remorse or considering the birth of a child as a burden on account of financial hardship, ill health or for any other reason.
4. Do not procure an abortion. Abortion or killing a child after birth are both acts of heinous barbarity, gruesome cruelty and extreme cowardice and entail ruination in this world and Hereinafter. Allah affirms:

   "Those who kill their children out of their foolishness are the great losers." *(6: 140)*

In an impressive condemnation of human shortsightedness, Allah has clearly forbidden the genocide of children:

"Slay not your children fearing poverty. We shall provide for them and for you. Lo! the slaying of them is great sin." *(17: 31)*

On one occasion a companion [R.A.A.] enquired from the Holy Prophet [S.A.W.], "O Prophet of Allah [S.A.W.]! Which is the greatest sin?" The Holy Prophet [S.A.W.] observed: "Polytheism." The companion [R.A.A.] again asked: "And what next" The Holy Prophet [S.A.W.] observed: "Disobedience to parents." The companion [R.A.A.] enquired the third time: "And which sin is the greatest next to it?" In answer to this, the Holy Prophet of Allah [S.A.W.] observed: "To kill you children fearing that they will share your sustenance."

5. At the time of delivery, recite Ayat-ul-Kursi and the following two verses of Surah Al-Aaraf near the pregnant woman. Recite also Surah 'Al Falaq' and Surah 'An-Nas' repeatedly and after each recitation blow your breath over the woman awaiting delivery:

   "Allah! There is no Allah save Him, the Alive, the Eternal. Neither slumber nor sleep overtaketh Him, unto Him belongeth whatsoever is in the heavens and whatsoever is in the earth. Who is that interecedeth with Him save by His leave? He knoweth that which is in front of them and that which is behind them while they encompass nothing of His knowledge save that what He wills. His throne includeth the heavens and the earth and He is never weary of preserving them. He is the Sublime, the Tremendous." *(2:255)*

The two verses of Surah Aaraf are as under:

"Lo! your Lord is Allah Who created the heavens and the earth in six days, and then sat upon the throne of His Kingdom. Who makes the night cover the day which is in haste to follow it and has made the sun and the moon and the stars subservient by His Command. His verily is all creation and commandment. Blessed be Allah the Lord of the worlds! (O mankind) Call upon your Lord humbly and in secret. Lo! He loveth not aggressors."

(7: 54, 55)

6. After birth, bathe the infant and say adaan in its right and Iqamat in its left ear. On the birth of Hadrat Hussain [R.A.A.], the Holy Prophet [S.A.W.] had said adaan and Iqamat in his ears." (Tibrani)

   The Holy Prophet [S.A.W.] is also reported to have affirmed: "Whenever someone begets a child and says Adaan in its right and Iqamat in its left ear, the child is immunised against the affliction of Umm-ul-Sibiyan *by this act."* *(Abu Yala)*

There is great wisdom in conveying the names of Allah and His Messenger [S.A.W.] to the ears of a new-born infant.

In his work entitled 'Tuhfa-tul-Wadud', 'Allama Ibn Qayyim observes: "The significance of this act is that the proclamation of the Greatness and Glory of Allah should be the first to reach the ears of a human being. And the affirmation of belief which he will render in full consciousness later in order to enter the fold of Islam should be conveyed to him in the very first day of his life as a man is prompted to recite Kalima-e-Tauhid (Affirmation of belief in One God) at the time of his death. Another advantage of saying the Adaan and Iqamat in the ears of the child is that the devil, who lies in ambush planning to entrap the human being in trials, flees on hearing the sound of Adaan and before the devil can draw the soul of the child towards himself, the child is called towards Islam and worship of Allah."

7. After the Adaan and Iqamat get a date chewed by some pious man or woman and paste its pulp on the palate of the infant and ask that man or woman to offer a prayer invoking grace and blessings of Allah upon the child. Hadrat Asma [R.A.A.] reports: "When 'Abdullah ibn Zubayr [R.A.A.] was born I put him in the lap of the Holy Prophet [S.A.W.]. The Holy Prophet [S.A.W.] asked for a date, chewed it and applied his sacred saliva inside the mouth and pasted the chewed pulp of date on the

palate of 'Abdullah ibn Zubayr. Afterwards, the Holy Prophet [S.A.W.] offered a prayer invoking grace and blessings of Allah upon the child."

Hadrat 'Aishah [R.A.A.] states: "Infants were brought to the presence of the Holy Prophet [S.A.W.]. The Holy Prophet [S.A.W.] used to Tehnik *and pray for the favour and blessings of Allah upon him."* *(Muslim)*

When Hadrat Imam Ahmad ibn Hambal [R.A.A.] was blessed with a child, he asked for Meccan date which was available in the home and requested a pious lady Umm 'Ali [R.T.A.] to perform the Tehnik.

8. Give your child a fine name, preferably a name resembling that of the Prophets [peace be upon them] or put a prefix 'Abd with some attribute of Allah, just as 'Abd-Allah or 'Abd-Rahman, to make up a name for your child.

The Holy Prophet [S.A.W.] has affirmed: "On the Day of Judgement, you shall be called by your names. So prescribe fine names for yourselves." *(Abu Daud)*

Furthermore, the Holy Prophet [S.A.W.] observed: "Among all your names 'Abdullah and, 'Abdul Rahman are the favourites of Allah." In addition, the Prophet [S.A.W.] affirmed: "Prescribe those names which resemble the names of the Prophets [A.S.]."

It is recorded in Bukhari that the Holy Prophet [S.A.W.] also observed: "Name your children after my name, but do not give them my 'Kuniyyat'."

9. If you have prescribed a wrong name due to ignorance, change it and prescribe some good name. The Holy Prophet [S.A.W.] used to alter wrong names. The name of one of Hadrat 'Umar's [R.A.A.] daughter was 'Asia. The Holy Prophet [S.A.W.] changed it and named her Jamila [R.A.A.]. (Muslim)

The original name of Hadrat Zainab [R.A.A.] the daughter of Abu Salama [R.A.A.] was 'Barrah' which means the pious one'. On hearing this name, the Holy Prophet [S.A.W.] observed: "Do you make a self proclamation of piety?" The people submitted, "What other name shall we prescribe then?" The Prophet [S.A.W.] observed: "Name her Zainab." *(Abu Daud)*

10. Perform the Aqiqa ceremony on the seventh day of the birth of a child. Sacrifice two lambs for a boy and one if the baby is a girl. However, it is not obligatory to slaughter two lambs for a

boy. You may sacrifice one animal also. Get the hair of the head of the baby shaved off and give away in charity gold or silver equal in weight to these hair. The Holy Prophet [S.A.W.] has observed:

"Prescribe a name for the child on the seventh day after birth and perform 'Aquiqa ceremony after getting the baby's head shaved off." (Tirmidhi)

11. Get the male child circumcised on the seventh day after birth. However, if for some reason the operation is put off, it is obligatory to get the circumcision performed before the male child reaches the age of seven. Circumcision is part of Islamic faith.
12. When the child learns to speak, teach him first of all to recite: *La Ilaha Illallahu.* (There is no god but Allah.) The Holy Prophet [S.A.W.] has observed:

When your offspring starts speaking, teach him to recite: La Ilaha Illallahu. *(There is no god but Allah) and never fear about his end. When the milk teeth are uprooted, order your child to observe prayers.*

The Tradition also records that whenever a child in the household of the Holy Prophet [S.A.W.] began to speak, the Prophet [S.A.W.] used to teach him the second verse of Surah al-Furqan in which the concept of the belief in One God has been beautifully expressed in a concise form.

"He unto Whom belongeth the sovereignty of the heavens and the earth, He hath chosen no son nor hath He any partner in the sovereignty. He hath created everything and hath meted out for it a role."

13. Feed the child on your breast-milk. The mother owes this obligation to the child. The Holy Quran has made repeated references to this favour of the mother to her child and has enjoined the pious to treat their mothers with extraordinary devotion in return for their favour. It is the duty of the mother to inculcate in the soul of the child belief in One God, devotion to the Prophet [S.A.W.] and love of religion along with the drops of her milk which she feeds to the child. She should make sure that the heart and soul of her child completely assimilates the spirit of religion. Do not ease your burden by transferring the duty of rearing the child to a nurse. Perform this pleasant obligation of religion yourself and enjoy spiritual satisfaction and ecstasy.

14. Avoid frightening the children. The fright instilled in the mind of the child in the early years overshadows his mind and intellect for the remainder of his life and these children usually prove incapable of achieving extraordinary success in life.
15. Make it a point not to shout at, reproach or rebuke children on every trifling matter. Make an affectionate endeavour to train the children to form good habits with devotion and good sense instead of expressing annoyance or contempt on the faults of children. However, act in such a way that children must remain in fear that you will not tolerate any of their actions which do not conform to the dictates of religion.
16. Always treat your children with affection, love and tenderness. Keep them happy by providing for their needs and requirements according to you means. Promote sentiments of loyalty and devotion in your children.

Once Hadrat Muawiyyah [R.A.A.] asked Ahnaf ibn Qais [R.A.A.], "Say, in what manner the offspring should be treated?"

Ahnaf ibn Qais [R.A.A.] answered: *'Amir-ul-Mominin,* the offspring are the fruit of our hearts, a support for our backs; we are like the sky providing a protective shade over them; we are like a soft and harmless ground on which they recline. It is they who give us the incentive to perform great deeds. Hence if they demand anything from you, fulfil their demand with a generous heart. If they are stricken with sorrow, alleviate their grief. Consequently they will love you and appreciate your paternal concern. Do not be an intolerable burden on them to the extent that they should in annoyance wish that you were better dead than alive and hate to come near you."

Hadrat Muawiyyah [R.A.A.] was deeply moved on hearing this wise speech of Ahnaf ibn Qais [R.A.A.] and remarked: "Ahnaf, [R.A.A.] I swear in the name of Allah that when you came and sat beside me I was burning with rage against Yazid."

Later, when Hadrat Ahnaf [R.A.A.] departed Hadrat Muawiyyah's [R.A.A.] anger had cooled down and he felt reconciled to Yazid. He at once sent two hundred dirhams and two hundred dresses as a token of love to Yazid. On receiving these presents, Yazid divided them into two equal portions and despatched one hundred dirhams and a hundred dresses as a gift to Hadrat Ahnaf ibn Qais [R.A.A.].

17. Pat the heads of children with affection; take them up and seat them in your laps, fondle them and treat them in good humour. Do not rule over them as an irate tyrant. Such an attitude stunts the growth of affectionate sentiments towards parents in the

hearts of children, destroys their self-confidence and adversely affects the development of their inborn faculties.

On one occasion Aqra' ibn Habith [R.A.A.] came to the presence of the Holy Prophet [S.A.W.]. The Holy Prophet [S.A.W.] was at that time engaged in fondling Hadrat Hassan [R.A.A.]. Aqra' [R.A.A.] felt rather surprised and submitted, "O Holy Prophet [S.A.W.] do you also fondle children. I have ten children and have never shown fondness to even one of them"—The Holy Prophet [S.A.W.] raised his eyes and taking a look at Aqra' observed: "If Allah has deprived your heart of kindness and affection, what can I do!"

Hadrat 'Amir [R.A.A.] held a high post in the government during the reign of Hadrat Umar [R.A.A.]. He once paid a call at the house of Hadrat 'Umar [R.A.A.] and was astounded to see that a few children had mounted the chest of the Caliph and were engaged in play. The Caliph realised the feelings of annoyance writ large on the face of 'Amir [R.A.A.] and enquired, "What manner of treatment do you show to your children?" 'Amir [R.A.A.] now got the opportunity to express his viewpoint on the matter. He said: 'Amir-ul-Mominin, as soon as I enter my house the people of my household are struck with terror and stand dumb with fear." On hearing this, Hadrat 'Umar [R.A.A.] said in a deep tone of sorrow:

"Amir [R.A.A.], you are a follower of the Holy Prophet [S.A.W.] and yet are ignorant of the important injunction that a Muslim should behave towards his family members with extreme love and deep tenderness."

18. Concentrate all your efforts to train and educate your children in piety and honesty and consider the greatest sacrifice too little to achieve this purpose. This is an obligation laid upon you by religion; it is a favour you owe to your children; and it is the greatest good that you can do to yourself. The Holy Quran affirms:

    "O Believers, protect yourself and the people of your household from the ire of Hell."

The only means of obtaining salvation from Hell-Fire is that man should be aware of all the requisite knowledge about religion and his life should pass in loyalty and devotion to the commands of Allah and His Messenger [S.A.W.].

The Holy Prophet [S.A.W.] has observed: "The best gift that a father can bestow upon his son is to arrange good education and training for him." *(Mishkat)*

In addition to this, the Apostle of Allah [S.A.W.] affirmed: "The actions of man cease with his death. But there are three deeds whose reward and blessing continue to reach him even after death: One that he should make a Sadaqa Jariah (Recurring Charity). Secondly, he should leave behind a legacy of knowledge from which people may continue to derive benefit; thirdly, pious offspring who continuously invoke mercy of Allah upon him."

(Muslim)

In fact the pious offspring are the only means of keeping alive your cultural traditions, religious doctrines and the concept of faith in One God, after you have expired. The believer prays for pious offspring so that the younger generation may keep the message of the old generation ever green and alive.

19. When the children attain the age of seven years, teach the 'Namaz' and urge them to observe prayers. Take them to the mosque with you to arouse their interest. If the children neglect to observe prayers when they have attained the age of ten, administer suitable punishment to them. By word and action make it absolutely clear to them that you will not tolerate their evasion of saying prayers.

20. When the children attain the age of 10 years, give them separate beds to sleep in. The Holy Prophet [S.A.W.] has observed:

"When your children are seven years old, urge them to observe prayers. When they attain the age of ten and neglect saying prayers, punish them, and after this age provide separate bedding to them."

21. Always keep your children neat and clean. Take care that they are clean, neat and bathed. Keep them dress pure and clean. However, avoid excessive adornment or ostentation in dressing up children. Keep the dress of a female child simple and clean. Do not spoil the nature of your children by dressing them up in gaudy and flamboyant clothes.

22. Do not point out the faults of your children in the presence of others and strictly abstain from degrading or hurting the self-respect of your children.

23. Do not express your dismay at reforming your children in their presence. Instead praise them generously even for their ordinary virtues in order to boost up their morale. Make constant endeavours to encourage them, and to foster self-confidence and boldness in them so that they may strive for the highest goals in the field of life.

24. Keep telling the children the stories of the Prophets [A.S.], tales of the pious people [R.A.A.] and episodes of the courageous feats

of the illustrious companions of the Holy Prophet [S.A.W.]. This must be considered an essential means of training, civilising, character-building and arousing love for religion among the young and despite countless other preoccupations you must find some time to talk on these subjects with your children. Recite to them the Holy Quran in a sweet rhythmical voice frequently and on occasions relate to them the stirring stories and traditions of the life and work of the Holy Prophet [S.A.W.]. In this manner, you should try to inculcate in the hearts of the young warm sentiments of true love and devotion to the Holy Prophet [S.A.W.].

25. Let the children distribute food or money to the poor with their own hands sometimes so that the virtues of liberality, generosity and charity to the poor may develop in their hearts. On occasions, let brothers and sisters distribute shares of food or other eatables among themselves without your aid. This will create in them an awareness of the rights of others and accustom them to fair-dealing.
26. Do not comply with each legitimate or non-genuine desire of the children. By means of patience and common-sense teach them to give up this habit. Be strict with them at times and do not turn them into obstinate and self-willed youngsters by showering excessive love upon them.
27. Avoid thundering and shouting at the highest pitch of your voice and urge the children to speak softly in a moderate tone and abstain from shouting or railing at each other.
28. Inculcate the habit of self-help in children. They should not look to the servants to do every little job for them. This habit makes the children lazy and crippled in some ways. Foster the habits of sturdiness, hard work and strenuous application among the children.
29. In the event of an altercation taking place among children, do not lend undue support to your own child. You must realise that the sentiments which you cherish in your heart for your child are exactly the same which other people have for their children. Keep in view the faults of your own child and in all untoward circumstances try to pinpoint the error and fault of your own child and then make an earnest endeavour to eliminate these childish shortcomings in a wise manner by exercising constant vigilance.
30. Show equal treatment to all your children and avoid going to extremes in the matter of behaving towards children. If you

are naturally drawn towards a particular child then, of course, it can't be helped. Yet in behaviour and dispensation of requirements you must show equal treatment and evenhanded justice. Do not show distinctive favour to a child to the dismay of other children. This will foster inferiority complex, hatred and frustration and all this will finally erupt into rebellious conduct. These evil sentiments greatly retard the development of natural faculties of a child and leave an adverse effect on the moral and spiritual growth of child's personality.

On one occasion Hadrat Bashir [R.A.A.] took his son Hadrat Noman [R.A.A.] to the presence of the Holy Prophet [S.A.W.] and submitted: "O Prophet of Allah [S.A.W.]! I possessed one slave and I have transferred that slave to the ownership of this son of mine." The Holy Prophet [S.A.W.] enquired: "Have you given a slave to each of your sons?" Hadrat Bashir [R.A.A.] submitted: "No." Thereupon the Holy Prophet [S.A.W.] commanded him: "Take the slave back from him. Fear Allah and show equal treatment to all of your children." Hadrat Bashir [R.A.A.] returned home and revoked the transfer of ownership of the slave to Noman. According to another tradition, the Holy Prophet [S.A.W.] had observed on that occasion: "Do not make me a witness of sin. I shall not be a witness to injustice." In yet another tradition it is reported that the Holy Prophet [S.A.W.] observed to Hadrat Bashir [R.A.A.]: "Do you wish that all your sons should behave equally well towards you?" Hadrat Bashir [R.A.A.] submitted: "O Prophet of Allah (S.A.W.]: Yes, why not!" The Holy Prophet [S.A.W.] observed: "Do not act in this manner then." (Bukhari, Muslim)

31. Always present a good practical model before the children. Your own life style serves as a mute and permanent precept for your children. Children constantly lean and adopt lessons from your own conduct in life. Do not tell a lie even as a matter of fun before the children.

Hadrat 'Abdullah b. 'Amir [R.A.A.] relates an episode from his own life as follows: "One day when the Holy Prophet [S.A.W.] was present in our house, my mother called for me and said: "Come here, I have something for you." The Holy Prophet [S.A.W.] was watching. He [S.A.W.] observed to my mother, "What is it that you want to give to the child?" My mother submitted: "I wish to give him a date." The Holy Prophet [S.A.W.] observed: "If you had called the boy on the pretext of giving him something and in fact did not give him anything on his arrival, surely this sin of falsehood would have been added to the scroll of your deeds." *(Abu Daud)*

32. Celebrate the birth of a female child with as much rejoicing as you observe on the birth of a male child. Boy or girl, both are a gift from Allah and only He knows better whether a boy or a girl is propitious for you. It does not behove a faithful of Allah to demure or feel crest-fallen on the birth of a girl. Such behaviour is the height of ingratitude and an insolence towards the Omniscient and Merciful Allah.

The Tradition records: "When a girl is born to someone Allah sends angels to his home who pronounce: "O inmates of this house! peace be on you." The angels take the baby girl under their wings and passing their hands on her head in a gesture of affection observe: "This is a weak creature born out of a weak creature. Whosoever protects and rears this infant girl, Allah shall sustain him till doomsday." *(Tibrani)*

33. Train and bring up your girls with a sense of great pleasure, spiritual satisfaction and in the spirit of religion. In return for this pious service anticipate from Allah that He will admit you to the uppermost level of Paradise. The Holy Prophet [S.A.W.] has affirmed: "The man who patronises three daughters or three sisters, educates them and teaches them good manners and behaves kindly towards them till they become independent of his care by the will of Allah, is entitled by Allah to enter Paradise." Thereupon a person submitted: "If there be only two daughters or two sisters?" The Holy Prophet [S.A.W.] said: "The same reward will be given for similar conduct towards two daughters or two sisters." Hadrat Ibn 'Abbas [R.A.A.] observes: "Had the people enquired about the reward for rearing one girl in this manner, the Holy Prophet [S.A.W.] would have given the same glad tidings." *(Mishkat)*

Hadrat 'Aishah [R.A.A.] narrates, "One day a woman accompanied by two small girls came to visit me and begged me to give her something. I had only one date which I handed over to her. The woman divided the date into two halves and gave one half to each girl, leaving nothing to eat for herself. Afterwards she stood up and went out. The same moment the Holy Prophet [S.A.W.]

entered the house. I related the whole matter to him [S.A.W.]. On hearing the case, the Holy Prophet [S.A.W.] observed: "Any man who is put to trial on account of daughters being born to him and he comes out of the trial successful by virtue of showing good treatment to his daughters, these girls will serve him as a shield against the fire of Hell on the Day of Judgement."

(Mishkat)

34. Do not look down upon the female child, nor show preference to the boy over the girl in any matter. Treat both with equal love and behave towards both in an equal manner. The Holy Prophet [S.A.W.] has affirmed: "Anyone who is blessed with the birth of a girl and does not bury her alive in the manner of the pagan days and does not look down upon her; neither shows preference to the boy over the girl nor considers the boy in any way superior to the girl, such a man will surely be admitted into Paradise by Allah."

 (Abu Daud)

35. Give the prescribed share to the girl out of your property will and with careful attention. This share is ordained by Allah and no one has the authority to increase or decreases the amount of this share. It does not behove a pious believer to make excuses in the matter of paying the share of the girl or to feel content by giving away some fraction of it according to his own personal views. Such an action is a breach of covenant with Allah as well as tantamount to offering an insult to the religion.

 (Allah forbid!)

36. Along with these practical measures, say prayers from the depths of your soul and with sincere devotion of heart for your offspring. We may trust the Munificent and Kind Allah that He will not let earnest prayers offered by the parents out of the depth of their soul go unanswered.

Making Contacts

1. Love your friends and become the object of love of your friends. The man who is held in deep affection by his friends and who cherishes feelings of love for his friends is the most fortunate person. The person who avoids the company of other people and whom the people regard with feelings of disgust is the most deprived man. The man who has no wealth is not poor. In point of fact great poverty consists in being friendless. A friend makes

life beautiful, acts as a supporter in the journey of life and is a gift of Allah. Make friends and become friends of others. The Holy Prophet [S.A.W.] has affirmed:

> *"The believer is an embodiment of love and affection. And the man who neither loves other nor is loved by others has no good or virtue in him."*
>
> *(Mishkat, Bab-ul-Shafqat)*

The Holy Quran has affirmed:

> *"The believing men and believing women are protecting friends of one another."* *(9: 71)*

The Holy Prophet [S.A.W.] used to cherish deep feelings of affection for all his illustrious companions [R.A.A.] so each one of them entertained the happy thought that the Holy Prophet [S.A.W.] loved him more than any one else.

Hadrat 'Amr b. al-Aas [R.A.A.] reports: "The Holy Prophet [S.A.W.] used to converse with me with such deep attention and sincerity and lavished such great care on me that I came to believe myself to be the best person among my people. And one day I submitted to the Holy Prophet [S.A.W.]: "O Prophet of Allah [S.A.W.]: Who is better - Me or Abu Bakr?" The Holy Prophet [S.A.W.] observed: "Abu Bakr is the better one." I submitted again: "Who is better-Me or 'Umar [R.A.A.]?" The Holy Prophet [S.A.W.] affirmed: "Umar is better." I submitted once more: "O Prophet of Allah [S.A.W.]: Who is better - Me or 'Uthman [R.A.A.]?" The Prophet of Allah [S.A.W.] observed: "Uthman is better than you." I then requested the Holy Prophet [S.A.W.] to explain the real matter in detail whereupon the Holy Prophet [S.A.W.] told me the plain truth. I felt greatly ashamed of myself and wondered what impelled me to ask such questions!

2. Maintain amicable social relations with your friends and try to develop sincere links and continue to cement friendships. Avoid adopting an attitude of annoyance with your friends or keeping aloof from them. When a man lives in the society of other men and has to participate in social matters, it is inevitable that he should suffer different kinds of shocks. Sometimes his sentiments are hurt; at other times his reputation is tarnished; one times his peace is disturbed, other times his usual activities are interfered with. Sometimes things are done against his temper and desires; at other times his patience and endurance are severely tried and at times he has to suffer great financial loss. In other words, he has to face all kinds of trials and tribulations. But when a man suffers these hardships, his heart

is strengthened and he gains in wisdom and experience. Good morals develop in his personality and passing through a natural process of training and purification he makes rapid spiritual and moral progress. He thus acquires the sublime virtues of patience, forbearance, selflessness, affection, sympathy, humanity, respect, loyalty, devotion and cooperation, sincerity and love, generosity and gallantry, kindness and favour to the highest degree and he becomes an instrument of goodness and blessing for the human society. Every man holds him in esteem and values his friendship; each man considers him a source of blessing in his favour. The Holy Prophet [S.A.W.] has observed:

"The Muslim who participates in social matters with other men and shows forbearance if he suffers any pain from them is a far better person than the one who isolates himself from the people and is dismayed at the hardships caused by others." *(Tirmidhi)*

3. Form friendships with the pure and righteous people. In the choice of friends do keep in mind the thought as to how far the people with whom you are forging bonds of amity and friendship can prove useful to you from the viewpoint of religion and morality. There is a famous maxim which says: If you wish to ascertain the moral state of a man, look at the moral condition of his friends." And the Holy Prophet [S.A.W.] has observed: "A man follows the beliefs of his friend. Hence each man should deeply consider the question as to what kind of a man is the person with whom he is striking a friendship."

(Musnad Ahmad, Mishkat)

The observation that a man will follow the beliefs of his friend implies that when a man keeps the company of his friend he will be affected by the sentiments, thoughts, taste and the mental outlook of his friend. He will inevitably begin to judge things to the standard of likes and dislikes adopted by his friend. Hence a man should exercise utmost care in choosing a friend and should establish bonds of affection and friendship with a person whose taste, temperament and activities conform to the tenets of faith and religion. The Holy Prophet [S.A.W.] has enjoined: "Develop a relationship of love and friendship with a believer only and eat and drink in his company only." Furthermore the Holy Prophet [S.A.W.] affirmed:

"Keep company with the believer and only the righteous should eat from the Dastar Khwan of a believer."

Eating together naturally stimulates sentiments of warm affection and love between friends and these links should only be developed with the believers who are Allah-fearing and righteous people always keep away from those who have forgotten Allah and are irresponsible and indifferent in carrying out the commands of religion and are immersed in immorality. The Holy Prophet [S.A.W.] has described the nature of relationship with a good and bad friend in a sublime allegory:

> *"The example of a good or a bad friend is like that of a dealer of musk-perfume and an ironsmith who stokes the furnace. In the company of the perfumer you will certainly derive some benefit i.e. you will buy musk perfume or at least its sweet odour will afford pleasure to you. On the other hand, the furnace of the ironsmith will burn your house or set your clothes ablaze or the foul fumes emitted by the furnace will give you a headache."* *(Bukhari, Muslim)*

The Tradition is recorded by Abu Daud in the following words:

> *"The example of a pious friend is like that of a muskperfumery shop-keeper. If nothing, at least the benefit of sweet smell can be derived from this friend. The example of an evil friend is like that of a furnace. Even if your clothes are not set ablaze, your dress will certainly be blackened by the fumes of the furnace."*

4. Love your friends for the sake of Allah. The favourites of Allah are those who join together on the basis of Allah's religion and struggle shoulder to shoulder with perfect unity of mind and soul to discharge their obligation of establishing the religion of Allah and stand like a solid wall in defence of their creed.

The Holy Quran affirms:

> *"Lo! Allah loveth those who battle for His cause in ranks as if they were a solid structure."* *(61: 4)*

And the Holy Prophet [S.A.W.] has affirmed:

> *Allah will ordain on the Day of Judgement: Where are those people who used to love their fellows for my sake only. I shall place them under My own shadow."*
> *(Muslim)*

The enviable state of dignity in which these people will find themselves on the Day of Judgement has been described by the Holy Prophet [S.A.W.] in these words:

> *"There are some loyal servants of Allah who, though they are not Prophets or martyrs, yet they shall be elevated to such high status by Allah on the Day of Judgement that*

the Prophets and martyrs will envy their good fortune." The illustrious companions [R.A.A.] submitted: "O Prophet of Allah [S.A.W.]! Who will be these fortunate persons?" The Holy Prophet [S.A.W.] affirmed: "These will be the people who loved each other on the basis of the religion of Allah- they were not related to one another by blood, nor had any commercial connection with each other. I swear by Allah, the faces of these people will be glowing with radiance nay they will be the emblems of pure light. When all the people shall be trembling with fear, they shall be free from fear. When all the people will be grief-stricken, they shall know no sorrow."

Afterwards the Holy Prophet [S.A.W.] recited this verse of the Holy Quran:

"Lo! verily the friends of Allah are (those on whom fear (cometh) not, nor do they grieve." (10: 62)

Hadrat Abu-Darda [R.A.A.] states that the Holy Prophet [S.A.W.] observed: "Some people shall be raised from their graves on the Day of Judgement in a state that their faces will be glowing with radiant light. They shall be seated on pulpits made of pearls. Other people shall envy their elevated state. These dignified people, however, will neither include Prophets nor martyrs." The companions submitted: "O Prophet of Allah [S.A.W.]! Who are these people? Tell us their distinguishing qualities." The Holy Prophet [S.A.W.] observed: "These are the people who love each other for the sake of Allah only." (Tibrani)

5. Consider the love of pious people as a source of salvation in the eternal life and a means of winning the favour of Allah. Pray to Allah to bless you with the love of righteous people and beseech His favour to admit you to the ranks of the pious. Hadrat 'Abdullah ibn Masud [R.A.A.] narrates: "A person came to the presence of the Holy Prophet [S.A.W.] and submitted: "O Prophet of Allah [S.A.W.], a person loves a pious man for his piety, yet himself does not emulate the good deeds of this pious man, how shall he be treated in the next world?" The Prophet of Allah [S.A.W.] affirmed: "It does not matter at all. Man shall find himself in the company of that person whom he loves."

(Bukhari)

One night the Holy Prophet [S.A.W.] was blessed with the vision of Allah. Allah said to the Holy Prophet [S.A.W.]: "Ask what thou wilt?" Thereupon the Holy Prophet [S.A.W.] said this prayer:

"Allah! I beseech Thy favour to perform good deeds and avoid evil deeds and I seek the love of the poor and implore Thee to grant me forgiveness and show me Thy Mercy. When you wish to send a calamity over a people, lift me in a state in which I may enjoy Your protection from the calamity. I implore Thy love and I beseech Thee to grant me love of that person who loves Thee and grant me the favour to perform deeds which may serve as means of obtaining nearness to You."

> *Hadrat Muadh ibn Jabal [R.A.A.] states that the Holy Prophet [S.A.W.] affirmed: "Allah ordains that I owe love to those people who develop links of love and friendship among themselves for My sake and assemble at one place to recite My name and meet each other for the love of Me and show good treatment to each other in order to win My favour."* *(Ahmad, Tirmidhi)*

The Holy Prophet [S.A.W.] giving an inspiring description of the meeting of two friends, observed:

> *"A man set out to call on his friend who lived in another habitation. Allah appointed an angel to await him on the way. The angel enquired of him: "Where are you going?" The man made the answer: "I am proceeding to that village to see my brother." The angel further enquired: "Does he owe you a debt of favour which you are now going to receive from him?" The man replied: "No, I am going to meet him only because I love him for the sake of Allah." The angel thereupon told him: "Listen then! God has sent me to convey to you the glad tiding that Allah loves you as much as you love your friend for Allah's sake."* *(Muslim)*

6. Make friendship with those who deserve to be your friends from the viewpoint of Islam and then by your utmost to maintain a loyal and devoted friendly relationship throughout your life. As the choice of pious people as friends is a matter of utmost importance, so equally is the continuous endeavour to maintain and strengthen these bonds of friendship.

The Holy Prophet [S.A.W.] has affirmed: "On the Day of Judgement when there will be no shade anywhere except under the heaven of Allah, only seven types of people will find place under the shade of Allah's heaven. Of the first type will be two persons who were friends of each other for no other purpose except for the sake of Allah. The love of Allah would have forged a common link of friendship between them and they would separate from each other in the same condition.

In other words, their friendship would be based on their common love of Allah and they would endeavour to maintain and cement this bond of friendship throughout their lives. And when one of them would be near the end of his life, their friendship would be intact at that time and they would part in this world as friends. Trust your friends. Behave cheerfully while you are in their company. Avoid being gloomy and making your friends gloomy. Be informal, frank and good natured amidst friends. Do not frown; nor stand on formality. Try to act as an informal companion, a good-natured mate and a cheerful comrade among your friends. Your friends should not feel bored with your presence; rather they should feel happy and alive in your company and should feel drawn towards you.

> *Hadrat 'Abdullah ibn Harith [R.A.A.] relates: "I have never seen a person who smiled more often than the Holy Prophet of Allah [S.A.W.]." (Tirmidhi)*

> *Hadrat Jabir b. Samrah [R.A.A.] narrates: "I was present in over hundred sittings with the Holy Prophet [S.A.W.]. In these sittings the illustrious companions [R.A.A.] used to recite verses and related stories and anecdotes dating back to pagan times. The Holy Prophet [S.A.W.] used to hear all this in silence and even joined in laughter himself at times." (Tirmidhi)*

> *Hadrat Shuraid [R.A.A.] reports that "on one occasion I was sitting behind the Holy Prophet [S.A.W.] on the back of an animal. During the journey I recited a hundred verses of Umayyah ibn as-Salt to the Holy Prophet [S.A.W.]. After each verse the Holy Prophet [S.A.W.] asked me to recite some more verses and I complied." (Tirmidhi)*

> *Similarly, the Holy Prophet [S.A.W.] sometimes himself used to relate stories in his company. Hadrat 'Aishah [R.A.A.] reports: "Once the Holy Prophet [S.A.W.] related a story to the members of his household. A lady submitted: "This strange tale resembles the stories of Khurafa." The Holy Prophet [S.A.W.] asked her: "Do you know the real story of Khurafa?" and then himself narrated the true story of Khurafa in great detail. Similarly, the Holy Prophet [S.A.W.] once related a very interesting story of eleven women to Hadrat 'Aishah [R.A.A.].*

> *Describing the informal conduct and cheerful temper of the illustrious companions [R.A.A.] Hadrat Bakr ibn 'Abdullah [R.A.A.] relates:*

"The illustrious companions [R.A.A.] used to throw the peelings of melon at each other in playful fun, yet when the time came for attack or defence the valour of the companions [R.A.A.] outweighed others in this field also."(Al-Adab-ul-Mufrad)

Hadrat Muhammad b. Ziyad [R.A.A.] reports: "I have seen the times of the righteous forebears. Several families of them lived in a single mansion. On many occasions it so happened that a family received a visit from a guest. At that moment food would be cooking in a pot in the quarter of another family. So, the host who had received a guest would go to the quarter of his neighbour and bring over the food without informing the family. The owners of the pot would then go about searching for their pot of food and would ask the people: "Who has taken away my pot?" The host who had taken the pot would then confess to him. "Brother, I had received a visit from a guest so I took away your pot of food." The owner of the pot of food would thereupon say, "May Allah bless you by increasing the quantity of this food." Muhammad ibn Ziyad [R.A.A.] also states that when these people baked bread, the same thing happened.

(Al-Adab-ul-Mufrad)

A saying of Hadrat 'Ali [R.A.A.] is as follows:

"Let your heart be free at time. Let your mind conceive pleasant notions, for mind also gets weary even as the body is fatigued."

8. Do not be dull and spiritless. Be of good cheer and keep your spirits high. Beware, however, that your cheerful temper and humour does not exceed proper limits. Along with a cheerful temper, fun and recreation, you should never forget to observe sanctity of religion, prestige and self respect, balance and moderation in your activities.

The illustrious companion of the Holy Prophet [S.A.W.], Hadrat Abdul Rahman [R.A.A.] reports that the illustrious companions of the Holy Prophet [S.A.W.] neither were devoid of humour nor talked about in a lifeless manner. They used to recite verses and narrate tales and legends of pagan times in their sittings. But when in any matter something was demanded of them which did not conform to justice and truth, the pupils of their eyes were inflamed with such intense anger as if they were seized with a fit of madness.”

(Al-Adab-ul-Mufrad)

Somebody remarked to the renowned traditionist Hadrat Sufyan b. Uyaina [R.A.A.] that humour is a nuisance. He answered: “No, humour is a Sunnah, but only for the man who knows the suitable occasion on which to practise it and has the ability to indulge in good jokes.” (Sharh Shamail Tirmidhi)

9. If you love someone, you must express your love to that person. Its psychological effect on that person will be that he will develop a sense of nearness to you. The exchange of feelings and passions on both sides will augment love and sincerity to an extraordinary extent. Love then will no longer be merely a feeling confined within the heart but will begin to play a potent role in practical life. Thus people will have an opportunity of taking deep interest in the individual lives of each other and coming nearer to each other.

The Holy Prophet [S.A.W.] has affirmed: “Any person who cherishes in his heart sentiments of love and sincerity for his brother, he should express these sentiments to his brother and tell him clearly that he holds him in love and affection.” *(Abu Daud)*

On one occasion a man passed in front of the Holy Prophet [S.A.W.]. Some people were at that time in attendance on the Prophet [S.A.W.]. One of them submitted; “O Prophet of Allah [S.A.W.]! I love this man for the sake of Allah alone.” On hearing this the Holy Prophet [S.A.W.] enquired from him: “Have you told this to the man?” The man submitted: “No, I have not.” Thereupon the Holy Prophet [S.A.W.] urged the man: “Go and tell the man that you love him for the sake of Allah.” The man stood up at once and approaching the passer-by expressed to him his sentiments. The passer-by made the answer: “May Allah love thee for whose sake you entertain feelings of love for me.”

(Tirmidhi, Abu Daud)

In order to cement the bonds of friendship and to bring friends closer to each other for their mutual benefit, it is essential that you should take proper interest in the individual and private matters of your friends and express to them your special feelings of devotion and concern.

The Holy Prophet [S.A.W.] has observed:

> *"When a man establishes ties of friendship and fraternity with another person he should ascertain from him his name, father's name and particulars about his family as this strengthens the roots of mutual friendship."*
>
> *(Tirmidhi)*

10. Adopt a moderate course in expressing your love and in the conduct of mutual relationship. Do not display such unconcern that your love and connection may appear doubtful, nor permit yourself to go to such extremes of passion that your love and friendship may assume the form of craziness and perchance you may suffer a shock at times (Allah forbid!) Always observe moderation and keep your feelings at balance. Adopt a moderate attitude which may be enduring and long-lasting. Hadrat Aslam [R.A.A.] states that Hadrat 'Umar [R.A.A.] observed: "Your love should not assume the form of madness, nor should enmity excite you to perpetrate torture on other." I submitted: Sir, how should we de so?" Hadrat 'Umar [R.A.A.] observed: "In this manner that if you love someone you start hugging him in a childlike fashion and display other forms of childish behaviour. And if you feel angry with someone, you resolve upon the destruction of his life and property and utter ruination."
   (Al-Adab-ul-Mufrad)

   Hadrat 'Ubaid Kindi [R.A.A.] reports: I heard Hadrat 'Ali [R.A.A.] observing: "Adopt a tender and moderate attitude towards your friend; he might turn your enemy tomorrow. Likewise, follow a tender and moderate course in your conduct towards the enemy; he might become your friend sometime later." (Al-Adab-ul-Mufrad)

11. Be loyal and devoted to your friends. The best form of devotion to your friend is that you should increasingly try to elevate his morals. You should be more concerned with his salvation in the eternal world than his advancement in the material world. The Holy Prophet [S.A.W.] observed: "Religion wholly consists in seeking the welfare of others." The real test of a well-wisher is that one should wish for his friend the same thing that one wishes for his own self, for a man can never be his own illwisher.

The Holy Prophet [S.A.W.] has affirmed:

"I swear by Him Who hath power over my life, no man can be truly pious unless he wishes for his brother the same thing that he wishes for himself."

Laying down six obligations which each Muslim owes to the other, the Holy Prophet [S.A.W.] observed: "And the believer should act as a well-wisher of his brother both in his presence and absence." Furthermore, the Holy Prophet [S.A.W.] affirmed:

> *"Without doubt Allah has ordained the ordeal of fire for that man and He has forbidden his entry into Paradise who forfeits the right of a brother Muslim after having sworn to fulfil his obligation." Someone from among the illustrious companions [R.A.A.] submitted: "What if that obligation relates to a very minor thing?" The Holy Prophet [S.A.W.] affirmed: "Yes, even if he owes an ordinary branch of the 'Pelu' tree to another Muslim."*

12. Share the grief and sorrow of your friends. Likewise, participate actively in their joyous occasions. The purpose of your sharing their grief should be to alleviate their suffering and the aim of your participation in their festivities ought to be to enhance their joy. Every friend rightly expects from his sincere associates that they will stand by him in times of trial and will never desert him in the hour of need. Similarly, he anticipates that his friends will add to his felicity by increasing the grace of his festive parties with their presence and active participation.

The Holy Prophet [S.A.W.] has observed:

> *"The Muslim fraternity is like a mansion. Even as each brick supports and cements the other brick, so does a Muslim act as a supporter and a source of strength for the other Muslim." So saying the Holy Prophet [S.A.W.] interlocked the fingers of his both hands and thus explained the mutual link and close connection that ought to subsist among the Muslim community.*
>
> *(Bukhari, Muslim)*

The Holy Prophet [S.A.W.] enjoined:

> *"In their sense of mutual love and affection and perception of common distress, you will find Muslims as one body; if one organ of this body is afflicted, the whole body is affected by fever and sleeplessness."*
>
> *(Bukhari, Muslim)*

13. Meet your friends in a cheerful, amicable, joyous and sincere manner. Greet them warmly and observe proper etiquettes in receiving them. Avoid showing an indifferent, cold and unconcerned behaviour. These evils create a rift in the hearts.

Say words of praise and thanks and joy and satisfaction during meetings with your friends. Abstain from talk which reveals sorrow, grief and low spirits. Behave in such a manner during meetings with your friends that they should be thrilled with feelings of joy and liveliness. Do not greet them with such a gloomy face that they may feel crestfallen and may come to regard your fellowship as intclerable nuisance.

The Holy Prophet. [S.A.W.] has affirmed:

"Do not look upon any pious deed as insignificant, may it be greeting your brother with a cheerful heart."
(Muslim)

On another occasion, the Holy Prophet [S.A.W.] observed: "Your smile on seeing a brother is also an act of sacrifice on your part." *(Tirmidhi)*

Tenderness, politeness and civility generate feelings of affection and love in the heart and it is on the basis of these virtues that a good society can be formed.

The Holy Prophet [S.A.W.] observes:

"I tell you the distinguishing marks of a person for whom the fire of Hell has been made unlawful and who is a forbidden person for the Hell Fire to consume: He is a man who bears a sweet temper, tender heart and is soft-spoken." *(Tirmidhi)*

The illustrious companions [R.A.A.] relate that the Holy Prophet [S.A.W.] used to be attentive with his whole posture towards the person with whom he was talking and listened to the talk in rapt attention. Once the Holy Prophet [S.A.W.] was sitting in the mosque. A man paid a call and the Holy Prophet [S.A.W.] shifted his posture and shrank a little. The man submitted: "O Prophet of Allah [S.A.W.]! there is ample room here." The Holy Prophet [S.A.W.] observed:

"A Muslim owes it to his brother that on seeing him, he should move for him a little." *(Baihaqi)*

Describing the virtues of the believers, the Holy Quran affirms:

"They are always very gentle to the believers."

The Holy Prophet [S.A.W.] has elucidated the same fact in the following words:

"The believers are forbearing and soft-hearted like a camel who is tied with a nose band; the camel is drawn

to whichever direction his nose-band is tugged and if he is made to sit on a stone, he complies." *(Tirmidhi)*

14. Whenever you differ among yourselves on any matter resolve it at once. Always take the initiative to seek forgiveness and to admit your fault.

Hadrat Abu Darda [R.A.A.] reports: "Once there was an exchange of hot words between Hadrat Abu Bakr and Hadrat 'Umar [R.A.A.]. Hadrat Abu Bakr [R.A.A.] felt it hard and went to the Holy Prophet [S.A.W.] in a very sad and sorry mood and submitted: "O Prophet of Allah [S.A.W.]! A difference arose between 'Umar and myself whereupon I flew into rage and we exchanged some bitter words. Later, I felt greatly ashamed of myself and solicited 'Umar [R.A.A.] to forgive me. But, O Prophet of Allah [S.A.W.]! 'Umar was not reconciled and declined to forgive me. I am feeling very much upset and uneasy so have I come to you.

The Holy Prophet [S.A.W.] observed: "Allah will grant you forgiveness and salvation". Meanwhile Hadrat 'Umar [R.A.A.] also realised his fault and rushed to Hadrat Abu Bakr's [R.A.A.] house. He was informed that Abu Bakr [R.A.A.] has gone to the presence of the Holy Prophet [S.A.W.]. Whereupon 'Umar [R.A.A.] also hurried to the presence of the Holy Prophet [S.A.W.]. Signs of anger and displeasure appeared on the countenance of the Holy Prophet [S.A.W.] on seeing Hadrat Umar. Noting the displeasure against Hadrat 'Umar, Hadrat Abu Bakr [R.A.A.] felt deeply perturbed. He fell on his knees and submitted to the Holy Prophet [S.A.W.] in great humility "O Prophet of Allah [S.A.W.]! 'Umar is not at fault. All blame rests on me. I committed the fault. It was I 'who spoke harshly to him." Thereupon the Holy Prophet [S.A.W.] observed: "Allah sent me as His Prophet among you and when in the early days you refuted me, it was Abu Bakr who affirmed his faith in me and stood by me at the cost of his life and property. Would you now aggrieve my companion?"

Do not lose time in making peace. The longer the delay in resolving quarrels, the deeper grow the roots of contention, and the wider grows the gulf of separation between the hearts.

The following precept of Hadrat 'Isa [A.S.] contained in the Bible is intensely heart-warming:

> *"So if you are engaged in offering sacrifice at the altar and you suddenly recall to mind that your brother has some complaint against you, leave your offering at the altar and return at once to your brother to make peace*

with him. Then go back to the altar and make your offering."

The Holy Prophet [S.A.W.] has observed:

"The deeds of the people are presented to Allah on every Monday and Thursday and every believer is granted pardon except the one who nurses a grudge against any of his believing brothers. Allah ordains: "Leave them so that they may resolve their quarrel."

Who knows whether the next moment will bring death or life! Who knows whether he will witness the next Monday or Thursday! Why and on what hope do you delay in purifying your heart and settling the complaints of your friends? Is any sensible person who believes in the Day of Judgement ready to present himself with an impure, dark and gruesome heart before the Almighty Allah?

Beware also that if your friend admits his fault and requests pardon, you should accept his excuse and forgive him from the core of your heart.

The Holy Prophet [S.A.W.] has affirmed:

"The Muslim who declines to accept the confession of his fault and a request for forgiveness from his brother Muslim is held guilty of a sin as grave as the sin of cruelty and oppression committed by an Octroi man who extorts an illegal cess."

15. Restrain your tongue even if friends talk or behave in a manner which is offensive to your temper or taste. Do not utter harsh or offensive speech in retaliation. Instead let the matter pass with tact and gentle conduct.

The Holy Prophet [S.A.W.] observed:

"Hadrat Moosa [A.S.] submitted to Allah: My Allah: 'Which one is the dearest to you among your creatures?' Allah affirmed: 'That one who hath the power to take revenge' yet forgives." *(Mishkat)*

In addition to this, the Holy Prophet [S.A.W.] observed:

"The heaviest thing put in the balance of a believer on the Day of Judgement will be his politeness. Allah looks upon that person with intense wrath who utters indecent and foul speech."

Hadrat 'Abdullah ibn Mubarak [R.A.A.] had defined the virtue of politeness in three ways:

ii(i) A person should meet others with a bright, smiling face.

i(ii) A man should spend his wealth on the destitute and needy persons.

(iii) A person should not cause harm to any one.

Hadrat 'Aishah [R.A.A.] reports: "The Holy Prophet [S.A.W.] observed: "The worst man in the eyes of Allah on the Day of Judgement will be the one whom the people avoid on account of his indecent and foul speech." (Bukhari, Muslim)

16. Do not shirk your duty to reform your friends and train them in righteousness. Do not let vanity and pride take root in the character of your friends which is the greatest hurdle in their reformation and moral uplift. Always try to persuade your friends to realise their omissions and errors and develop moral courage to confess their faults. They should always be mindful of the fact that failure to realise one's shortcomings and insistence upon one's faultlessness mars one's spiritual development.

As a matter of fact it is very easy to show off false humility, to call oneself as insignificant and to display submissiveness in style and manners, but it is extremely difficult to sustain an injury to your feelings, to listen to and admit your shortcomings with a cool mind and to tolerate the criticism directed by your friends against your personal faults. Yet true friends are those who keep an enlightened eye on the conduct of their friends and are always alert and alive to the task of protecting each other from the evils of vanity and pride by sincere counsel and practical example.

The Holy Prophet [S.A.W.] affirms:

ii(i) The passion which is allowed to prevail upon one's good sense.

i(ii) The greed and lust which is allowed to become the guiding principle of one's life.

(iii) And vanity-the most dangerous of the three ills." (Baihaqi, Muslim)

Criticism and accountability are lancets which purge the moral existence of man from all undesirable elements. They augment moral strength and infuse new life into the individual and the society. To take offense, to get irritated and to consider oneself as above the criticism and accountability of friends is detrimental to one's moral being as well as to evade healthy and constructive criticism of one's friends to check and protect them from moral degradation. Do feel uneasy if you find hideous faults and shortcomings in your friends and take wise measures to eliminate those blemishes on the characters of your friends. Similarly, give a chance with genuine humility and urge to your friends that they should expose to you your own foibles and faults. When your friends discharge this unpleasant duty towards you, do not be vainglorious, but welcome their criticism with large heartedness, cheerfully and with a grateful heart. Express your gratitude to them for their sincerity and kindness. The Holy Prophet [S.A.W.] has described this exemplary friendship in a most eloquent allegory.

> *"Each one of you serves as a mirror to his brother. Hence if your see any fault in your brother, eliminate it."*
>
> *(Tirmidhi)*

There are five illuminating points in this allegory which can make your friendship exemplary in genuine terms:

(i) The mirror reflects the spots and stains on your person when you stand before it with the intention of locating these spots and stains. When you stand aside, the mirror ceases to reflect these blemishes. Similarly, you should expose the foibles of your friend only if he willingly presents himself before you for criticism and chastisement with an open mind. At the same time, make it sure that his mind is receptive to your criticism and that his heart is eager to accept suggestions for the correction of his faults. In the absence of these conditions, you should keep silent and put off the matter wisely for a later occasion. In the absence of your friend especially you should exercise the utmost care not to utter a single word pointing to any shortcoming of your friend, for this would be counted as back-biting and backbiting divides the hearts rather than uniting them.

(ii) The mirror reflects very honestly all such spots or stains which are really present on the face; it neither hides their number nor makes an addition to them. Furthermore, the mirror reflects only those deformities which are outwards and apparent; it does not expose the hidden blemishes, neither probes inward, nor presents an illusory picture of your demerits.

Likewise, you should also present a genuine and true picture of the inadequacies and faults of your friends. Moved by sentiments of undue politeness and flattery you should neither suppress the exposure of a few foibles of your friends nor exaggerate their dimensions or add to their number in the heat of your passionate oratory and declamation. Moreover, point out only those faults of your friends which are exposed in the normal conduct of life. Do not display curiosity or an eagerness to spy into the secrets of others. To expose the secret faults of your friends is no moral service, in fact it is a perilous and immoral act on your part.

The Holy Prophet [S.A.W.] once ascended the pulpit and warned the congregation in a very high tone of his holy voice:

> *"Do not pry into the vices of Muslims. Allah exposes the hidden vices of a person who seeks to expose the faults of his brother Muslims; and when Allah decides to expose the faults of someone, He inevitably reduces the man to disgrace, even if such a man hides himself in the inner recesses of his home."* *(Tirmidhi)*

(iii) The mirror discharges its duty unaffected by any sort of motives. Any one who faces the mirror, the mirror shows him his true image without any reservations. The mirror nurses no grudge or vendetta against anyone, nor wreaks vengeance on anybody. You should also chastise your friends unaffected by personal motives, feelings of vendetta grudge, pique, or dishonesty. Your only motive in criticising your friends should be to enable him to reform himself, as a man adorns himself by eliminating spots and stains from his person by locating them through their reflection in the mirror.

(iv) No one feels annoyed at seeing his true image in the mirror, nor commits the blunder of breaking up the mirror in a fit of rage. Instead most people on looking into the mirror begin to adorn themselves by removing the apparent defects on their persons and in fact realising the valuable services of the mirror in this regard are thankful to it in their hearts. They are fully conscious of the fact that the mirror has proved extremely helpful to them in the task of embellishing their persons. They believe that the mirror has done its natural duty remarkably and they put it away carefully for use at another time. Similarly when someone presents your true picture before you in his own words, do not retaliate in annoyance. Instead express your gratitude to him for his sincere performance of the obligation of friendship. Feel grateful to him in your heart also, apart from offering him thanks in words and set about reforming yourself at once. Realising the value and greatness of your friends with an open mind and with a sense of extreme gratitude, request your friend to continue to show you the favour of his valuable suggestions.

(v) The final point is that "every Muslim selves as a mirror unto his brother Muslim." A brother is an emblem of sincerity and love for his brother. A brother is loyal, devoted, sympathetic a well-wisher and a helper in grief to his brother. He feels restless on seeing his brother in trouble and is overjoyed at his happiness. Hence the criticism of a brother and a friend if motivated by feelings of extreme sincerity, devotion, sympathy and love. It will be characterised by a desire for the welfare and extreme concern for the best interests of his friend. Every word of this friendly criticism will reflect the spirit of reformation. Such a form of criticism may be rightly expected to unite the hearts and correct the wrongs.

17. Exchange gifts in order to express your feelings of sincerity and love for your friends and to deepen the relationship of love and affection. Mutual exchange of gifts unites the hearts and cements the bonds of love. The Holy Prophet [S.A.W.] has observed:

"Exchange gifts with each other. This will generate mutual feelings of love and eliminate feelings of animosity and estrangement from your hearts."

(Mishkat)

The Holy Prophet [S.A.W.] himself often used to send gifts to his illustrious Companions [R.A.A.]. The Prophet's Companions [R.A.A.] also frequently exchange presents and gifts among themselves. In the matter of exchanging gifts always keep within your means. Whatever the status of the receiver, do not think that your gift should necessarily be a costly one. Give according to your means and whatever is easily available. The real worth of your gift depends on your sincerity and the nature and depth of feelings with which you have presented the gift. It is the feelings of sincerity and deep passions of love and devotion which unite the hearts and the cost or value of the gift is insignificant in this regard. Do not regard the gift of your friend as insignificant, however cheap in cost it may be. Instead put a high value on the feelings of love and sincerity reflected by the gift of your friend.

The Holy Prophet [S.A.W.] observed:

"Even if someone offers me the leg of a goat as a gift, I shall accept it and if someone invites me to a dinner

consisting of a cooked leg of goat, I shall certainly join the feast." *(Tirmidhi)*

You must answer a gift with a gift. The Holy Prophet [S.A.W.] used to observe this rule strictly. The Holy Prophet's [S.A.W.] favourite gift was perfume. You should also consider the present of a perfume as a propitious gift. In the present-day circumstances, the presentation of a book can also be regarded as a propitious gift. In this connection, you should hold common feasts at times. Invite your friends to dinner at home. When friends invite you to functions at their homes, make it a point to join their parties. Mutual entertainment promotes feelings of love and affection, and bonds of fraternity are further cemented. However, on these occasions instead of observing excessive formalities and laying out lavish quantities of food and drink, you should put more emphasis on displaying and augmenting the feelings of love and sincerity.

18. Look after your friends. Stand by them in their hour of need, even at the cost of your own life and property. Asbahani relates in a tradition: "A person came to Hadrat 'Abdullah b. 'Umar [R.A.A.] and asked: Which one is the most favourite of Allah among the people?" Hadrat 'Abdullah b. 'Umar [R.A.A.] answered: "The most favourite person of Allah among the people is he who affords the greatest benefit to his fellow men. The deed which wins the greatest favour of Allah is that you should make a Muslim happy in such manner that you should alleviate his suffering or hardship or make a provision of food to satisfy his hunger.

    I would go out with a brother Muslim in order to help him in his need rather than sit in the mosque of the Holy Prophet [S.A.W.] and perform Itikaf. Allah shall fill the heart of that man with His favour on Doomsday who controlled his rage at a time when he could give vent to his fury, if he so wished. And the person who accompanied his brother in order to help satisfy his need and actually provided for his need shall be rewarded with the favour of Allah on Doomsday when the other people will be staggering, this person will walk with a firm gait."

The Holy Prophet [S.A.W.] has affirmed:

"Any man who provides for the need of his brother, Allah shall always keep fulfilling the need of that man. And any person who alleviates some hardship of a Muslim, Allah on Doomsday shall remove one of his hardships out of the many hardships of that day."

(Bukhari, Muslim)

The Holy Prophet [S.A.W.] also affirmed:

> *"Allah continues to help a man as long as he continues to help his brother."* (Tirmidhi)

Hadrat 'Abdullah b. 'Abbas [R.A.A.] has reported that the Holy Prophet [S.A.W.] observed:

> *"The reward and blessing for the act of providing for the need of a brother Muslim exceeds the reward and blessing for performing an I'tikaf for a period of ten years."* (Tibrani)

Hadrat Anas [R.A.A.] states that the Holy Prophet of Allah [S.A.W.] observed:

> *"A Muslim who conveys a message of felicity and happiness to a brother Muslim and thus affords him happiness, Allah shall, on Doomsday, make this messenger happy."* (Tibrani)

19. Be a trustworthy confident. If a friend, relying on your good faith, confides his secret to you, you should safeguard his secret. Do not betray the confidence of your friend. Make your heart an iron vault for the safe keeping of secrets, so that friends may take counsel with you without hesitation and also in order that you may proffer good advice to your friends and extend your full cooperation to them.

Hadrat 'Umar [R.A.A.] narrates:

> *"When Hafsa [R.A.A.] was widowed, I called on 'Uthman [R.A.A.] and said to him: "If you are agreeable I should give Hafsa in marriage to your." 'Uthman [R.A.A.] answered: "I shall think over the matter." I waited for his message for many nights. Later 'Uthman [R.A.A.] met me and said: "I have no intention of marrying at the moment." I then went to see Abu Bakr [R.A.A.] and proposed: "If you wish you may take Hafsa [R.A.A.] as your wife." Abu Bakr [R.A.A.] kept silent and make no answer. I was offended at the silence of Abu Bakr. I was more deeply offended with him than even at the response of 'Uthman [R.A.A.]. Many days passed and one day the Holy Prophet [S.A.W.] sent me a proposal to marry Hafsa [R.A.A.]. I accepted the proposal and gave Hafsa [R.A.A.] in marriage to the Holy Prophet [S.A.W.]. Later one day Abu Bakr [R.A.A.] met me and said: "You talked to me concerning Hafsa [R.A.A.] and I kept silent. My response*

might have caused you some pain." I replied: "Yes, I did feel sore at your silence." Abu Bakr [R.A.A.] thereupon told me: "I knew that the Holy Prophet [S.A.W.] himself intended to send a proposal for marriage with Hafsa [R.A.A.]. The Holy Prophet [S.A.W.] had confided this secret to me and I did not intend to reveal it. If the Holy Prophet [S.A.W.] had not expressed his intention concerning Hafsa [R.A.A.], I would certainly have accepted your proposal." *(Bukhari)*

Hadrat Anas [R.A.A.] relates: "One day I was playing with boys of my age when the Holy Prophet [S.A.W.] arrived and blessed us with 'salam' [peace be on you]. The Holy Prophet [S.A.W.] told me his need and sent me on some errand. The errand took rather a long while. When it was over and I reached home late my mother enquired: "Where have you been for so long?" I answered: "The Holy Prophet [S.A.W.] had sent me on an errand." She asked: "What for?" I said: "It is a secret matter." Thereupon my mother advised me: "Look, do not reveal the secret of the Holy Prophet [S.A.W.] to anyone."

(Muslim)

20. Your moral conduct towards the people should be characterised by a cosmopolitan, vast, comprehensive, and tolerant outlook, so that people of every taste and temper, thought and ideal may feel an uncommon sense of attraction towards you. Keeping in view the particular taste, viewpoint and temperament of every one, behave towards each person so wisely that no one's feelings are hurt. Do not adopt the unwise attitude of measuring everyone according to your own particular standard of propriety, nor make an absurd and unsuccessful attempt to mould every one according to your own taste and temperament. The variety of tastes and temperaments is a beauty of Nature. Do not deform the beauty. Keep your relations according to the nature of acquaintance and the temperament of your friends, give them respect and importance accordingly and keep them attached in bonds of friendship with you by means of your own liberal behaviour and good character.

An all-round genius as the Holy Prophet [S.A.W.] was, men of all tastes and temperaments found consolation and contentment in his august company. Nobody felt any uneasiness due to the magnanimous toleration and extraordinary charitable nature of the Holy Prophet [S.A.W.]. The august company of the Holy Prophet

[S.A.W.] included embodiments of toleration and affection like Abu Bakr [R.A.A.] and men of iron nature and courage like 'Umar Farooq [R.A.A.], pacifists who trembled at the prospect of war like Hassan b. Thabit [R.A.A.] as well as the gallant victor of Khybar Hadrat 'Ali [R.A.A.]. There was Abu dhar Ghifari [R.A.A.] a saintly, gloomy figure as well as 'Abdul Rahman b. 'Auf [R.A.A.], sumptuously rich and elegant in person. It was by virtue of the cosmopolitan outlook, excellent conduct, deep love for humanity and the highest degree of statesmanship of the Holy Prophet [S.A.W.] that men of divergent personalities were extremely devoted to the person of the Holy Prophet [S.A.W.] and the Prophet of Allah [S.A.W.] himself treated everyone of them with such deep .consideration that every one thought himself the most favourite friend of the Holy Prophet [S.A.W.].

Again, it was owing to this cosmopolitan moral view-point, statesmanship, wisdom and unique selflessness that the Holy Prophet [S.A.W.] formed that matchless group of illustrious companions [R.A.A.], who despite their variegated natures and temperaments, were welded together in a unique combination characterised by uncommon unity, cooperation and enviably deep mutual love and affection. The mankind as a whole may rightly consider this era as the essence and substance of its long existence so far.

Your friendships, in fact, can only be successful and longlasting when your collective attitudes and behaviour reflect rationality, liberalism, patience and tolerance, forbearance and magnanimity, forgiveness and selflessness, mutual understanding and humility, submissiveness, mutual accommodation of each other's sentiments and due consideration of each other's interests in every day life. You may judge from the following few references from the life of the Holy Prophet [S.A.W.] how considerate, magnanimous, liberal, forbearing and tolerant was the Prophet of Allah [S.A.W.] towards the natural needs, feelings and frailties of human beings:

> *"I come to offer prayer and wish to prolong the prayers. But I hear some infant crying on the woman's side and I shorten my prayers, for I cannot afford to put the mother of the child to inconvenience by prolonging the prayers." (Bukhari)*

Hadrat Malik bin al Huwarith states:

> *"Some of us young men of the same age group paid a visit to the Holy Prophet [S.A.W.] in order to learn religion from him. We stayed with the Holy Prophet [S.A.W.] for twenty days. The Holy Prophet was very kind*

> *and tender in his dealings. At the end of our twenty days' stay, the Holy Prophet [S.A.W.] felt that we were anxious to return home. The Prophet of Allah [S.A.W.] enquired from us: "Tell me about the people you have left behind at home." we related to him [S.A.W.] the affairs of our households in detail. Whereupon the Holy Prophet [S.A.W.] commanded us: "Go back to your wives and children. While living among them teach them everything you have learnt here and urge them to observe piety. Tell them the proper timings for offering prayers. When the time for prayer comes, one of you should call the people for prayers by saying Adaan and he who excels in knowledge and good morals among all of you, should act as leader (Imam) in the prayer."*
>
> *(Bukhari, Muslim)*

Hadrat Muawiyyah b. Hakam Sulami [R.A.A.] relates one of his own experiences as follows:

> *"I was saying prayers behind the Holy Prophet [S.A.W.] when a man sneezed. Forgetting that I was saying my prayers I spontaneously replied* Yarhamukallah *whereupon the people started rebuking me. I said to them: "May Allah protect you, why do you stare at me?" I felt, however, that the people wanted me to observe silence, so I kept mum. When the Holy Prophet [S.A.W.] had finished the prayers-May my father and mother be sacrificed for him, for never had I seen nor saw afterwards anyone who was a better teacher and guide than the Holy Prophet [S.A.W.] he did not reproach me, neither beat me, nor rebuked me. He [S.A.W.] only observed: "This is worship and it is not proper to talk in the prayer. Prayer is meant to announce the purity of Allah, to acknowledge His Greatness and to recite the Quran."* *(Muslim)*

21. Be very much particular in prayers. Pray for your friends and request them to remember you in their prayers. Pray for your friends in their presence as well as in their absence. Think of your friends and pray for them by name in their absence. Hadrat 'Umar [R.A.A.] reports: "I requested leave of the Holy Prophet [S.A.W.] to perform 'Umrah. Granting the leave, the Holy Prophet [S.A.W.] observed: "O My brother, do not forget us in your prayers." Hadrat 'Umar [R.A.A.] said: "I felt so happy on

hearing this observation of the Holy Prophet [S.A.W.] that I would not have felt happier had I been offered the whole world."

The Holy Prophet [S.A.W.] has affirmed:

> *"When a Muslim says a prayer for his brother Muslim in absentia, Allah accepts his prayer and appoints one of his angels on the Muslim who is offering the prayer so that when this Muslim prays for his brother Muslim the angel says: "Amen, you shall receive from Allah for yourself too what you are asking for you brother."*
>
> *(Muslim)*

Beseech Allah in your sincere prayers: "Allah, clear our hearts of all grudge, vendetta, enemity and misunderstanding and tie us with bonds of sincerity and love. Make our relationships pleasant by means of mutual cooperation and love." Say this prayer of the Holy Quran also:

> *"Our Allah! Forgive us and our brethren who were before us in the faith, and place not in our hearts any rancour towards those who believe. Our Allah; Thou art full of pity, Merciful."* *(59.' 10)*

Role of the Host

1. Express your joy and love on the arrival of a guest. Greet him with a cheerful heart. Welcome him with open arms and show him every mark of respect and honour. Do not display stinginess, indifference, cold attitude or resentment.

The Holy Prophet [S.A.W.] has observed:

> *"The people who believe in Allah and the Day of Judgement should show hospitality to their guests."*
> *(Bukhari, Muslim)*

Hospitality includes all those matters which are essential for showing due respect and honour to the guest and to make provisions for his comfort, peace, happiness and fulfilment of his needs. Showing respect to your guest means treating your guest with politeness and in good cheer; to entertain him with pleasant conversation, to make provisions for his rest and relaxation; to introduce him to your other respectable friends; to look after his needs, to arrange provisions of food and drink for him with a liberal and generous mind and to give personal service and attention to all the requirements of your friend.

"Whenever respectable guests paid a visit to him, the Holy Prophet [S.A.W.] used to attend to their hospitality himself."

"Whenever the Holy Prophet [S.A.W.] served meals to his guest he [S.A.W.] used to prompt the guest repeatedly to partake more of the food. When the guest had taken to his fill and expressed inability to eat more, it was then that the Holy Prophet [S.A.W.] ceased urging him to take more.

2. When a guest arrives, say Salam [peace be on you] to him and pray for him. Then enquire about his health.

The Holy Quran affirms:

> *"Hath the story of Ibrahim's honoured guests reached thee (O Muhammad) when they came in unto him and said: "Salam" Hadrat Ibrahim answered salam."*
> *(51: 24-25)*

3. Show generous hospitality to your guests and offer them the best that is readily available. On arrival of his guests, Hadrat Ibrahim [A.S.] at once got busy in making arrangements for their dinner. He [A.S.] had a fat calf in his home, which he slaughtered and got it roasted for his guests.

> *"Then he went apart unto his house folk and brought a fatted calf roasted for the guests; and presented it before them."* *(51: 26, 27)*

Faragha ila ahlihi also bears the meaning that Hadrat Ibrahim [A.S.] went inside his home to make arrangements for the feast without informing any one lest the guests should feel informal or forbid preparation of food for them for fear of causing inconvenience to the host. In that case, it would not be possible for the host to entertain his guests.

Hadrat Abu Shariah, in his report of the manner in which the Holy Prophet [S.A.W.] has urged the Muslims to show hospitality to their guests, states as follows:

> *"I saw with my two eyes and heard with mine two ears when the Holy Prophet [S.A.W.] was delivering this counsel: "The people who believe in Allah and Day of Judgement should show hospitality to their guests. The first night and first day of his stay is the prized day and night for you."* *(Bukhari, Muslim)*

To attribute 'Inam' (reward) to the first night and first day of the guest's stay implies that as the munificent feels spiritual contentment on giving away (reward) with deep sentiments of joy and love, similar behaviour should be displayed by the host towards the guest on the first night and first day of his stay with him. Likewise as the beneficiary receives the (reward) with joy and happiness deeming it as his rightful due and appreciates the munificence of his benefactor, a similar attitude should be adopted by the guest towards his host during the first night and first day of his stay with him. The guest should not stand on formality and ought to accept the offerings of the host with sentiments of joy and close fellowship considering the host's hospitality towards him as his rightful due.

4. As soon as the guest arrives, think first of his natural human needs. Make discreet enquiries as to whether he wishes to use the toilet or bathroom. Arrange a bath for him, if it is required. Even though it may be a late hour for meals, ask your guest if he wants to eat or drink in such a discreet manner that he should not decline as a matter of formality. Show your guest his bedroom where he is to stay.
5. Do not pester your guest with your constant company. Similarly do not keep him awake late in the night talking or discussing matters. Allow him sufficient time to rest so that he may not feel inconvenient. When the guests paid a visit to him, Hadrat Ibrahim [A.S.] left them alone for a while and went inside his home to prepare a feast for the guests.
6. Do feel pleasure when the guests are dining with you. Do not show any signs of stinginess, annoyance or weariness. The guest is not a burden, but a source of blessing, grace and Divine favour. Whomsoever Allah sends to you as a guest, He sends provisions for the guest also. The guest eats with you whatever was decreed for him; he does not eat your share of the Divine bounty. The visit of a guest adds to your honour and dignity.
7. Protect the honour and dignity of your guest and consider his honour and dignity as vital as your own. In case any one poses a threat to the honour of your guest, you should consider it a challenge to your own honour and conscience.

The Holy Quran affirms that when the people of the habitation assaulted the guests of Hadrat Lut [A.S.] with evil intentions, Hadrat Lut [A.S.] rose up in their defence and declared: "These people are my guests. Do not disgrace me by treating them offensively. I hold their disgrace as an offence against my own person."

"He said:

> *Lo! they are my guests. Affront me not! And fear Allah and shame me not."* *(22: 68-9)*

8. Observe all the etiquettes of hospitality with deep enthusiasm and eagerness for three days. The guest has a right over you to

entertain him for three days and a believer should always be extremely generous in discharging their obligations. On the first day the guest should be shown special hospitality. Hence make sumptuous arrangements for the entertainment of your guest. On the subsequent two days it does not matter if that level of sumptuous entertainment cannot be maintained. The Holy Prophet [S.A.W.] has observed:

"And hospitality is ordained for three days. Later whatever entertainment the host offers to his guest is a charity on his part." (Bukhari, Muslim)

9. Consider rendering service to the guest as your moral duty. Do not consign your guest to the care of your servants and children. Instead devote yourself personally to the service of your guest. The Holy Prophet [S.A.W.] used to look after the entertainment of the guests personally. When Hadrat Imam Shafii [R.T.A.] paid a visit to Imam Malik [R.T.A.] he was received with every mark of honour and respect due to a guest and was lodged in his bedroom to sleep for the night. At dawn Imam Shafi heard a knock on the door and a voice said in affectionate tones: "May Allah show you His Mercy! Arise, the hour of prayer has come." Imam Shafi at once got up and found Imam Malik standing on the door with a vessel full of water in his hand. At this, Imam Shafi [R.T.A.] felt some embarrassment, noticing which Imam Malik [R.T.A.] remarked in deep affection "Never mind, brother, it is my obligation to look after the guests."
10. Having lodged the guest, tell him the location of the toilet; provide him with a vessel of water; point out the direction of the Qiblah, and supply him with a prayer-mat. The servant of Imam Malik [R.T.A.], having lodged Imam Shafi [R.T.A.] in a room submitted to him: "Hadrat! This is the direction of the Qiblah; the vessel of water is placed here and the toilet is located this way."
11. At dinner time wash your hands first and reach the table before your guests wash their hands. When Imam Malik [R.T.A.] observed this etiquette, Imam Shafi [R.T.A.] asked him the significance of this gesture. Thereupon Imam Malik [R.T.A.] observed, "Before starting the meal the host should wash his hands first and reach the dining place before his guests in order to greet them at the meal. At the end of the meal, however, it is the guests whose hands should be washed first and the host should wash his hands last of all lest some more guests should drop in before the host gets up from the dinning place."

12. The quantity of food and the number of plates should be somewhat in excess of the actual number of guests. It is possible that someone might turn up during the meal. In that case, the host will have to get up and take the extra trouble of making further arrangements. If the provisions and plates are already there the new guest will be saved from embarrassment and will rather feel happy and honoured.
13. Show selflessness and sacrifice in the case of a guest. Provide comfort to him at the cost of your won convenience.

One day a person came to the Holy Prophet [S.A.W.] and submitted: "O Prophet of Allah [S.A.W.]! I am in a terrible agony of hunger." The Holy Prophet [S.A.W.] sent word to one of his holy wives [R.A.A.]: "Send whatever food is available," The answer he [S.A.W.] received was: "In the name of Allah Who has sent you as His Apostle, there is nothing except water available here." The Holy Prophet [S.A.W.] thereupon sent the same message to a second wife and received the same reply. The Holy Prophet [S.A.W.] made enquiries from each of his wives, but answer was invariably the same. The Holy Prophet [S.A.W.] then turned towards his companions [R.A.A.] and observed; "Who among you will accept this man as his guest for tonight?" A companion [R.A.A.] from among the Ansar submitted: "O Prophet of Allah [S.A.W.], I accept this man as my guest."

> *The Ansari [R.A.A.] thereupon took the guest to his house and told his wife: "I have brought a guest from the Holy Prophet [S.A.W.] with me. Show him some hospitality." The wife answered: "I have just enough food for children and no more." The illustrious companion said: "Put the children to sleep by diverting their attention to some thing else and when you serve the meal before the guest, extinguish the lamp on some pretext and sit down beside the guest so that he may feel we are sharing the meal with him." In this manner, the guest ate to his fill, but the hosts passed the night on an empty stomach. Next morning when this illustrious companion [R.A.A.] reached to the presence of the Holy Prophet [S.A.W.], the Prophet [S.A.W.] on beholding him observed: The goodness both of you displayed towards your guest has won you the immense pleasure of Allah."*
>
> *(Bukhari, Muslim)*

14. Even if your guest has treated you with bad manners and given you a cold shoulder on some occasion in the past, behave towards him with generosity, liberality and magnanimity.

Hadrat Abul Ahwas Jashmi [R.A.A.] relates about his father that once he submitted to the Holy Prophet [S.A.W.]: "If I come across someone and he does not perform his duty of hospitality and entertainment towards me and later if he happens to meet me, is it obligatory upon me to show him hospitality? Or should I act towards him in the same impolite and indifferent manner? The Prophet [S.A.W.] observed: "No, you should perform your obligation of hospitality towards him in any case." *(Mishkat)*

15. Make a request to your guest to offer a prayer invoking the favour and grace of Allah on you, especially when the guest is a man of piety, a devotee of religion and a person of excellent faith. Hadrat 'Abdullah b. Busr [R.A.A.] reports: "The Holy Prophet [S.A.W.] once stayed as a guest with my father. We presented to him a dish of 'Harith'. The Holy Prophet [S.A.W.] ate some of it. Afterwards we offered some dates. The Holy Prophet [S.A.W.] ate the dates and taking the kernels between the two forefingers of his hand, cast them away. Finally we presented a drink. He [S.A.W.] took some draughts of it and passed it on to the next person sitting on his right. When the Holy Prophet [S.A.W.] got up to leave, my father took hold of the bridle of his horse and submitted: "O Prophet of Allah [S.A.W.]! Pray for us." Thereupon the Holy Prophet [S.A.W.] prayed for him.

    "O Allah! Bless the provisions you have vouchsafed to them with Thy increased bounty, grant them salvation and show them Thy Mercy." *(Tirmidhi)*

Attending the Guests

1. When you pay a visit to someone as a guest, do take some gifts for the host or for his children according to your means. Keep in mind the taste and liking of your host while choosing gifts for him. Exchange of presents and gifts augments sentiments of love and promotes intimate relationship. The gift creates a soft corner in the heart of the receiver for the donor.

2. Do not stay for more than three days as a guest with any one, save under special circumstances or when the host insists on your staying with him for a longer period. The Holy Prophet [S.A.W.] affirms:

> *"It is not permissible for a guest to stay so long with the host as to cause him trouble." (Al-Adab-ul-Mufrad)*

'Sahih Muslim' reports:

> *"It is not permissible for a Muslim to stay so long with his brother as to make him a sinner." The people submitted: "O Prophet of Allah [S.A.W.]! How will a Muslim make his brother a sinner in this manner?" "By staying so long with his brother that his brother may be exhausted of all means of entertaining him."*

3. Do not always be a guest of others. Invite others also to be your guests and entertain them liberally.
4. When you go to stay as a guest with somebody, take necessary baggage and bedding etc. according to the season along with you. In winter, especially, never forget to take the bedding with you, otherwise the host will be put to extreme hardship. It is highly improper that the guest shall in any way become an unbearable burden for the host.
5. Keep in mind the engagements and duties of your host. Take care that your host's occupation, duties and engagements are not in any way disturbed by your presence as a guest with him.
6. Do not make all sorts of demands on your host. Be content with whatever provisions he makes for your comfort and entertainment and thank him for this. Do not put him in any extraordinary trouble.
7. If your host's women are not your close or blood relation, avoid entering into conversation with them without reason. Do not eavesdrop on the mutual conversation of your host's women. Behave yourself in such a manner that your conversation or conduct does not become a nuisance for them. Do not violate the privacy and the limitations of Purdah in any case.
8. If for some reason you do not wish to eat with your host, or you are observing a fast, excuse yourself politely and say a prayer invoking the Grace and Blessings of Allah upon your host.

When Hadrat Ibrahim [A.S.] presented a sumptuous meal to his venerable guests and the guests would not partake of it, Hadrat Ibrahim [A.S.] said to them: "Gentlemen, why don't you eat?" In a bid to put Hadrat Ibrahim at ease the angels submitted: "Please do not take it ill. As a matter of fact, we cannot eat. We have come only to convey the glad tidings of the birth of a talented son to you."

9. When you attend a feast, say a prayer at the end of the meal invoking Allah to bless the host with extensive means, grace, favour, salvation and His Mercy. Hadrat Abu Athhim b. Tahan [R.A.A.] once invited the Holy Prophet [S.A.W.] and his illustrious companions [R.A.A.] to a feast. When the meal was over, the Holy Prophet [S.A.W.] observed: "Reward your brother." The illustrious companions [R.A.A.] submitted: "How can we reward him, O Prophet of Allah [S.A.W.]?" The Holy Prophet [S.A.W.] observed:

    "When a man pays a visit to his brother and eats and drinks there, he can reward his brother by praying for Allah's favour and blessings upon his brother:

    (Abu Daud)

The Holy Prophet [S.A.W.] once visited the house of Hadrat Saad b. 'Ubadah [R.A.A.]. Hadrat Saad [R.A.A.] presented to the Holy Prophet [S.A.W.] bread and olive oil. The Prophet of Allah [S.A.W.] took the meal and then prayed for him:

> *"May the fasting people break their fasts with your provisions! May the pious partake of your meals and may the angels pray for Allah's Mercy and forgiveness for you."* *(Abu-Daud)*

Description in Holy Quran

Importance of Family Ties

> *He causes many to (go) astray and many He leads into the right path; but He causes not to (go) astray except those who transgress; those who break Allah's covenant after it is ratified and sever (the relations) which Allah has ordered to be joined; and so do mischief on the earth; those are the losers.* *(Baqara 2:26-27)*

The right guidance in life comes only through the blessings of Allah. Moreover, Allah gives this guidance to those who seek for it sincerely, and not to those who transgress His set limits. Joining of family ties is a commandment of Allah. The Quran states that those who sever these ties, transgress Allah's limits are deprived of receiving Allah's guidance. Thus maintaining family ties is one of the prerequisites for receiving Allah's guidance in life. Those who are guilty of severing family ties, deprive themselves of receiving Allah's guidance. It is for this reason that the verse states: those are the losers.

Rights of the Relatives

> *Allah commands justice, Ehsan and giving (their due) to near relatives.* (Nahl 16:90)

The practice of justice and *Ehsan* in Islam is as important a duty as praying *Salat* or observing *Siyam*. This is because of the fact that Islam is a *Deen* and provides guidance in one's social as well as personal life. It is evident from the above verse that the practice of justice and *Ehsan* should start with the near relatives. The importance of this commandment is evidenced by the fact that this verse has been incorporated as the last part of Friday sermon and is recited in each and every mosque throughout the Muslim Ummah. Every Muslim is thus reminded every Friday to remember his duties towards his relatives and to treat them with kindness and *Ehsan*.

> *Serve Allah, and join not any partners with Him; and do Ehsan with parents, kinsfolk, orphans, those in need, neighbours who are near, neighbours who are strangers, the companions by your side, the wayfarer (you meet), and what your right hands possess.* (Nisa 4:36)

The essence of Islam is not only to serve Allah, but also to serve our fellow human beings. It also calls for achieving a level of *Ehsan*, i.e. excellence in our attitude and practice. This is a wider and more comprehensive concept than the Western concept of: "Love God and love your neighbour". The above verse commands us to do *Ehsan* not only with parents but with all persons whom we come across in our lives. Furthermore, the verse also shows that doing *Ehsan* with relatives is a duty next to that of parents and supersedes the rest of our social obligations. And give to the relatives their due rights, as well as to those in want, and to the wayfarer, but waste not (your wealth) in the manner of a spendthrift. The verse makes it clear that helping a relative, a needy person or a traveller is not just an act of charity but a commandment of Allah. Each member of a Muslim community has certain rights upon us and we have to honour these rights. It should be noted that this commandment starts with the rights of relatives.

> *So give what is due to relatives, the needy, and the wayfarer; That is best for those who seek the favour of Allah, and it is they who will prosper.* (Rum 30:38)

The verse states clearly that those who desire the pleasure of Allah should fulfill their social obligations, especially those concerning to the relatives. The verse further states that only those who fulfill these obligations shall prosper in life. It thus follows that no matter how righteous a person is in his personal life, he cannot receive the good pleasure of Allah unless he also fulfills his family and social obligations.

Spending on Relatives

> *They ask you: What they should spend (in charity). Say: Whatever you spend that is good, is for parents and relatives and orphans and those in want and for wayfarers; And whatever you do that is good, Allah knows it well.* (Baqara 2:215)

Islam is the *Deen* of nature. It sets the human rights according to their respective needs and positions. The parents in this hierarchy of rights occupy the first position. Next to them comes the position of the nearest relatives. This is then followed by the other social obligations towards the community.

Admonition to the Rich

> *Let not those among you who are endowed with grace and amplitude of means resolve by oath against helping their relatives, those in want, and those who have left homes in Allah's cause; Let them forgive and overlook; Do you not wish that Allah should forgive you? For Allah is Oft-Forgiving, Most Merciful.* (Noor 24:22)

Each family has a few persons who bear some personal dislikes or disputes with a few other members. The Quran commands that these differences should not stop a person from meeting his family obligations and that the rich in the family should always help the poor members of family. The Quran then reminds us that each one of us wishes for Allah's forgiveness. Hence, we should also practice forgiveness in our mutual dealings. It is not appropriate to wish forgiveness from Allah unless we forgive others.

Bibliography

Alfieri, Binaca Maria : *Islamic Architecture of the Indian Subcontinent,* Lawrence King, New York, 1989.

Ali, Asghar : *Theory and Practise of the Islamic State,* Lahore Pak. Vanguard Books, 1985.

Arberry, A.J. : *The Islamic Art of Persia,* Goodword Books, New Delhi, 2003.

Ayoub, Mahmoud: *The Quran and its Interpreters,* Albany: State University of New York Press, 1984.

Berkey, Jonothan P. : *The Formation of Islam : Religion and Society in the Near East,* Cambridge University Press, New Delhi, 1990.

Bukhsh, S. K. : *Contribution to the History of Islamic Civilization,* Kitab Bhavan, New Delhi, 2000.

Chaudhri, Sajedul Bar : *The Profile of an Islamic State,* Dhaka, Islamic Foundation Bangladesh, 1984.

Daniel Pipes : *In the Path of God: Islam and Political Power,* New York: Basic Books Inc., 1983.

Engineer, Asghar Ali : *Islam : Challenge in Twenty-first Century,* Gyan Books Pvt. Ltd., New Delhi, 2004.

Fred M. Donner: *The Early Islamic Conquests,* New Jersey: Princeton University Press, 1981.

Glasse, Cyril : *The Concise Encyclopedia of Islam,* San Francisco: Harper & Row, 1989.

Heyworth-Dunne : *Religious and Political Trends in Modern Egypt,* Washington,1950.

Ikram, S.M. : *Muslim Civilization in India,* Oxford, New York, 1981.

Islahi, M.A.A. : *Islamic Faith and its Presentation,* Adam Publishers, New Delhi, 2002.

John F. *Science and Religion: From Conflict to Conversation.* Mahwah, NJ: Paulist, 1995.

Keddie, Nikki R. : *Roots of Revolution: An Interpretive History of Modern Iran.* New Haven: Yale University Press, 1981.

Kirmani, M. Zaki : *The Quran and Future of Science,* Global Vision Pub, 2001.

Lewis, Bernard : *Islam and the West.* New York: Oxford University Press, 1993.

Manzuruddin, Ahmad : *Islamic Political System,* Kitab Bhavan, New Delhi, 1991.

Marmaduke, Pickthall : *The Meaning of the Glorious Qur'an,* Published by Taj Company, Delhi, 2005.

Mian, S. Khalid : *The Quranic Verses,* Adam Publishers, New Delhi, 2002.

Michael A : *Approaching the Qur'ân: The Early Revelations.* Ashland, Ore.: White Cloud Press, 1999.

Mujahid, Al Sharif: *Muslim League Documents 1900-1947,* Quaid-i-Azam Academy, 1990.

Nasr, Seyyed Hossein : *Science and Civilization in Islam,* Cambridge, UK: Islamic Texts Society, 1987.

Peters, Rudolph : *Jihad in Classical and Modern Islam,* Princeton, NJ: Markus Wiener Publishers, 1996.

Quddus, Syed Abdul : *The Challenge of Islamic Renaissance,* Atlantic Publishers, New Delhi, 1989.

Rauf , Muhammad Abdul : *The Concept of Islamic State,* Kuala Lumpur, 1988.

Sardar, Ziauddin : *Explorations in Islamic Science.* London: Mansell, 1989.

Siddiqi , M. Mazheruddin : *Development of Islamic State and Society,* Lahore, Institute of Islamic Culture, 1956.

Syed, Qutub : *Islamic Approach to Social Justice,* Royal Pub., Lahore, 1978.

Taha, Mahmud Muhammad: *The Second Message of Islam,* Syracuse, N.Y.: Syracuse University Press, 1987.

Toshihiko Izutsu : *God and Man in the Koran,* Weltansckauung. Tokyo, 1964

Trimingham, J.S. : *The Sufi Orders in Islam,* Oxford, New York, 1920.

Underhill, E. : *Mysticism : a Study in the Nature and Development of Man's Spiritual Consciousness,* Oxford, New York, 1956.

Voll, John Obert : *Islam, Continuity, and Change in the Modern World.* 2d ed. Syracuse, N.Y.: Syracuse University Press, 1994.

Walker, Benjamin : *Foundation of Islam : the Making of World Faith,* Rupa & Co., New Delhi, 2001.

Index

❑❑❑